George D. Zollers

Thrilling Incidents on Sea and Land

The prodigal's return

George D. Zollers

Thrilling Incidents on Sea and Land
The prodigal's return

ISBN/EAN: 9783337034139

Printed in Europe, USA, Canada, Australia, Japan

Cover: Foto ©ninafisch / pixelio.de

More available books at **www.hansebooks.com**

THRILLING INCIDENTS

ON SEA AND LAND:

THE PRODIGAL'S RETURN.

By GEORGE D. ZOLLERS.

MOUNT MORRIS, ILL.:
THE BRETHREN'S PUBLISHING COMPANY.
1892.

Entered according to Act of Congress, in the year 1892, by

GEORGE D. ZOLLERS,

In the Office of the Librarian of Congress at Washington.

To

MY WIFE,

My Ever Faithful Help-Mate,

A Christian Woman,

Whose Sympathy and Fidelity have been a

Source of Consolation,

and to

MY CHILDREN,

For whose Welfare I have much Concern,

This Volume

Is Affectionately Dedicated.

PREFACE.

"OF making books there is no end," said the wise man, and many, in glancing at this work, might be at a loss to know why another volume should be added to the many already before the reading public.

There have been many books of travel published heretofore,—most of them pandering to the sensational desires of man, without attempting to elevate the nobler qualities of the soul. Feeling that something should be provided that would be helpful to a higher, Christian life, I have tried to measure the great responsibility of this undertaking, and trust that the Spirit of God "has helped my infirmities." The Brethren's Publishing Company, as well as many other brethren and sisters, have placed me under obligations for favors shown me in the preparation of this work, and efforts in the successful circulation of the same. I hereby express to them my heart-felt thanks.

In preparing these pages it was my purpose to relate, in a simple manner, the wanderings of my earlier years, embracing my life in the army, and especially my experience on the rolling deep. While these scenes are faithfully depicted, I have aimed to bring out the more important part of my work,—the spiritual applications drawn from that which I witnessed or experienced. If I have suffered, in the days gone by, through my own folly and disobedience, I am nevertheless glad that, by the lessons thus learned, I am able to point out the reefs and breakers on life's troubled sea to others, and thus direct others to a higher and better life.

How far I have succeeded in this, I leave others to judge. It is enough for me, to have been an humble instrument in the hands of God, to cite my fellow-travelers to that great school of discipline, in which we must all take lessons, and in which the course of instruction will not be finished until we receive our diploma from the Great Teacher. Written in letters of love and sealed by the atonement of Calvary, we will indeed realize that our life has not been in vain.

That this work may give vigor to the Christian pilgrim and a nobler aim to life, is the wish of

THE AUTHOR

Mt. Carroll, Ill., Aug. 1, 1892.

CHAPTER I.

Our Happy Home. — A Loving Father Consigned to the Tomb. — Among Strangers. — "No Place like Home." — Early Trials. — Influence of Maternal Teachings. — A Serious Struggle. — A Terrible Contest. — President Lincoln's Call for Volunteers. — Heart-rending Scenes in the Parting Hour. — A Last Farewell. — Departure for Norristown. — Reception at Harrisburgh, Pa. — Military Drill at Chambersburg, Pa.

MY birth-place was Skippack Township, Montgomery Co., Pa. Of the seven children in the old homestead,—four sons and three daughters,—I was the fifth. My father was a farmer. He died before I had reached my fourth year, and his decease caused a dark cloud to rest upon our happy home. Though yet in the tender years of childhood, when father's death occurred, it is fixed on my memory to-day. The death scene in the home circle is ever sad and impressive. Mother was weeping bitterly and the neighbors were vainly endeavoring to console her. Although my mind could not realize death's separating power, I received an impression that will never be forgotten.

The consignment of a loving father to the grave occasioned the separation of our once happy and united family. One by one all, with the exception of the youngest, left the home circle to be reared in the homes of strangers.

As our dear father had not accumulated much of this world's goods, my mother was necessitated to form habits of strict economy. With her slender means she purchased three acres of ground and on this small tract built a humble cot and earned her bread by the sweat of her face. Only those who know of the dark and dismal way of poverty can appreciate the situation of a widow bereft of her bosom companion.

In our dreary homes among strangers the thoughts of home and its fond endearments often caused the tears to start. When the day of reunion would draw near, the gloomy shadows would leave the heart, and home, with all its beauty and attractiveness, would rise before our youthful vision. Sad experience taught us the force of those beautiful words, "There's no place like home."

Many a time in the twilight, when the labors of the day were ended, did I resort to an elevation from which I could view my fondly-cherished home. Though less than eight years of age I would gladly have wended my way through the darkness of night to my home, there to receive the solace for my aching heart, which that familiar spot alone could afford. Then I would retire to my couch and pray God to protect the dear inmates of my home.

At such times I experienced a relief by invoking God's blessing upon everything that pertained to that cherished spot; and, then, amid tears, and sobs, and heartaches, I would seek to forget my grief in silent slumber. These early trials were conducive to pious inclinations, and my heart yearned after God. The precepts which my mother inculcated, amid the woes and sorrows of her life, began their silent influence at an early period of my life. Mother taught us two prayers which we never forgot amid all the vicissitudes of our career. One was, "Now I lay me down to sleep," and the other, the "Lord's Prayer." These invocations were so indelibly fixed on my memory that, invariably, I uttered these prayers before falling asleep.

Mothers should not grow weary in teaching their children the ways of God. The seed they sow in tears may not spring up and grow at once, it may not seem to flourish in the *sunshine* of life, but the clouds that intervene and the reverses that attend their journey will cause the seed, that was sown in early years, to germinate. In maturer life will recur to the mind the wooings of maternal love. The good deeds, entreaties and prayers, in behalf of the son or daughter, will be ratified and blessed by a faithful and loving God.

I formed an attachment for the Bible in the morning of my life. It was my principal school-book. I read its wonderful truths with pleasure. At the age of twelve years I read the Bible with still greater regularity, and many serious thoughts were awakened in my mind by the diligent perusal of God's Sacred Book. I became so absorbed in its sublime truths that, when I was toiling through the day, I could scarcely wait till the evening would arrive, so that the longings of my soul might be satisfied by perusing my cherished Bible.

How dear to my recollection is the golden period of my youth! The Lord was very near me. My innocent heart longed for my Creator. I prayed to him often. I greatly admired his visible creation and gazed with fondness at the murmuring stream, as its crystal waters reflected the image of groves, arrayed in their vernal foliage. The song of the birds disclosed to me the Creator's love and power.

Had I known just how to proceed in the service of my Lord at that time, I would gladly have walked in his ways, but I lacked the proper teaching. I was sincere, honest and true, as far as I went, but I needed some human agency, by divine appointment, to teach and direct me, and explain to me the plan of salvation. When the eunuch was perplexed as to the way of salvation, Philip came to his assistance and preached unto him Jesus. The willing auditor soon believed and was baptized, and went on his way rejoicing. Oh, for more Philips to be thus instant in season!

In course of time my zeal and love began to relax. By improper associations my hilarity and youthful glee gradually suppressed my serious thoughts and, as a result, I grew cold and indifferent. But notwithstanding my lethargy, I still formally uttered the prayers which my fond mother had taught me.

At the age of seventeen I had a serious struggle under the convicting power of Divine Truth. I was then laboring for an aged brother whose heart and affections were absorbed in the work of God. His exemplary life, his fervent prayers, and godly conversation had a powerful influence over me; but notwithstanding my strong convictions, and contrition of heart, I found it needed a much stronger will-power to conquer the opposing forces of sin than it would have required when I felt the gentle wooings of the Divine Spirit in earlier life. I was almost persuaded but, sad to relate, I did not make the good choice. The longer the work of grace is delayed, the more difficult it is to become reconciled to God. Let the dear friends, young or old, who peruse this book, profit by my sad experience. Let them not slight the precious opportunities of grace, lest they suffer a loss which can never be repaired.

I lived with this pious old brother about three months. Then, for a number of years, I was thrown into the society of non-professors, with the exception of about one year when I served an apprenticeship at the plasterer's trade with my cousin, who was a God-fearing man. His amiable qualities and religious tendencies had their salutary influence upon me, but still the charms of the world were more attractive, and the "strong man armed" was occupying the palace of my heart. The terrible contest, in which the Great Conqueror would dethrone the infernal antagonist and assume the legal sway, was a matter for future development.

In the year 1861 occurred the cruel war in the United States which threw the entire country into commotion. I, like others, was animated with the spirit of patriotism and, when the call was made by President Lincoln for sixty thousand soldiers, to defend the rights of the country, I responded and, in company with a number of my youthful associates, entered the service of the Government at Norristown, Pa. Many heart-rending scenes were witnessed at this time of our country's peril. I shall never forget the dismal moaning of my own grief-stricken mother, when, at the hour of midnight, I announced to her my intention of taking my departure in the morning for the scene of war and carnage. It was a new phase in my youthful career, and the painful beatings and gloomy emotions of my own heart, in that lone and dreary night, are easier imagined than described. At night the horrors of war arose before my vision. The doleful thought impressed itself upon me that, perhaps, I was about to bid farewell to home associations and endearments, and, that, from the scenes of bloodshed and misery, and the din of battle, I might be hurled into the gloom of eternity.

Morning came, but everything wore a dismal aspect. Mother's eyes were suffused by tears and her visage appeared troubled and sad. She entreated me not to go, but I had given my comrades my word that I would meet them that morning, and I felt too brave to break my promise.

I had to nerve myself for the parting scene, and utter in a suppressed tone the sad farewell, but the severest task was to say that saddest of all words to mother. Her parting look was one of anxiety, her feeble response was expressed in a sad and burdened tone.

A dismal cloud rested on my heart,—a result of the dreary parting scenes. Before me was a life of cruel conflicts, unpleasant exposures, and the hardships of the soldier. As I journeyed along, I cast a lingering gaze at the familiar scenes around me. As I passed the neighboring houses, the friends came to take their leave, and in sadness we thought that, perhaps, we should never see each other again. In the spirit of sympathy they wished me success in my prospective military life.

I met some of my comrades at their homes and witnessed the same painful separation between mothers and sons, and brothers and sisters, that I, a little while before, had experienced at my own home. The spirit of war was prevalent and the entire country seemed to be in an uproar. The once tranquil homes of America were overshadowed by the sable cloud.

At Norristown, Pa.,—our rendezvous,—our names were enrolled on the army-lists. Here there was a great commotion, and when the raw recruits, whose names were entered upon the regimental rolls, were marched forth to board the waiting train, parents, wives, and children, with sad feelings, bade us farewell, lamenting over the painful separation and the approaching desolations of war. It was heart-rending to observe the last fond embraces of husbands and wives, fathers and children, brothers and sisters, mothers and sons. At last all was in readiness and the train slowly rolled away from the weeping crowd, and we looked back to see the hundreds of white handkerchiefs, waving the last farewell. We were soon borne away from loving friends, but the ties of home endearments and amiable associations were still entwined around our memories. We were now hurrying on to Harrisburg. In a few hours we reached our destination and met with a welcome reception by the citizens of Harrisburg. We were marched through the city to the soldiers' quarters, where we obtained, for the first time, a slight idea of what the soldiers' life in camp would be. Some of us occupied sheds, carpeted with straw, others dwelt in tents.

Our experience soon proved to be a change from weal to woe, from peaceful pursuits and the charms of home to a life of hardships and the dismal forebodings of war. We tried to accommodate ourselves to our new surroundings, but the inuring process, though very gradual, was altogether incongenial. In spite of all our efforts to be of good cheer an undercurrent of gloom and sadness pervaded our hearts. The citizens treated us kindly and plenty of edibles were brought to the camp for our sustenance.

To increase my dissatisfaction, I was separated from my home companions. My name having been inscribed near the close of the list, and the names having been taken in the order of their enrollment, the company was formed ere my name was reached. This pained the hearts of my comrades, as well as my own. One of them pleaded with me to return home, because of this sad disappointment. I shall never forget his look of concern and anxiety as we parted. I had seen the separation in his humble home, near the waters of the Skippack. His mother wept, when she exclaimed, "Farewell, my dear Harry." After kissing his hand she turned aside and wept bitterly. This poor mother's two sons were subsequently imprisoned at Libby Prison and starved to death.

I did not follow the advice of my friend, but enlisted in a Berks County Company, under Captain George Herbst, and was incorporated into the Seventh Pennsylvania Regiment, commanded by Col. Irvin. Having sworn allegiance to the Government of the United States, we were conducted in military order to Chambersburg, Pa., where we were brought under army discipline and accustomed to military drills and regulations. We now had to adapt ourselves to our surroundings, and make strong efforts to cultivate and imbibe the spirit of war,—no matter how contrary to our former training in an atmosphere of serenity and peace. With all this, I could not fully counteract the undercurrent of Biblical training and culture.

CHAPTER II.

The New Testament Teachings Opposed to War. — God's Plans and Dealings. — Christ's Example. — Reconciling Myself to the Life of a Warrior. — "The Powers that Be." — Military Training and its Results. — A Start for Old Virginia. — Long Marches. — "Nature's Beverage." — Martial Music and its Effects. — Reclining by the Wayside. — A Fluent Speaker. — Two Kingdoms. — At Williamsport. — Rebel Picket Guard. — On to Martinsburg. — The Destructiveness of War. — Charleston. — A Midnight March. — General Patterson's Failure. — Returning Home. — Arrival at Hagerstown.

AN honest Biblical student will not be slow to determine that the spirit of carnal warfare and the spirit of the Gospel widely differ. Paul says that the "weapons of the Christian's warfare are not carnal but mighty through God, to the pulling down of strongholds, casting down imaginations, and every high thing that exalteth itself against the knowledge of God." But the question arises, Did not God command his people in ancient days to engage in war? Did he not bid them slay their enemies with the edge of the sword? I answer, Yes. But there is a marked contrast between the dispensation of Moses and the economy of grace. Even under the former dispensation the Lord did not always destroy the enemies of Israel solely by means of carnal weapons. He reveals to us, by the various methods of showing his destructive power, that he can consult his own pleasure as to the means and methods of carrying out his purposes.

Every Bible student remembers that simple and peculiar procedure to effect the downfall of the massive walls of Jericho. The Israelites were commanded to go around the city, each day, with the utmost regularity in marching. Never were military forces better controlled than when Jehovah himself moved in the van. There was no visible manifestation of power, save the prompt and precise march each day. No battering rams were used. There was no manipulation of swords and bows, no effort to scale the towering walls, but steady and timely was the march and unceasing was the music discoursed by the simple rams' horns. With the seventh day a change was made in the order of marching. Instead of going around the city once, they were commanded to march around it seven times. Though the onward march of this peculiar, God-fearing army was more continuous, the opposing forces discovered no demonstrations of conquest; but God selects his own time for the disclosures of his vengeance and destructive power. When the seventh circuit was effected, the priests were commanded to blow their rams' horns, and the whole army of Israel was commanded to shout. No doubt the welkin rang with the sound of their voices. After their obedience to God had been shown, he brought into requisition his resistless power, and the mighty walls of Jericho crumbled to the ground.

No military skill or ingenuity can disclose the secret of this divine force. "God moves in his own mysterious way his wonders to perform." If his children are obedient, he will grant them triumph over all their enemies. God's power is in his word. The duty of his children is to be submissive to his rule, and his conquering might will be sure to follow their obedience. Under the New Covenant there is a change from a secular to a spiritual kingdom. Christ says, "If my kingdom were of this world, then would my servants fight." It is a spiritual kingdom that admits of spiritual culture and attainments, and the carnal weapons can not perfect the more refined part of our being.

The prophet Isaiah understood the character of this spiritual warfare when he said, "Every battle of the warrior is with confused noise, and garments rolled in blood;" but Christ's kingdom he represents as a kingdom of peace. Christ himself exemplified this peaceful spirit in his life. "When he was reviled he reviled not again, when he was persecuted he threatened not," and he exhibited a disposition of kindness to his most inveterate foes. He prayed for his malignant persecutors and bore their cruel insults with calm submission. He taught his followers to love their enemies and pray for those who persecuted them, and then enforced his instructions by his own hallowed example.

Now, although God controls the destinies of armies and nations and consummates his vast designs through human hostilities and military achievements, yet he does decidedly declare to his own children, under the present spiritual dispensation of mercy, that they shall not resist evil or use the weapons of carnality for their defense. According to the teachings of Christ, as revealed in the Gospel, I was not able to imitate his life and example and at the same time serve the Government in a carnal warfare. Thus I was compelled to consider my situation aright and make the best of it. Others explained it differently, and chaplains, who were employed by the Government, endorsed the carnal strife. So, by degrees, I was inured to war principles and my tender sensibilities were gradually hardened. Yet I would secretly read the Bible and pray God to spare my life.

As I had sworn allegiance to the United States Government, I endeavored to cultivate a spirit of bravery, wrest my conscience into the current of popular Christianity and thus educate myself to harmonize the two elements,—carnal warfare and spiritual salvation. I can readily discover how thousands of professing Christians evade the cross of Christ. I tried to lean on God's unbounded mercy, thinking that if I would show a little respect to the Lord by reading his Word in secret and calling on his name occasionally, his mercy might perchance prevail in the critical hour; but while I endeavored to cultivate military valor I was, in the Christian warfare, reconciling myself to a life of timidity and cowardice.

It is impossible to be the friend of the world and the friend of God at the same time. The Bible tells us that plainly and I learned it, too, by my own experience. I went the rounds of military discipline and army regulation. I tried to be a soldier in reality. I respected my officers and implicitly obeyed their commands, but I thank God that the little spark of vitality, which may be compared to the smoking flax, referred to in the Scripture, was not quenched beneath the pressure of the strong carnal forces, but that, in God's own good time, it was fanned into a flame.

No person, however eminent and talented he be, can persuade me that war and bloodshed do not have a tendency to demoralize our being. I believe that God is preparing his people, through the ordeals of spiritual renovation, for the millennial age, when the swords shall be beaten into plowshares, and the spears into pruninghooks.

The spiritual power with which his chosen people are clothed is paramount to all the manifestations of military prowess and grandeur; and in proportion as the Government respects these peculiar, non-resistant people whom God acknowledges to be the salt of the earth, it will prosper, and their humble prayers to God, in behalf of those in authority, are indeed more acceptable with the Most High than is commonly conceded. Their spiritual power is hidden from the world. Let the people, who value their security from the outpouring of divine vengeance, not despise the few lights that the Lord still permits to shine upon this benighted world.

Had the kings of the earth known that Christ was the Savior of the world, they would not have crucified the Lord of glory. Their carnal prosperity and self-reliance, and their confidence in their military resources blinded them and concealed the superior power and glory from them. Having elevated their human standard above the divinely-appointed test or criterion, they effectually lost their latitude and, as a result, ignored and crucified the purest and most lovely Being that ever graced the earth. Christ's own chosen people were removed from the doomed city of Jerusalem before its terrible desolation. The Savior had disclosed to them the signs of its approaching downfall. They had no hand in defending its fortifications and they knew by the prophetic announcements of their Master that the renowned city was doomed to destruction. The besieging forces, under Titus, revived the force of the prophetic statement and in compliance with his divine command the Christians fled to the mountains and escaped the overwhelming catastrophe.

The powers that be, are to be respected; they are ordained of God to protect the good and punish the evil, and they bear not the sword in vain. To resist this power brings upon the offender the judgment of the sword. Therefore let the magistrates, in their responsible positions, be honored and let their dues be rendered to them. Let that divine principle—love—be the controlling characteristic of God's peculiar people and let their life manifest the superior spiritual power by which they are influenced! May they be kept untainted by the fleshly power, and thus continually have a salutary bearing upon those around them.

But I must return to my military experience. Day after day we practiced the manual of arms so as to become expert and dexterous in the art of war. We made grand displays in military tactics and so prompt and exact were the army regulations and so constant the exercises in the daily routine of duty,—the guard-mounting, stationing of sentinels at their respective posts, exercise in drills, dress-parade, etc.,—that the mind was directed and educated in this new and warlike channel. As the constant dropping wears away stones, so the incessant training in this military school suppressed gradually all former convictions, and by degrees habituated us to our new life.

The method of training, alluded to, was continued at Chambersburg, Pa., for about six weeks. Then we started for Old Virginia. There were almost daily rumors of war, and though we did not come in contact with the opposing forces, we were obtaining experience in the more stern realities of the soldier's life. We learned the tediousness of long marches, bearing the luggage apportioned to each soldier. This consisted of a knapsack, containing blanket for bed and the actually necessary clothing, a haversack with apportioned rations, and a canteen for water. "Nature's beverage" is very useful to slake the soldier's burning thirst, while sweltering beneath the heat of the noonday sun, and enduring the fatigue of the long marches.

Now and then the martial music would awaken energy in the drooping soldier, by discoursing harmoniously the national airs. During the marches some of the weaker ones would become faint and discouraged. They would drop from the ranks and recline along the highway, till accosted by some officer in the rear, who would urge them to continue the march to the destination. He would entreat them ardently, but, if they would decline making the needed effort, he would change the tone of his voice to the severity of an imperative command. If marching was an impracticability, they were placed on the ambulance wagons and conveyed to their destination.

Since I have become enlightened in the Christian warfare, I have been enabled to deduce many practical illustrations from the incidents occurring in army life. How often must weak professors of Christianity be entreated to activity, when they grow weary and faint on the spiritual marches, to repel the intrusions of their hostile enemies! The unruly must needs be reproved sharply, while the helpless and infirm must be tenderly supported by the strong.

The earnest singing of the redeemed of the Lord often relieves the monotony of the journey, and revives their languishing spirits. The persistent zeal and perseverance of the brave soldier should spur the Christian warrior to untiring activity in the contest before him.

Col. Irvin, who commanded our regiment, was a competent military commander, but Lieut. Col. Ripley was the most fluent speaker, and whenever the troops were to be entertained by an oration, the latter officer was appointed to address the soldiers. On one occasion he delivered an address, when he tried, with all his power of eloquence, to make a practical exposition of the two swords, spoken of by Christ, near the time of his apprehension. His purpose was to impress the minds of the soldiers, with the idea that, by the selection of the two swords, Christ designed the carnal warfare or military power. But we have learned, in the course of life, that the most eloquent speeches do not always afford the clearest expositions of truth and that, through human weakness, we are inclined to accommodate the evidences of truth to the support of our favored enterprises. After Peter, by the sword, had severed the ear of the High-priest's servant, Christ, after having healed the ear, commanded Peter to put up his sword into the sheath, "for he that taketh the sword shall perish with the sword." I am constrained, by the influence of Divine Truth, to deduce a practical illustration from this incident, and that is this: The command of Christ to Peter, to put up the sword, reveals the fact that it should be put up by all the followers of Christ, and hence their non-resistant qualities are evinced and enforced by this memorable circumstance. But what became of the other sword?—for there were two swords prepared. My conclusion is that the latter may be the one assigned to the secular power, for the punishment of evil doers. So, then, the manifest distinction of the two kingdoms can be observed at this juncture, —the spiritual and the natural. These two kingdoms, therefore, cannot blend, for Christ, the Savior of mankind, has separated them, and they can only serve their appointment of God when they operate in their respective spheres.

We, at length, arrived at Williamsport, on the Potomac River, and were then in close proximity to the enemy. One morning, ere the dawn, as I was serving as sentinel in the town of Williamsport, a regiment of soldiers passed me, and soon after they fired a volley at the rebel picket-guards on the opposite side of the river. At daybreak we received marching orders and were soon at the riverside, and commanded to wade across the water at the fording. Soon the river was filled with the boys in blue. After we had forded the Old Potomac, we were hurriedly advanced, driving the rebel pickets before us, in the direction of Martinsburg, Virginia. Before reaching the town we anticipated a battle with the "boys in grey," as they were called,' and I remember, as the supposed crisis was drawing near, that Lieutenant Colonel Ripley interrogated us as to our willingness to meet them in mortal conflict. The soldiers who marked his coolness and presence of mind on the verge of a military contest, signified their readiness to follow wheresoever their brave officers would lead them; but no battle occurred. The rebels, feeling, I presume, inadequate to the forces coming upon them, fled, and left Martinsburg in our possession. We found the place considerably damaged by our enemies. Among other deeds of demolition, the Baltimore & Ohio Railroad was torn up and quite a number of locomotives destroyed.

We now began to discover the destructiveness of war and were made to feel the reality of the hardships it imposes, rather than a presentation of it in theory and romance, while sitting at ease by our comfortable firesides. Yet this was only the beginning of sorrow. How terrible are the desolations of war! Homes that were once in the glow of prosperity, are now dilapidated and wear an aspect of dreariness and gloom. War arrays man against man in deadly strife and brands the human heart with hatred and revenge. It hardens the finer sensibilities of our being, and gives vent and force to the baser propensities. We may endeavor to conceal its hostile ravages by sanctimonious efforts but it is war and bloodshed still, in all its horror, ever resulting in the destruction of life and property.

In about two weeks from the time when we entered Martinsburg, we again received marching orders, and our next halt was at Charlestown, W. Va., where the radical, enthusiastic John Brown was executed. Many things revolved in our mind as we entered the place where the dismal and fatal tragedy was enacted, and we procured, as we supposed at least, relics of the gallows upon which this gallant champion was executed.

One night, as I was stationed on picket duty, I was, in the midnight hour, summoned from my post, and conducted, under official orders, to the ranks of the regiment, in readiness to march. We left Charlestown hastily, under the cover of night, without any clear conception of what we were wanted to do, but we marched along in the lone and dismal night. Fatigued and burdened, hungry and sleepy we trudged along the weary way, not knowing whither we went, or what would be our destination. Sometime, ere the dawn of day, we halted upon the side of a high, but gradually-sloping, hill. Exhausted by our nocturnal march, we sank to the earth and were soon wrapped in deep slumber, unconscious of the dangers to which we might be exposed. I never slept a more profound sleep than I did in that morning watch, and to the third hour of the day. When I awoke I was lying in the heated rays of a Southern sun. I could hardly comprehend the situation, nor did I spend much time in contemplation, for the first thing that taxed my somewhat recuperated energies was, to satisfy the gnawings of hunger. Not far from the place where we bivouaced, on the hill-side along the Shenandoah River, I found a mill, and there I purchased some flour and corn meal for my breakfast. Never did I relish a meal more than this one, and nature's wasted powers were again recuperated. We learned afterwards that the purpose of our being forwarded to this place was to arrest General Johnston and his army on the way from Winchester to Bull Run. Having failed in the attempt, for some cause or other, General Patterson was, I believe, severely censured for the failure. At all events, our efforts were foiled.

The three months, for which time we were sworn in the service of the Government, having expired, the matter of returning to Hagerstown, Md., was taken under advisement by the officials, that is after Col. Irvin had pleaded with us to prolong our time, or enlist for a longer period; but after three months' experience in army life, we were yearning for at least a brief respite, and the privilege of seeing our friends once more. The Colonel felt somewhat chagrined at his regiment, for declining his earnest request, but it now being the prerogative of the men to decide, their almost unanimous decision was in favor of returning home; so we began our homeward march in the direction of Hagerstown. We arrived at our destination at about ten o'clock the following night, exhausted in strength and energy. We forded the Potomac near Shepherdstown and the march, though a homeward one, was, in its taxations, severe enough throughout. Most of the soldiers slept in the open air, and I, for one, had blistered feet. We learned by experience that a soldier's life is not one that is enjoyed on flowery beds of ease, and evidently the Christian, who is engaged in a far superior enterprise, should not expect to arrive at the terminus of his career without losses and crosses, turmoils and tribulations by the way. If professors of the Christian religion would exhibit the same comparative energy in their spiritual warfare, that the natural soldier does in his carnal warfare, they would be, to a larger extent, successful in conquering the infernal powers. But how we squirm and recoil at the cross of Christ, when a little more fortitude and courage would bring about the achievement of great feats. The martyrs of old suffered, and prior to the excruciating pains of death, their feet were no doubt often blistered by long and weary journeys. Often, no doubt, their bodies were chilled by the dampness of the mountain caverns. O, blessed martyrs, how noble your characters and how faithful were you to your Commander!

Terrible Ravages of the War Fiend.
Plantation Ruins on James River.

CHAPTER III.

What Christian Soldiers Should Be. — More Devotion Needed. — Enjoyment of Home Associations After the Three Months' Campaign. — Renewal of the Conflict. — Leaving Home Again. — Attached to a Music Corps. — Winter Quarters at Camp Pierpont. — Rigors of Army Life in Winter. — Benefits of Peace. — Routine of Camp Life. — Martial Music. — Marching Orders. — Difficult Creek. — A Fierce Encounter. — Scenes of Death and Carnage. — Return to Place of Encampment. — "Halt, Boys, We Are Right Among Them!" — A Pell-mell Retreat. — Ineffectual Command to Stand Up Bravely. — Effects of a False Alarm.

NATURAL soldiers in their warfare show a more determined and resolute character than thousands of professing Christians who claim to be marching under the banner of the cross. If the zeal and courage shown by the natural army were shown by the spiritual army, stupendous indeed would be the achievements of the spiritual warriors. The church of Christ would appear as wonderful and powerful as she is represented in the Volume of Truth, "Fair as the moon, clear as the sun and terrible as an army with banners."

There is nothing that appears more magnificent to a trained military eye than a well-disciplined army, with banners floating in the breeze over the deep columns of soldiers, bearing the weapons of their warfare, and dexterously changing positions at the command of their officers. But how divinely fair to the experienced spiritual warrior appears the church of Christ, achieving her spiritual conquests in the fear of God. No wonder that the poet, after having witnessed the decline of the power of the church, intensely yearns to see her as she was when clothed with celestial glory and power.

> "I've seen thy glory and thy power,
> Through all thy temple shine,
> My God, repeat that heavenly hour,
> That vision so divine."

The Jewish people, God's representative nation of yore, forfeited their pre-eminence by affiliating with the heathen nations. The divine appointment of the Jewish nation, with all its peculiar characteristics and distinct form of government, is a clear prefiguration of the church of Christ, distinct from the governments of the world; and in proportion as she retains her identity and progresses in love, exhibiting her distinctive features in her external and internal life, she will disclose her pre-eminence and reveal herself as the illuminating power of the world. She will move from conquest to conquest in her spiritual sphere, bringing the weapons of her warfare to bear "against spiritual wickedness in high places," casting down "imaginations, and every high thing that exalts itself against the knowledge of God." But in proportion as the church sacrifices her immunities, and compromises with the world, she will forfeit the power with which the God of heaven has clothed her. Does not this mournful picture meet our vision now? So indistinct and confused are the teachings and examples in Christendom to-day that it is difficult to discriminate between the world and the church.

I do not make these statements out of a feeling of prejudice or disrespect, but simply to evince my loyalty to truth as it is revealed in God's Word. I believe that when

Christ makes his second advent, the churches will have lost their latitude as utterly as the Jews had lost theirs at the time of his first coming. My testimonials will show my life to have been loyal to the Government of the United States in my military course before my spiritual vision was fully unsealed; and now I trust that my attachment to Christ's spiritual kingdom will be so great that I may ever show allegiance to all its sacred rites and demands.

After our three months' campaign had expired, the troops were conveyed to Harrisburg and mustered out of service. We hurried home with light hearts to greet our friends once more. I joyfully met my mother, brothers and sisters again. Never did they seem dearer, and my home more precious. I did not want a soft bed to repose in but wanted to keep myself, to some extent, habituated to hardships. I slept (and soundly too) for many nights in succession on mother's carpeted floor. My military experience had to a considerable degree alienated my affections, and military science and the spirit of war seemed to be the leading characteristic. There were wars and rumors of wars all over the country, and, though the three months volunteers had returned, thousands were still offering their services to the Government to crush the cruel rebellion, which bid fair to continue longer than had at first been anticipated.

Preparations were now being made for a terrible conflict between the North and South. My friends enlisted all around my native place. This filled me with uneasiness and suggested to my mind the propriety of re-enlisting. My band comrades had just tendered their services as musicians, and were pleading with me to come and unite with them. I concluded that this opportunity was as suitable as any that would be offered me. I began to expostulate with mother and the home inmates. I was hopeful, and endeavored to bend the inclinations of my kindred so that they would think as I did. I told them that if I declined this privilege, I would be running the risk of being drafted; and, thus pressed into service, I should be deprived of my comrades, and besides have a smaller compensation for my services, as musicians were given better wages by the Government than soldiers.

In the month of August, 1861, I again broke away from home associations and started for the army. My sensibilities were more callous at this period of my career, and the second departure was not quite as difficult as the first, but yet it required firmness of resolution, and bracing up of the will-power. Instead, however, of shouldering the deadly weapon, now I carried my musical instrument to animate and cheer the soldiers. I met my comrades at Hightstown, near Washington, D. C. We were in the Second Regiment of the Pennsylvania Reserves, commanded by Col. Mann; then in General McCall's division, and General Banks' corps. We were rejoiced to meet. Under the dismal aspect of affairs, we seemed to be more dear to each other than ever before. There is nothing else in our journey through life that so endears friend to friend as suffering the woes of life, and enduring special hardships together. We were wrapped up in each other's welfare, the continuance of life being more uncertain than it is in the absence of mortal strife. We endeavored to accommodate ourselves to the warlike element, and cultivated a spirit of hilarity and merriment, however dark the hour.

Music lends enchantment, and disperses the gloom of life, and music with us was a specialty. We were almost constantly in the spirit of melody, but not in tuning our hearts and lips to sing the spiritual songs of Zion. Had Zion's children been drawn into this uncongenial element, they would have had to lament the digression from their spiritual sphere; and, as of old, must have hung their harps upon the willows. Instead of cultivating our vocal organs in song, we made our horns the mediums of discoursing the national airs and such strains as would best adapt us to the life in which we were engaged. So we whiled away the precious hours of our brief life, and passed through its bright as well as dismal scenes.

Winter came on, and we took up our winter quarters at Camp Pierpont, ten miles from Washington. This inured us to the severer part of army life, so far as the rigors of climate were concerned. We pitched our tents, and shaped our camp for winter. We were near timber, and so felled trees for fuel and constructed beds in our tents, so as to raise ourselves from the dampness of the earth. On this hard frame structure we had no chaff-tick or mattress, but simply our blankets. Two or three of us would bunk together, and thus have blankets to lie upon, and to cover ourselves with. The Government furnished us with small sheet-iron stoves to keep us as comfortable as soldiers needed to be kept. Thus we managed to survive the bleak winds of winter. While we were passing through this most dreary portion of the year, we often thought of the time in our past lives when peace and plenty reigned.

We, as a rule, are inconsiderate, and often very ungrateful in the time of peace and prosperity, and fail to appreciate what we have until we are deprived of it. We enjoy the blessings of the home circle; we gather in the familiar places; we are nourished by the rich bounties which a merciful God provides for his dependent creatures. Think of these benefits in the time of peace; then contrast this scene of serenity and plentitude with war and its terrible ravages, its destruction by sword and flame, depopulated regions, desolated homes and sorrow-riven inmates. And then ask the question, with the inspired James, " From whence come wars and fightings? Come they not even of your own lusts?" If we, as a nation, would try to answer more fully the end and design of our creation, and try to be humble rather than to aspire to fame, these terrible hostilities would be done away with. When one of us is becoming popular, another envies him; and when the dross of our corrupt nature is compressed, it must explode, and is poured out in storms of human passion. Streams of blood must flow to correct us for our transgressions, for our violation of that precious law of divine love which was procured with blood that was purer and more precious than human blood.

Let me illustrate farther. Scientific discoveries reveal the fact that gases accumulate in the interior of the earth. Terrible explosions occur, and the volcanic eruptions are evidences of compressed matter that must have vent. In that respect volcanoes may be regarded as the safety-valves of the earth. So, when the carnal propensities predominate, and human passion burns in the heart and circulates in the veins of humanity, war gives vent to the fire of wrath. Many who fought in the cruel war of 1861, and a few who held prominent positions in it, are among the peaceful followers of Christ. Some are heralds of the Lamb that was slain but liveth again. I know one to whom I listened with pleasure while he enumerated the distinctive characteristics of Christ's kingdom. He was once absorbed in political issues, and was two or three times in the legislature. He went with the secessionists in the civil contest, and evinced his firmness and resolution in many a battle. But ultimately he discovered the impropriety of such a course, laid down his carnal weapons, and vowed allegiance to the government of Christ. I can refer to Federals and Confederates who opposed each other in the deadly strife when the contending armies confronted each other, but who have now yielded to the peaceful measures of the Christian economy. Their hearts have been purified in obeying the truth; hatred and wrath have been subdued; love to God and man now sways their hearts and they are humble, loving, and inoffensive.

Here, again, we recognize the superior excellence of the divine means in subduing enemies. In the carnal warfare they are subdued by physical force, and it is by superior power alone that they are kept in restraint. The feelings of revenge may be deep and dire, and an opportunity to transcend the authority and repel the physical power that restrains, will disclose the retaliatory disposition in all its violence. But divine love, that attribute of heaven, once so beautifully exemplified in Christ, eradicates every vestige of hatred and revenge, melts the human heart to deep contrition, and moulds it after the example of Christ, "who when he was reviled reviled not again, when he was persecuted he threatened not," who loved his enemies, and prayed for them that despitefully used him. They spit in his face, they pierced his sacred temples with the crown of thorns, they scourged him, they buffeted him, they mocked him, and, in his excruciating agony on the cross, they wagged their heads in scorn; and though the sun was veiled, and the rocks were rent, and the earth quaked, yet the dying Son of God submitted to the opposing powers of sin without a murmur, or feeling of resentment towards his inveterate foes. Here is, indeed, a divine precedent which should draw out our strongest efforts to imitate and follow. Oh, to be a humble soldier of Christ, with courage and fortitude to endure hardships and repel by his mild yet powerful means, the forces of sin, is far more than to be a warrior in the carnal strife, wielding a sword of burnished steel, parading in military pomp and splendor, and obtaining the honor and renown attending military achievements.

The winter passed slowly by and the daily routine of labor was performed. In the morning the bands were heard in all directions, as the signal to rise from slumber and begin the work of the day. The next thing in the order of military regulation was guard-mounting, when the bands were employed. During the greater portion of the day the soldiers were usually exercised in drills. In the evening we had dress parade, when the bands were all employed. After dress parade we all repaired to our tents and ate the last meal of the day. About 9 o'clock at night the bands again performed and made the camp resound with their harmonious airs. Then the entire camp was replete with melody. This closed the program, and was called the tattoo. After this all but the sentinels retired. In this manner proceeded the daily routine of military duties. Order and regulation must necessarily be kept up to keep the men prompt and active. An air of vigilance is everywhere present, so as to be in readiness for the sudden assaults of the enemy. The guards retain their positions and are on the alert, however dark the hour. Amid falling snows and beating rains, in torrid or frigid climes, however cold and bleak the storms of winter, the sentinel walks his beat.

On Dec. 20, 1861, two brigades received marching orders; namely, the first and third. Our brigade, the first, was commanded by General Reynolds; and the third, by General Ord. The two brigades belonged to the Division of Pennsylvania Reserves. The march was made in the direction of Drainsville. At Difficult Creek our brigade halted and the third brigade advanced. About two hours after their departure we heard sharp cannonading in the direction of Drainsville, and we received orders to re-inforce the advance brigade in double-quick time. We began our hurried march with the vivid prospect of an ardent engagement with the opposing forces, who had secreted themselves in a pine woods in order to hold the vantage ground. But notwithstanding their advantageous position they were routed before we reached the scene of conflict. This was our first sight of anything like a real battle. The shock and storm of the engagement were over before we reached the ground, but the bloody effects of it were visible.

The first sad spectacle that met our gaze was three of our own men stained with blood, two of whom were dead; the third had the top of his head terribly fractured, disclosing his brains, and his life was almost extinct. We next repaired to a large farmhouse situated between the two contending forces; and after the deadly missiles ceased to be hurled, the wounded rebels were carried into this house. Among the number of the boys in grey, who were writhing in the throes of death, was a mortally-wounded rebel officer, who was lying upon a lounge. He was endeavoring to make the best of his injuries, and his close proximity to that dreaded and mysterious monster,—death. The loss of blood awakened a burning thirst, and when he discovered our canteens suspended by our sides, he pleaded for the cooling fluid to refresh his languishing powers. We gladly complied with his dying request; but his wretched condition suggested painful thoughts concerning the misery and burning anguish of the damned in the infernal regions, where the request for but one drop of water to cool the parched and burning tongue cannot be granted.

We next repaired to the pine timber where the showers of bullets and the bursting bombs were, in the main, directed; and there horrid and ghastly scenes met our vision. The effects of war could be seen in all their horrible aspect: mangled human forms could be observed in almost any direction; from the youth in ruddy glow on through the different stages of human life; bodies of those in whom the life blood quickly flowed one hour before. But now the complicated machinery had stopped and the soul had taken its unknown flight. These were the first horrid scenes of death and carnage that we had witnessed, and they made deep impressions on our minds.

After the tumult was over we were ordered to return to our place of encampment. We had about fifteen miles to travel, and most of the march was made under cover of night. Our minds were full of the day's terrible disasters, and in our brains hundreds of thoughts revolved. When we reached Difficult Creek, where our halt had been made the same day, prior to the conflict, we were marching along rather promiscuously. We had crossed the bridge and were ascending a hill when, for some cause, one of the officers uttered a startling command. He must have been startled, judging from the tone and character of his command: "Halt, boys! My God, here we are right among them!" The order seemed to emanate from a terror-stricken heart, and it sent a thrill of terror through the unsystematized ranks. To increase the confusion, there was a gun fired by some soldier whose nerves were perhaps unstrung; and that, together with the wild and eccentric command, was a sufficient basis for demoralization and a pell-mell retreat. I, with a number of my comrades, rushed beneath the high embankment for protection from the expected assaults of our enemies and the volley of deadly missiles that might be hurled into our confused ranks. I frankly admit that I was frightened, and even the hairs of my head were disturbed. I shall long remember the horrid and hurried sounds of the retreating feet, down the acclivity and over the bridge that spanned Difficult Creek. The last command that I heard amid the consternation was, "Don't run, boys; stand up to them!" But the running pressure was too great to effect a stand.

It was a false alarm. I never learned who the officer was, or what occasioned his untimely orders. I concluded that perhaps he had fallen asleep on his horse and these terrible visions confronted him in the form of dreams. I there learned the injurious results of a false alarm, and the little service that can be expected of troops when not properly regulated and retained in orderly positions. Here let me deduce an illustration to impress the necessity of good discipline in the spiritual army. A church cannot prosper without good government. God is a God of order and his spiritual army must harmoniously respond to Christ the Captain of their salvation. False alarms in the spiritual ranks have occasioned great havoc and utterly incapacitated the soldiers for their spiritual conquests. No wonder an eminent spiritual officer said: "For if the trumpet give an uncertain sound, who shall prepare himself for the battle?"

CHAPTER IV.

Constant Vigilance Required. — Characteristics of the Lord's Army. — Return to Camp Pierpont. — Advance Toward Manasses. — Exposed to the Fury of a Rain-storm. — My Confinement in the Hospital in Alexandria. — My Ride, after Partial Recovery, to Manasses, on the Tender of a Locomotive, unprotected from the Wintry Blasts. — Some Reflections.

WE have shown to you, by an experimental knowledge, that the drills and manipulations of the natural army must be prompt, accurate and timely. If they are not similar in a spiritual army, how can there be success? I have seen, comparatively speaking, more looseness and inactivity in the spiritual army than I discovered in the natural; and it is indeed mortifying to see such relaxation in church government. It ever indicates weakness and ultimate defeat. It requires constant exercise of the spiritual weapons and incessant vigilance upon the part of every soldier to retain zeal, dexterity and tact in our spiritual achievements. The cross is the criterion and the animating power of the child of God. Every principle of religion and every mandate in the economy of grace is permeated by the power of the cross. It sometimes imposes long and weary marches, night vigils, and fatiguing toil, exposure to inclement weather, painful struggles in order to gain a conquest over the malice, hatred, scorn and revenge of men and devils. The opposition of these forces but spurs the live soldier of the cross to earnest zeal and powerful diligence in the noble and heaven-ratified feats of the spiritual warfare.

> "Am I a soldier of the cross,
> A follower of the Lamb,
> And shall I fear to own his cause
> Or blush to speak his name?"

But how must a confused, demoralized, and flesh-conquered spiritual army appear to the trained eye of its Great Commander, Christ, who confronted the Arch-enemy himself in the gloomy trial in the desert, who withstood his charges and subterfuges, and evinced his conquering might by defeating the infernal designs of his antagonist? He could impart to his followers no easier terms than he himself met. He said, "In the world ye shall have tribulation: but be of good cheer; I have overcome the world." Therefore in his strength we should meet the storms of battle and endure the hardships of our spiritual warfare, being ever animated to active diligence in the heated contests with the opposing powers. O wonderful army of the Lord, as you value your spiritual conquest over earth and hell and your glowing reception by the Divine Commander and his celestial retinue at his bright appearing, retain your equilibrium now by the power of faith, and your orderly positions in the spiritual ranks! Let there be no false alarms, and no disgraceful retreats! Let there be no carnal ease, or pandering to the unhallowed lusts of the flesh, but endure hardness as good soldiers of Jesus Christ, and, like a well-disciplined army, imitating the life and character of your worthy Commander, press your way so that you may take part in the grand reunion in eternity, and experience the effulgent manifestation in glory which will surpass in excellence and beauty all military prowess and grandeur. But I must return again to the narrative of my army life.

After the fright and confusion at Difficult Creek, we were collected, in order to continue our march to Camp Pierpont. We arrived in camp about the third watch of the night, fatigued by the march and our minds absorbed in the impressive scenes and experiences of the battle. We now resumed the ordinary routine of camp life. There was nothing notably unusual in our immediate line of operation till the breaking up of our winter quarters. This occurred about at the end of winter, and was an event worthy of note in the military movements of the army of the Potomac. The Confederates were occupying Manasses, and the Union forces were advancing in the direction of the enemy's lines. A laborious and hazardous march was before us. Each soldier was furnished with a gum blanket to protect him from the elements. And surely the rains descended, and the storms beat upon us, and our strength and endurance were tested to the utmost. I shall never forget our long and weary day's march when the rain was rapidly descending. We marched along, bearing our luggage, which was heavy, for everything was saturated with rain. When night overtook us, we lodged in the woods. The rain was still pouring down, and, amid the damp and chill, we had nothing but our gum blankets to shelter us. We were wet to the skin, and the rapid descent of the rain made it impossible for us to kindle fires. About midnight the rain ceased and it blew up cold. Fires were then, with difficulty, kindled and we crowded so close to them that we burned the stockings on our feet.

I caught a severe cold, which settled on my lungs. It resulted in pneumonia, which almost ended my mortal career. When we reached Alexandria I was confined to the hospital for a time. My sickness made quite an inroad on my constitution, and I did not recover from the shock during my life in the army. I fought hard against being prostrated by the malady, but with all my efforts to overcome it, I failed. My inability to conquer disease was manifest. It preyed upon my vitals, till I was rendered weak and helpless, and my condition was pronounced dangerous. But at the same time I did not feel much alarmed, for the reason, perhaps, that I did not realize that my case was critical. When I became convalescent I urged my restoration to the regiment, but was decidedly unfit. The doctor told me so, and even proposed to procure my discharge from army service. He knew more of the injurious effects it would have upon my system than I did, and had I taken his council I presume my health would have been better in subsequent life. It was then rumored that regimental bands would soon be dismissed from the service by an act of Congress, and as I had already endured many hardships with them, I desired to have the honor of returning home with them.

Our division was soon transferred from Alexandria to Manasses. The day in which the transfer was effected I shall not soon forget. My physician offered me conveyance in an ambulance, but I was so anxious to be with my comrades that I was willing to assume the responsibility of the trip. We were conveyed on the Orange and Alexandria R. R. to Manasses. The day was very inclement, rendered so by cold and sleet. My position was on the locomotive tender, every available place in the cab being occupied by officers. I would far better have taken the doctor's advice, and had a comfortable place in an ambulance.

But because of my strong will in determining the course I had, weak and indisposed as I was, I had to abide the consequences. We arrived at night, and knew not but that our night's lodging would be under the open canopy of heaven. Fortunately for us, in this extremity, the rebels had not succeeded in demolishing their winter habitations, and we became the occupants. Never was shelter from the storm more appreciated than by us soldiers at that time. We were contented with our comforts, but did not know how long we should enjoy them.

If soldiers in the natural army must undergo such severities, and forego the comforts and pleasures of life, what should the soldiers of the cross of Christ not be ready to endure to gain an immortal crown? Christ never promised his followers ease and comfort in this life. To be a soldier of Jesus Christ and march under the Christian banner means reverses, disappointments, crosses, losses, but also many joys and consolations. The brave soldier in his life of hardships should cause the formal and flesh-indulgent professor of religion to hide his face in shame. How many thousands are there in our day and age who say, Lord, Lord, but are far from obeying his commands? It is one thing to present a crucified Christ in the glow of oratory, and quite another to obey him and live as he did. It is easier to theorize than to practice, and a large proportion of the so-called Christian religion to-day, I fear, is only theory—covenants without sacrifices, "having a form of godliness but denying the power." But genuine religion, the kind that shows its fortitude in the shock of battle, and stands undaunted when the infernal forces are raging and combinations of human powers are charging in the contest, is rare indeed and, I think, will ever be.

It is said that when a certain military officer read the poem, "Why should the Spirit of Mortal be Proud?" he was so impressed by the beautiful sentiment, that he said he would rather be the author of that poem than to be the famous conqueror of an army. That poem was also President Lincoln's favorite. But I say, in all sincerity, that I would rather be a true, self-denying, and valiant soldier of the cross than to be either the author of the poem, or the world-renowned conqueror of an army with banners. True and faithful warriors of the cross are not so plenty as persons might conclude by giving the matter only a superficial examination; but where they exist they are very precious in the eyes of the Lord. They will one day appear in a splendor that all the grandeur of military display cannot compare with, and I should like to be associated with the Crucified One, that I might share the victor's crown.

The natural soldier is content with food and raiment and a shelter from storm and rain. He asks for no mansion, beautified and adorned with costly materials and fitted for the gratification of the flesh. Yet he lives in anticipation of the final conquest over his enemies, and talks and sings of the time when the cruel war shall end. Being inured to the hardships of this life, he contents himself with his present inconveniences in the hope of future relief and restoration to his friends and home, however much his prospects may be involved in uncertainty. But look at the professors of the religion of the humble, crucified Savior, the "man of sorrows and acquainted with grief," that humble Jesus who laid aside his glory voluntarily, and though he was rich, yet, for the purpose of redeeming the lost, became poor, that they by his poverty might be made rich, who exposed himself to the elements, observed vigils, and wrestled with God in the night watches, labored amid the bitter retorts, frowns, sneers and insults of his enemies, bore the cruelties, and braved the hardships of this life, and erected a standard by which sin, that bane of humanity, is to be conquered by God's powerful means of grace. How do the pomp, ostentation and ease of professing Christians compare with the humble aspect and life of Christ in his course of self-denial and trial? How does their life of ease and prosperity, their gaudy attire, their costly and magnificent edifices, reared for the purpose of worship, compare with the life of the lowly Christ? Is there any comparison? Can they reconcile the two ways by any process of reasoning? I know these interrogations will seem very impertinent, and my argument will grate upon their finely-cultured ears; but it is true, nevertheless, and with their polished arguments they cannot gainsay it. If the dying thief were to afford a precedent for God's mercy in the painful extremity of human life, I could see more propriety in presenting it in the form of a solace to the mangled, bleeding, dying soldier, regretting the errors of his life, and pleading with God for mercy when about crossing to the mysterious bourne, than to those who have prayed and argued fluently through life.

I assert that, if the world was not so overstocked with sham religion, the lusts and propensities of carnality would not be so prevalent as they are, and as a result, there would not be as much bloodshed and misery. It will be a wonderful and awful judgment when all sins are traced to their origin; and perchance many a sanctimonious religionist will be disclosed as the person through whom great and dire offences have come. "In the world there must needs be offences, but woe unto that man through whom the offence cometh;" that is, the condition of the world is such, since sin wields almost universal sway, that, as a result of its prevalence, there will be offences; but woe to the man who, to enhance his carnal interests and become famous, will secure God-dishonored advantages, "having men's persons in admiration because of advantage," and gild them over with a form of religion, so as to conceal what they really are. That man will be pointed out to his blind adherents in the Judgment Day as being the notorious one through whom the offence came, and by whose hell-controlled influence they have been led to a miserable end, and to endure punishment as God's justice may see fit to measure to each one for his offences. In proportion as the leaders in offensive channels occupy positions of prominence and renown, so will they be rendered conspicuous in enduring the greater punishment in the avenging day of God Almighty. This world is a stupendous arena, and we are all playing our respective parts. But there will be an inspection in the future, when the character and deeds of each will be fully known. When I place before me the grand and awful disclosures of that day, this world with all its busy scenes of pomp and show wanes into insignificance; and though the almost dominant sway of a formal religion seems to be beating back every humble and vital effort of the Crucified, yet, with my cross-enlightened faculties I feel like utilizing all my ransomed powers in the unpopular channel of self-crucifixion, where my Exemplar trod life's lowly way, in prospect of the joy set before him, so let all the votaries of the cross bear the shame and hatred and revenge of the opposing forces of sin until relieved at the crowning day.

CHAPTER V.

Description of War Scenes by Prof. Snyder. — A Visit to the Battle Field of Bull Run. — Review of Troops by Pres. Lincoln. — The Army of the Potomac. — Terrors of Peninsular Campaign. — Gen. Reynolds amidst a Shower of Bullets. — Serious Reflections while on the Field of Carnage. — Attacked by the Rebels at Gaines' Mill. — Carrying away the Wounded. — Some Thoughts Suggested by the many Dismal Scenes Connected with Carnal Warfare.

I DIGRESSED from my description of our movements in the army at our arrival at Manasses, and I will now insert the description as given by Prof. W. H. Snyder, of Oxford, Chester Co., Pa., who was my true friend and associate during my connection with the Band of the Second Pennsylvania Reserve Regiment. We both played B-flat cornets. His description is as follows: "While encamped in the vicinity of Manasses, a few of the Band one day visited the scene of the first Bull Run battle field. We noted all the points of interest, the place where Col. Cameron fell, where the Rhode Island battery was charged upon, the pike down which the army retreated, and the famous stone bridge that caused so much confusion, the shallow graves in many places, where, even then (less than a year after) the bones of many protruded through the scanty earth that covered them. All this we saw and returned to camp, musing on the rude hand of war that caused the soil of the 'Mother of Presidents' to drink the blood of brothers and citizens of our common country, who had now become enemies. From the vicinity of Manasses a series of movements and marches followed until we found ourselves on the north bank of the Rappahannock, near its source, and opposite Fredericksburg. All the bridges here had been burned, and steamboats too, the remains of which were visible. We crossed the river on pontoons and occupied the place for a short time. We were now in the command of Gen. McDowell. It was while encamped here at Fredericksburgh that our whole force was called together on one occasion to be reviewed by President Lincoln. I can see them yet as they rode down the line, Gen. McDowell in full uniform, making a fine appearance, and the President in citizen's dress, with pale and weary look, riding awkwardly along, seeming as if he did not feel at rest amid the martial display. Along with the reviewing party and in contrast to the bright uniforms of the staff officers, was another citizen from our own State, Hon. Galusher A. Grow; then speaker of the National House of Representatives.

The last of Maj. McCall's Division, composed of the Pennsylvania Reserves, were all placed on steamboats and taken to re-inforce McClellan's army before Richmond. We landed at White on the Pamunky river, marched to the extreme right of the Union lines and took position at Mechanicsville, from which point we could see the spires of Richmond. About the last of June, 1862, Gen. Lee suddenly withdrew Stonewall Jackson from McDowell's front and he threw himself with all his characteristic vigor against McClellan's right wing, and that, of course, struck the Pennsylvania Reserves. Mechanicsville, Gaines' Mill, Charles City, Cross Roads and Malvern Hill followed in quick succession, which gave us some experience of the terribleness of war. This series of engagements was known as the 'seven day's fight,' and doubtless was not exceeded in hardship and endurance for the same length of time, by any in the war. The sights, incidents, and dangers of that memorable campaign will live in our memories as long as life shall last. The 4th of July, 1862, we spent at Harrison's Landing on the James River. In the last of that month an order, in obedience to a recent act of Congress, came to muster out all Regimental Bands, and so we left the army just before its return to Alexandria, to take part in the second battle of Bull Run. Though returning home thus early in the contest, many members of the Band re-entered the service of the Government and served in various ways during the war."

This affords a condensed but correct description of our various operations in the Army of the Potomac. But if we were to give a detailed account of the terrible slaughter and horrid scenes of suffering during that campaign, it would surely demonstrate, as Prof. Snyder indicates, that we experienced the terribleness of war. The forces were gradually concentrated, and the clouds were gathering for the storm of battle. An uneasiness pervaded the hosts prior to the outpouring of vengeance. There was a feeling of dreadful suspense before the thunder of battle was heard. One feels, to some extent, relief when the spell of anxiety is broken by the explosion of the deadly storm that is inevitable. The contending armies are ranged in battle array. Soon the huge artillery introduces the direful work of carnage and death. Cannon balls are hurled in every direction. Bombs are bursting in the air over the charging columns of soldiers. Everywhere the scene is enlivened by active movements. Military skill and ingenuity are taxed to the utmost, and death and sorrow reign. Amid the din of battle, the shrieks of the wounded and dying are heard. Mutilated and mangled forms are seen all around; the blood oozes from the veins of the unfortunate victims, and while one tries to rescue them he is all the time in the storm of deadly missiles. There is no telling who will be the next to agonize in death. One moment one's body is unharmed and active, the next it is dreadfully lacerated, and the blood is streaming from his veins. The adage, " Death is no respecter of persons," is here verified. The rich and poor, the wise and ignorant, fall alike under its resistless sway. Oh what a scene of waste and desolation! To a serious, candid thinker how awful the thought of eternity, and the possibility of being launched into it at any moment! If we would prepare for death, let us do it before destruction comes as a whirlwind. How much better to prepare when all is calm and serene than to do otherwise! Man's period of probation is precious, so let him not fail to utilize the means and opportunities of grace. A "God save me" has but little influence with him who holds the destinies of men, if there has been no effort made to lay hold of the means of salvation. "Be ye therefore ready," is a vitally important and pertinent command. Let us heed the signals of warning in the acceptable time. We musicians were employed in the ambulance corps and our business was to secure the wounded while the battle was raging, and bear them on stretchers to the surgeons. The awful spectacles of bleeding misery that met our eyes, and the piercing groans, filled us with horror. But we were in it and must make the best of our situation. My thoughts were serious, and prayerful too. I desired a prolongation of life, for I knew, by my early conceptions of the Bible, that I was unprepared for a sudden departure to the eternal world. In this time of desolation and jeopardy I could vividly see my forfeited opportunities. How sweet to learn truth in the time of our youth! It will guide us safely through all the dangers of life, and save us when the powers of earth are in strife.

The first day was one of sorrow and gloom, surpassing any I had ever before witnessed. I saw Gen. Reynolds in the midst of a spirited fire, when cannon balls on their mission of death and destruction, were demolishing trees and ploughing the earth in their fury, when musket balls were incessantly whizzing by on their swift mission of death: amid this furious storm of battle I saw the General in the line of his duty, exhibiting courage before his men at the very critical juncture when such a manifestation was required. A brave officer can wield great influence over his men in such an hour of peril, by being self-possessed, composed and courageous, and Gen. Reynolds evidently was courageous, composed and self-possessed. He was an expert rider and a thoroughly-drilled soldier in every respect. I shall never forget his calm and brave appearance at the battle of Mechanicsville. I have thought of him many times since he was killed at Gettysburg. He had trained himself by an elevated military standard and there was a natural influence wielded by his personal presence in the storm of conflict. Such men, were they Christianized to the same extent, could be utilized, by the grace of God, in any and every emergency of the Christian conflict. They would be prepared to meet the outbreaks of human malice and revenge, and with their noble characteristics of endurance and fortitude, they would meet the fate of imprisonment and the most cruel torture of men to evince their loyalty to truth and equity. Such were the characteristics of heroic Paul and Peter. Had their training been in the military school they doubtless would have been in the van of the army and would have evinced a spirit of bravery and adroitness that would have served as a precedent for others. But God recognized in them the proper constituents of character to subserve his own righteous purpose, and hence trained them to be leaders in his more refined and superior army, the weapons of whose warfare are of a more exquisite temper and grade, and operate upon the finer sensibilities of man. The noble feats of this mighty warfare are not accomplished in blood and the demolition of the exterior organism, but the darts of death, which kill and destroy sin in all its direful phases, are directed to the interior or spiritual heart, in order to overthrow the Satanic influence.

We digressed in our remarks from the battle scene at Mechanicsville. Our object is to deduce some practical illustrations from what we saw and experienced; for there is nothing that can impress incidents so indelibly on the mind as personal observation. That dark, tumultuous day at Mechanicsville will impress our memories while life endures. The Reserve Division, in all its burdened marches, privations and military duties had never before been in such a strain of anxiety as when engaged in the ardent contest of this dismal day. When the curtains of night were lowered, the shrieks and groans of the wounded writhing in the throes of death were still heard.

Many mothers' sons were crossing in intense agony to the mysterious bourne of death, and the dreary tidings, reluctantly borne to those bereaved mothers, caused their hearts and homes to be draped in mourning. Oh, who can measure the grief a fond and affectionate mother must feel at the reception of such tidings? The gloomy thought that she shall see the visage of her darling boy no more in this life, constantly pervades her mind. Oh, could she have been there in the dying hour, to soothe his anguish by her presence, and administer to his dying wants! She could with her loving hands have given him the cooling draught, so commonly pleaded for by the dying soldier,— the draught needed to allay the thirst caused by the loss of blood. She could have gently wiped the cold sweat from his brow, and she would have been the last to linger and to bend over him with intense anxiety, to see the flickering light become extinct. She would, with all her maternal sympathy and affection, have noticed the final effort of the heaving lungs, the last pulsations of the fainting heart. But in the absence of a mother's care and personal administration, how many a son in anguish died on the lone and cruel field of contest!

The booming of cannon was heard during the night. Now and then the darkness was dispelled by a fiery stream that issued from the cannon's mouth. Amid all these gloomy horrors we felt as though we were standing in the presence of grim Death. I shall never forget my position in a potato patch beneath an apple-tree, after dismal and hurried toils of the day and night were over, when the wounded and dying, so far as they could be procured, were in the surgeon's care. My mind was active, and my thoughts were serious. I felt as though I would like to be a humble Christian and knew that I was not one. I felt persuaded that I might have been one, had I obeyed my early convictions of truth and right. But how to be a soldier and a Christian, I could not see. I never could reconcile the two warfares, as my sentiments all through this work indicate. Hence my only wish and prayer would be that the mercy of God might prevail in my behalf and that I might be spared until a future opportunity might be afforded me to become reconciled to my Maker through his own divinely-appointed means. If we would frankly confess, we would be apprized of the fact that many serious thoughts are in the human mind in such hours of peril. .

The night of dismal anxiety passed away. Whether the scenes of life be prosperous or adverse, time is ever on the wing. The band members were commanded to assist in caring for the wounded. We were not instructed as to the military movements of the day, and when summoned away on duty, some of us hung our instruments in an old cabin, expecting to attend to loading the wounded in the ambulances and then return and secure them. But we had no occasion to return, for the rebels secured them for us.

We retreated to Gaines' Mill, where we were again attacked by the Confederates. A hot engagement and great slaughter followed. We were now experiencing the dread realities of a soldier's life. It was one woeful contest after another until everything seemed to be enveloped in the dire calamities of war. There seemed to be comparative stillness before the assault was made, but we were quickly ushered into the storm and thunder of battle. We followed the charging columns and in advance of us arose dense columns of smoke. On stretchers we carried from the field the wounded soldiers, lacerated and bleeding, to the surgeons, who might give them timely, surgical assistance. It was only a repetition of the horrors of war; we again witnessed some painful sights. Some were slightly, and others mortally wounded. There was no evading the gloomy disaster, and at times our chances for surviving the conflict seemed almost hopeless. We heard the shouts of triumph as the charging hosts advanced in the storm of battle. To have a clear conception of the disastrous effects of two contending forces in battle, it must be personally observed.

It is not the design of this work to give a detailed account of the army movements in this series of engagements, called the seven days' fight, but only some of the general characteristics. I saw many terribly-mangled forms. I helped to bear to the surgeons a lieutenant officer, who was struck in the breast by a fragment of a bombshell. In respiring, the air seemed to escape through the bleeding aperture. In his zeal for conquest over the opposing forces his eye seemed to scan the movements of his men, and he appeared to be more interested in their attainments than in his own life. There was bravery in the highest degree. Men, animated by the spirit of patriotism, sacrificed their lives for the sake of their country. It showed their honesty and loyalty to the Government, and their respect for the oath of allegiance which they had taken. This suffering officer disclosed his integrity, too, in a dangerous crisis, when it was done at the hazard of his life. This courage was often exhibited by men who had more respect for their country than for God. Officers and soldiers, who would take God's name in vain and violate the higher and purer laws of heaven, would stand undaunted before the cannon's mouth and curse their enemies in the storm of battle. I have heard men speak of the brave spirit of the soldier in the critical contest, as palliating all disloyal deeds in the sight of their Maker, and make the sacrifice of their life a condition of acceptance with God. Now, while I always admired a spirit of bravery and loyalty to the Government, yet I cannot endorse making that a ground of acceptance with God. A soldier will only obtain the honor and the renown incident to his life; and when he is used by the Almighty as an agent to punish the lawless and disobedient, he can only anticipate the glory and remuneration that accrue in the line of his military achievements. But the soldier of the cross should evince the same zeal in suffering and the same self-sacrifice for the cause he has solemnly espoused and the allegiance he has promised to the superior spiritual government, and retain his loyalty and faith even to the sacrificing of his life.

Our sympathies often warp our judgment in the effort to discriminate between these two elements, and if we had no higher standard than our own mind, we might be excusable. But God has given us a criterion and the only real assurance of acceptance with him is to be controlled by his appointed means. When he says, Employ the carnal weapons, do so; when he says, "Put up the sword into his sheath, for he that taketh the sword shall perish with the sword," do not try to make his command doubtful and appeal to the authority of the law to justify your course. That would be like King Ahab going to Ramoth-Gilead. He consulted the three hundred false prophets and they ratified his course. But Jehoshaphat, who was more God-fearing, desired the predictions of a despised prophet of the Lord. His testimony conflicted with the testimony of four hundred prominent men, and the prophecy of the man of God was rejected. But Ahab failed; the testimony of his four hundred prophets was scattered to the winds and he perished with the sword because he did not bear it in obedience to the Divine command. And I say (with no feeling of disrespect to the Government) that Christ says to his followers, "My kingdom is not of this world, else would my servants fight;" and it required much training by him to give his disciples a clear conception of the spirituality of his kingdom. Just prior to his ascension they questioned him with reference to this matter. "Wilt thou at this time restore the kingdom to Israel?" They looked for the restoration of a temporal kingdom. But they were fully established on this question after the descent of the Holy Spirit on the day of Pentecost. Then they looked at his example and his instructions, relative to such a life from a spiritual stand-point. No doubt Peter could see the propriety and realize the force of the Savior's command to put "up the sword in his sheath." Whoever endeavors to establish Christ's kingdom by the power of the sword, will fail.

Night again came on and ended the day of weary contest. Many hundreds had taken hurried flight into the dismal regions of death. O what a subject for thought for the mind that has some degree of candor and seriousness! Who can ever obliterate from memory these mortal agonies? While the field is strewn with the ghastly dead, others are continually crossing the turbid waters. We are confronted on every side by the horrible prospect of blood, pain, and death. This awful experience certainly impresses on our minds the terribleness of war.

I saw a young soldier under the resistless power of death, who dreaded very much to die. It was right in the heat of the contest, when we were busy bearing the wounded to the surgeons in the rear of the contending forces. The jugular vein was severed and the blood was streaming from his throat. His nearness to death threw him into consternation and in his anxiety to live he cast his wistful eyes toward the surgeons. Anguish looked out of his eyes that were darkening in the shades of death and his visage was stained with the blood that was rapidly escaping from his veins. While many mangled forms lay before me, this young man, so reluctant to leave this life, arrested my attention more particularly. But leaving him to meet his gloomy fate, I had to go again into the smoke and storm of battle to convey more of the wounded and helpless to the rear for surgical assistance, thinking all the while that I might soon be lying among the wounded or dying.

CHAPTER VI.

Retreat from Charles City Cross Roads to Malvern Hills. — Fierce Assault by the Confederate Army. — End of the Peninsular Campaign. — Musicians Mustered out at Harrison's Landing. — Sorrowful Separation from our Late Comrades. — Down the James River to Fortress Monroe, and on to Baltimore. — Suffering from Disease Contracted while in the Swampy Regions of the Peninsula. — Our Departure from Baltimore to the Perkiomen Bridge. — Music and its Charms. — A Siege of Small-pox. — Attendance at Collegeville Seminary. — Determination to Enlist on a Man-of-War.

SUPERIOR numbers of the Confederates assaulted us in the retreat at Charles City Cross Roads; another fierce engagement followed and the same horrible aspect of blood and carnage met our gaze. Nearly everywhere we saw mutilated forms, all stained with blood, some ghastly in death's cold embrace: men whose visages bore the marks of intelligence, but they could no more utilize it on earth; they could take no part in the things of this life. Life was extinct and they were ready for the soldier's grave. Night again came on and ended the bloody contest.

The army kept falling back to Malvern Hills, where the Confederates gave us another fierce assault. We were under the protection of the gunboats on the James River, and their terrific bombardment threw consternation into the enemy's ranks and held them at bay. We were held in reserve during this engagement. From the hilltops we observed the armies advancing in battle array and saw the wounded carried back from the arena of cruel contest. The soldiers entered the scene of battle fully equipped. Regularly and orderly the columns poured into the shock of bloody contest, bearing the flags of their respective regiments. Those flags designate the nation's power, and never is there a stronger demonstration of this than in the storm of battle.

Here another forcible illustration can be deduced to impart instruction to the spiritual army and show the strength of her equipments, when orderly retained in her efforts to achieve her spiritual conquests. There evidently should be a distinction in the external appearance of the church and the world. The church should be known as well as an army with banners. The church that appears as gorgeously decorated as those who dwell in kings' palaces, has lost her latitude. The Gospel prescribes modest apparel for Christians, and when these humble requirements of the Gospel are discarded, the power of the church is weakened. If she would conquer pride in others, she must be humble. To be assured that we have Christian humility in the heart, we must have the signs on the exterior. In this respect the natural army is more precise than the so-called spiritual army. It is more difficult to regulate spiritual than secular government. The flesh incessantly wars against the spirit, and by indulging its carnal desires for show and worldly emolument the greater part of the so-called Christian world is overcome. But if the distinctive characteristics are retained, there will be good execution; and though the great work, ratified by heaven, is hidden from the wise and prudent, yet the result of her humble mission will be disclosed in the crowning day.

The battle of Malvern Hills ended this series of military contests in the Peninsular Campaign. We, as musicians, were mustered out of service at Harrison's Landing on the James River. After warfare rest was pleasant. The prospect of seeing our friends and home, and of a respite after cruel hardships was indeed an enjoyable one. But to go and leave our friends, endeared to us by hardships and adversities, was sad and painful. Our separation was effected at Harrison's Landing, and as our comrades came to take their leave, we felt sad to think that scenes of horror like those we had witnessed together in the past, were awaiting them in the future. Many of our fellow-soldiers had suffered such intolerable anguish that they desired death as a relief from their woes, and it was probable that some of our surviving comrades would share the same gloomy fate. The prospects of this life are very uncertain and especially when human hostilities rage. I had a special concern for my brother younger than myself who had taken quite an active part in the series of engagements, but, like myself, had escaped from every bloody contest uninjured. I feared that I should never see his face again. It was sad to think that I could return to the home so dear to us both and see our mother and brother and sisters, who were all so anxious for our welfare and the prolongation of our lives, while he must be left behind, exposed to cruel hostilities and the hardships incident to the life of a soldier. With such feelings I left him.

We boarded the steam-boat and were carried down the James River to Fortress Monroe, then across the Chesapeake Bay to the City of Baltimore. I returned worn and emaciated by sickness and exposure, my constitution having been shocked by the siege of pneumonia which I passed through at Alexandria, which disease was contracted during the tedious march from Camp Pierpont to the above-named place. In addition to this I had a severe attack of diarrhœa during the Peninsular Campaign, occasioned by drinking the surface water in that low and swampy region. Many a poor soldier died of the disease in that gloomy, sickly place, but I had so far escaped the grim monster, death, and was crossing the Chesapeake on my homeward trip. Not one of the number composing our band was killed or wounded. A soldier selected from the military ranks and employed in the band as drummer was taken prisoner by the Confederates during the succession of battles but had been restored to Federal lines prior to our departure; but was remanded to the company from which he had been taken. Not having entered the Government service as a musician, the act of Congress to release from the United States service all regimental bands did not reach him. Two of our number had been discharged because of sickness, and the rest of us were all homeward bound. Most of us had secured instruments again and were solicited to play our military strains as we journeyed toward home. Having had one year's steady practice, we had become somewhat proficient in the science and could perform our parts well.

We went home with deep emotions, because we were released from the woes of military life and had the prospect of home associations. I might illustrate from this event the entrance of the soldiers of the cross into the land of rest. The Prophet Isaiah depicts the scene in triumphant splendor: "Then shall the redeemed of the Lord return with singing and everlasting joy upon their heads; the mountains shall break forth from before them into singing and all the trees of the fields shall clap their hands." This is a figurative representation of the universal joy that shall attend the triumphant admission of the victorious soldiers of the army of Christ to the glory world. The strains that will grace that celestial reunion must be learned amid the hardships, self-denials, crosses, losses, disappointments and everything incidental to our spiritual warfare in this life. He who does not experience the contests against sin in its diversified operations and the Prince of the power of the air wielding his Satanic wiles, will never know the thrills of ecstatic joy that shall permeate the souls of the redeemed when Christ in his glory shall appear to release them from the warfare. Martial music will animate the soldier in military life, but it does not embolden the spiritual soldier in his spiritual campaign. That requires music that is finer and sweeter,—music that tends to inspire the spiritual senses. That music must be tuned from the world above. O that the soldiers of the cross would learn the strains well! Let there be no discord in the melodies.

We made the welkin resound with our national airs in the City of Baltimore after the waters of the Chesapeake were crossed. We were conveyed from there to Philadelphia by rail. At each prominent place we gave notice of our arrival by the music of the band. I do not believe we ever performed our parts more enthusiastically than when we were nearing our old familiar landscape. This was the second time that I was spared to return from the army. At Norristown, the place of rendezvous of my first enlistment, we were furnished with a stage coach drawn by four horses and thus were escorted to the old familiar place called Perkiomen Bridge, to the residence of Judge Longaker. Many of our friends were there to welcome our return and we saluted them with several of the choice airs which we had frequently discoursed in the army service.

If I could now interest the people with the Gospel trumpet as we amused them then, it would afford me much consolation. But finely-cultured musicians, just as finely-cultured orators, have the preference in this world. It is much easier to stir up our passions by the artistic movements on an instrument and impress the sentiment of some war-like or romantic air than to thrill the soul and impress it with the deep sense and spiritual meaning of the sacred songs that are tuned from the world above. The senses of the soul must be refined and purified before they can appreciate the spiritual melody.

David, the sweet singer of Israel and an excellent performer on stringed instruments, exclaims, " Blessed are the people that hear the joyful sound." The joyful sound alluded to does not have reference only to the external ear and its attraction to the melody of song, or the harmonious accents of the finely-tuned instrument, but it is the music of heaven, thrilling the soul through this charming medium, thus renewing the spiritual life and bringing it back to its normal faculties. Our music had often made light and buoyant the hearts of the weary soldiers, on their long and fatiguing marches, and dispelled their gloom when the din and horrors of battle were over. The divine music lends its sacred charms to the soldiers of the cross amid hardships and perils, and animates them in their warfare against sin and the powers of hell. Our band-master had an exquisite ear for music, and was a good composer, so we had choice selections, and under his competent teachings discoursed some good music; we threw all our spirit into it on our return to the Keystone State.

Music has become the charm and attraction of the popular churches of our age, and, in connection with oratory and ostentation, is made a specialty. Unregenerated persons, and even skeptics and infidels, are often employed to do the singing and playing, and I am forced to the conclusion that spirituality is neglected. What a deep gloom will be felt in Babylon when her downfall occurs, when her traffic ceases, and her wealth, beauty, culture, magnificence and fame are all swept away. It is then that the superior music of heaven will be heard, the melodious song of the redeemed, who were trained in the hardships of the spiritual warfare, "and washed their robes and made them white in the blood of the Lamb." That celestial music will supersede the music of earth, and lead the redeemed soul into the higher strains of rapture and bliss. Oh that our hearts may be tuned to sing that beautiful song of the redeemed of the Lord in the land that is free from sorrow and death!

Well, we met our friends once more on the shores of time. It was wonderful to reflect upon the past, to review all our ups and downs in military life, the perils that attended us, and then realize that we were home again. But, although I was home with everything that seemed to aid my consecration to the Lord, yet I was too prone to say, like Felix of old, "Go thy way for this time, when I have a more convenient season I will call for thee." My jovial disposition and attachment to friends absorbed my attention, and the work of grace was still excluded. I, like many others, respected religion in others but was not yet willing to make the sacrifice required to obtain it. My heart was hardened: military life and music seemed to hold sway. O how our higher and native sensibilities can be fettered down to flesh and sense!

I soon after passed through a siege of small-pox, which disease was prevalent in our vicinity. Its ravages were loathsome, and it hurried many to eternity. This aroused my thoughts and reminded me of the uncertainty of life and my liability to leave the world unreconciled to God. My constitution was considerably broken down by the disease. I attended the seminary for a time at Collegeville, then under the supervision of Mr. Henry A. Hunsicker. But I was restless and discontented. I was not satisfied in the army and I was not satisfied out of it.

In the spring of 1863 I had quite a pleasant interview with Bro. Isaac Kulp on religion. In the course of our conversation he observed that I had been thinking more on that subject than he supposed, and I was much impressed with his zeal for the cause, and his concern for me, a poor wandering soul. But the burden with me was to start, and I presume that is the burden that many have to contend with. I went to live in Philadelphia, soon after this conversation with Bro. Kulp, and there followed my trade. But army intelligence, and the absence of many of my comrades in the war, filled me with uneasiness and discomfort. I had no pleasure in anything. And no wonder I was restless, knowing my duty to God and not doing it. That is what makes many a soul uneasy and wretched. In this my apparent extremity I concluded to enlist on a man-of-war.

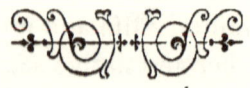

On the Dark Blue Sea.

The sailor boy, in our picture, has a fine view of his surroundings from his elevated
position on the mast-head. While many hardships fall to his lot, he has
also his happy hours, and we here see him in all his glory.

CHAPTER VII.

Deciding to Enlist on a Whaler. — Breaking the News of my Determination to the Home Circle. — On to New York and later on, to Bedford, Mass. — Initiated to my new Duties on Board the "Oriole." — My Feelings, as Expressed in a Poetic Effusion. — The Gulf Stream. — A Wise Dispensation of Providence.

ONE morning I started to the wharf to carry out my project; but I was interrupted in my course, and I subsequently regarded it as a divine interposition. I accosted a recruiting officer who was mustering men for the whale fishery. He spoke of his business and asked me if I did not feel like taking a voyage over the dark blue sea. At first I declined, not being willing to be turned from my purpose of enlisting on board of the war-vessel. But he persisted, as agents generally do, and thus drew my attention to his enterprise. I began to question him about the business, and after receiving some information I placed before my vision the romantic part of the enterprise, its roving character, novel features, and the great amount of knowledge and experience to be obtained, and I concluded to undertake the voyage. The agent tried to be sure of his victim and entreated me to repair at once to New York City at his expense; but I declined, intending to return home and apprize my mother, brother and sisters of my project.

I went home and was heartily welcomed by them all. They all seemed as anxious as ever for my welfare and prosperity, and were joyous and happy with my presence again in the circle of home. I was loath to mar their peace, hence had not the courage to break to them the doleful tidings of my early departure for the stormy ocean. Night came on, and still the gloomy project was not divulged. At last I disclosed the matter to my oldest brother, John, and requested him to submit it to mother after I had retired. Another troubled night was experienced. When morning dawned I reluctantly arose to behold my mother's countenance changed from joy to sorrow. Her feelings were sadly disturbed, and her restless and discontented son was the cause of it. The Prophet Isaiah says, "The wicked are like the troubled sea which cannot rest." I was truly in the sinful element of unrest and was destined soon to learn by experience the force of the prophet's language in reference to the troubled sea. I felt that I was the cause of the gloomy aspect of things at home, and as a result soon took my leave. Mother did not say much this time to have me change my purpose, for she knew by sad experience that I was determined to execute my projects when once they were fixed in my mind. I bade them all adieu at home and left for Perkiomen Bridge, where I took the stage-coach for Norristown. I sat on the top of the stage and on the way played several lively airs on the B-flat cornet, to dispel my gloom and drown my sorrow.

I met the recruiting officer in Philadelphia and boarded the train in the evening for New York. I felt lonely and sad as I swiftly rolled toward the famous city. This was my third separation from home and friends to engage in adventuresome enterprises; and no one could tell whether I would be permitted to return. We short-sighted creatures fail to measure the worth of privileges and blessings till they are forfeited and gone. Many a poor mortal is controlled and deceived by the power of sin and the prospective pleasures of life, until death and separation occur and leave him forlorn, his heart riven with anguish. Then he would give worlds to be restored to the blessings and golden opportunities of life once more.

I ate my breakfast in the City of New York the next morning with a man to whom I had been directed by my recruiting officer at Philadelphia. All faces were strange to me now and as I wandered off, perhaps my feelings were similar to those of the prodigal when he repaired to a far country. But I had made my choice as he did his, and I must abide the consequences. I could have repented in New York and turned back from my rash undertaking, but I was too resolute to do so. I left the great city in the evening on a steamer, and was conveyed down Long Island Sound on my way to Bedford, Mass.; from which port I expected to sail over the bosom of the great Atlantic. We reached Bedford the next day and I was soon accosted by men who appeared to be deeply interested in raw recruits. They proposed to furnish me boarding, lodging, clothing for the voyage, and, in short, the entire outfit. They seemed to be willing to grant all these without money and without price; but the money was expected out of the proceeds of the trip, and the price, I judge, was fixed at twice and, perhaps, three times the value of the goods.

I met many sons of the ocean here, and heard their thrilling tales of ocean life. I soon learned that the ship on which I was to sail was anchored in Buzzard's Bay, and having signed the articles of agreement, the raw recruits were all taken aboard the bark Oriole, anchored in the bay about one mile from shore. This introduced us to a new life, and we were left to look and wonder.

We took an observation of our strange residence. The existence of thirty-five men on such a limited craft seemed hardly possible. But I had given myself up to nautical authority, and it was not my prerogative to complain of the size of the family or dimensions of our home on the rolling deep. A colored man had charge of the ship riding at anchor, and we interrogated him in regard to the character of the life we were about to begin. His delineations were not very flattering, and we concluded that experience would disclose more of the reality of ocean life than ever we had learned by theory. We experimented on climbing the masts at our leisure, while the ship was still anchored; for it was a question whether we could effect a safe arrival at the top when our bark was liberated from her cable and was tossing on the sea. We found our floating home too unstable, even when stayed by the anchor, to scale the masts to the royal yard; and in consequence we had not much pride in our ability as seamen.

A few days after we went on board, the officers and the remainder of the crew came. We were now afforded a view of our whole family together. Different nationalities were suddenly ushered into our midst: quite a number of Portuguese and Americans, an Austrian, a German, a Spaniard, etc. The captain's name was Mr. Jernigan, of Martha's Vineyard; chief mate, Mr. Apes of New London, Connecticut; second mate, Mr. March, of New Hampshire; third mate, Mr. Ross, of New York; fourth mate, Mr. Silvia, a Portuguese. This afforded an officer for each whale-boat. There were four harpooners: one American, one Sandwich Islander, from Honolulu, Oahu Island,

and one Portuguese from Bruno Island, Cape Verde group; he was black as jet, with sharp features and long, straight, black hair; one white Portuguese, from the Azores Islands. This completed the corps of harpooners. There was a Spanish steward to wait on the officers, an African cook, black as jet, full of antics and resembling a clown; a ship-carpenter; a cooper, a German; a cabin-boy, about fourteen years of age, to wait on cabin officers; a steerage boy, to wait on harpooners, coopers and carpenters, who all occupied the steerage. The rest of the crew served before the mast.

We eyed our officers with much anxiety, for we knew that they were the main factors in the government of the floating craft. Nearly half of the men before the mast were able seamen, and the others were men who had had no experience in nautical life. The captain was an intelligent-looking man, and his looks did not belie him. He had an athletic movement, a commanding appearance, and a quick and ready speech. Leonard Apes had a bold, daring appearance; his eye was piercing, he had high cheek bones; in short, he was of grim and resolute mien. To become refractory under his rule and authority, indicated a recantation of rebellious ideas or extinction of life. Mr. March was a corpulent man; rather a pleasant-looking fellow so long as his equilibrium was not disturbed; but if his temper was ruffled, a storm of indignation was sure to follow. Mr. Ross was rather inclined to be good-natured, but long and continued familiarity with the rough usages of a mariner's life, and the temptations to debauchery surrounding him, tended to destroy his naturally good traits and rendered him depraved. He was skeptical, and would good-naturedly taunt and deride a professor of religion. Mr. Silvia was of a jovial disposition, but firm and decisive in duty and straightforward in the line of his duty. He was a full-blooded Portuguese and an expert and able seaman. Ability in seamanship is characteristic of the Portuguese race.

The officers and crew being aboard, all was animation and business, and when orders were given by the officers, the seamen having knowledge of the methods of operation, led off and the uneducated portion of the crew followed, with the prospect that they might live and learn. The first thing on the program was to heave the anchor. This was effected by a large windlass around which was wound the strong cable, attached to the anchor, sunk in the earth at the bottom of the bay. The command being given by the officer to heave the anchor, we worked vigorously, and soon the anchor began to slacken its firm hold in the earth beneath, as the ship moved to a position directly over it, and the crew was at the windlass. The heavy and powerful instrument rose, as the strength of the crew continued to be applied. In this operation the main dependence was on physical force, not on ingenuity. It served as a fair introduction to nautical labor and impressed us with the idea that our muscles must be firmly adapted to hard toil. The anchor having been raised and suspended at the bow of the ship, the steam tug-boat drew us out through the channel, marked by buoys, into the open sea. A pilot attended us through the difficult passage who was responsible, and not the captain, for the safety of the vessel. Beacon lights along the shore illuminate the passage at night and guide the mariner from the stormy main.

Once launched on the broad Atlantic, the steam tug left us and returned to the harbor. We were on the briny waters and the distance between us and the receding shore kept getting greater. The experienced mariners ascended the masts and went out upon the yard-arms to unfurl the sails, while we unskilled fellows assisted in hauling home the sheets, thus spreading the sails to the wind. We kept looking back to get the last glimpse of the shore before it disappeared from our vision and left us naught but the watery waste and the firmament. How novel the scene and how strange the experiences of this new life to which we were about to be inured! We were about to experience that which we knew by theory only, which we had read about in our comfortable homes, "A life on the ocean wave, a home on the rolling deep." The vessel moved along over the disturbed element, yielding to the swell of the sea. The unnatural motion began to make us landsmen feel as though we had departed from our natural element, and we had fearful apprehensions of suffering the consequences of the transition. The heaving surges soon made our stomachs heave, and we were rendered miserable and sick. Our life surely was unstable as water, and felicity, if any more there might be in reservation for us, was concealed behind the dismal clouds of the future.

>   In the prime of my life I wandered from home
>   About twenty-eight years ago,
>   To sail on the sea where the proud waves foam,
>   And the winds in their fury blow,
>
>   I soon was ploughing the wide-rolling deep,
>   Perchance to return never more.
>   I tell you, my friends, it makes a boy weep
>   To take his last look at the shore.
>
>   The golden sun set 'neath the far-swelling tide,
>   And the dark shades of night soon came on,
>   While the billows kept beating the ship on her side,
>   And I kept thinking of home.

A landsman at best is awkward at sea
  When the vessel is driven and tossed;
A surge from the windward will send him to lee,
  And he's ever afraid he'll be lost.

Our lesson on ropes was a study so new,
  And nautical phrases are strange:
Our words of address to the learned of the crew
  Would doubtless admit of some change.

Unfurling the Sails.

My ascension at first to the top of the mast,
  How I scaled the rope-ladder with care;
What a look of deep sadness my visage o'ercast,
  As I tremblingly rose in the air.

In sorrow I sat on the fore-royal-yard;
  My physical courage was low,
I thought, sure a mariner's life it is hard,
  'Tis a life of peril and woe.

This poem expresses the sentiments of one thus forlorn and distressed, thrown into a life and element new and untried, and endeavoring to perform difficult labor, in which he is unskilled. I had to be urged vehemently to the mast-head, and I shall not soon forget the command of the mate, and his angry frown as he scanned my uncouth movements in my perplexed condition and extremity of woe. I finally gained the summit with much difficulty, and to me it seemed to be a wonderful feat.

Had I tried as hard to counteract my carnal propensities and avail myself of the grace of God for the culture of the Christian traits of character, I might before then have made considerable progress in the divine life. How hard it is for us to learn the way of truth, especially in the days of our youth! But we all must learn sometime, that the yoke of the world is more galling, than the humble yoke of Christ. An acceptation of the yoke of Christ would have obviated all these heavy woes, and though I might have been contending against the opposing elements without, yet I should have been free from these stings of a guilty conscience within. We may rove over the earth and traverse the trackless main from pole to pole in pursuit of worldly enjoyments or fame, but they impart no peace to the mind or rest to the soul that is burdened with guilty fears. But the yoke which Christ imposes will afford the sure and solid peace and the glory which the world can neither give nor take away.

I had to remain two hours at the mast-head to become accustomed to the high position. When the time came for me to descend to the deck, fears were in the way again. In everything pertaining to ocean life and duties, I was untutored and unskilled. We even could not walk and retain our equilibrium until we got our sea-legs on. It was indeed sport for the trained mariners to behold the awkward efforts of the raw recruits. We were born and reared where the foundation under our feet was firm and stationary; but to become accustomed to a foundation that was incessantly moving was the lesson to be learned, and it required much effort to adapt ourselves to the motion of the ship so as to keep our equilibrium every time she careened over either on the starboard or larboard side. When the movements of our bodies were not adapted to the movement of the ship, which was constantly rolling from one side to the other, we would lose our balance and the result was a ludicrous fall.

Every evening we received lessons on the ropes and rigging of the ship. These were lessons almost similar to learning Latin terms in school. Our task was assigned us every evening by the mate, and the following evening we were expected to recite, and be prepared to fix upon the tablet of our memories the names of another new set of ropes. Thus we went through the routine of study and recitation until every rope was fixed on the mind. After they were indelibly impressed on the memory in their regular order, then we were required to discriminate. It was like learning the scale in music: after we learn to run the scale up and down, any one note in the scale is incidentally referred to, and thus the human voice is trained to give each note its exact sound. It is as necessary to be familiar with the ropes on a ship as a skillful performer on an instrument is with the different strings or keys of his instrument. Every rope has its importance and wields its power in the controlling of the ship. So, comparatively speaking, every command of the Bible has its influence in the saving of the soul. And any professed religious teacher who discredits the utility of any of the simple commands of Christ, and argues before his congregation that they are non-saving or obsolete, is just as inconsistent and nonsensical as a man who professes to be an able seaman and stands before nautical men and argues the non-utility of any of the ropes that are so orderly and systematically arranged. But he would not stand long before such intelligent beings and argue such nonsense, for they would not believe it. Neither will a professed spiritual teacher pursue such an unwise course before a spiritually intelligent audience, because they will discredit his teaching. God has not laid down a command in the Bible that is not designed to impart spiritual life to the soul. Hence, to be a genuine follower of Christ signifies to obey from the heart the entire form of doctrine which he has delivered to us in his revelation. It is without force, signification, or reason, to cry Lord, Lord, and not do the things which he commands. Christ means just what he says and we are to do just what he says, if we would be saved.

Practice makes perfect, the old adage says, and there is truth in the expression. We experienced it in our life at sea: the more we practiced the duties on board the vessel, the more expert we became in their accomplishment. But we had to accommodate ourselves to our condition and circumstances, and manifest a disposition and willingness to learn. Our awkward movements and blundering efforts were in course of time overcome, and we became more dexterous on the ropes and rigging. We could ascend the masts with confidence, occasioned by our improved ability. The fear that brought timidity was gone, and we realized the apparent severity of our officers to have been proper in its time and place. But any person with a reasonable amount of intelligence will not live long on board a vessel before he discovers that there is much to be learned in nautical science.

It is true that we find men in all the departments of life that are wise in their own conceits, and they are a class of people who are hard to instruct, for they always live in blissful ignorance of many important things that they might learn to their profit, if they were not afflicted with the enlargement of the brain. All along the pathway of Biblical times the truly wise and humble were molested more or less by this self-important class. Paul admonishes the early Christians "not to be wise in their own conceits." The wisdom alluded to has but a shallow foundation, is generally self-supporting, and being reared on a superficial conception of things, it falls of its own weight.

We passed along the stormy coast of Cape Hatteras and opposite the West Indies crossed the marvelous Gulf Stream and steered in the direction of the Cape Verde Islands near the coast of Africa. The Gulf Stream, issuing from the Gulf of Mexico and tending northward along the coast of the United States, designates its current through the deep by the warmth of its waters, and exerts a modifying influence upon the climate.

Here is one of the peculiar features of the Divine arrangement in the creation and preservation of this world. We need not advance far over this immense body of water before its currents and tides excite our admiration and wonder. There are many things a sailor does not know about the land, and there are many things a landsman does not know about the sea. Any candid and intelligent mind is thoroughly convinced of the wisdom and power of an overruling Providence. "They that go down to the sea in ships, see God's wonders on the deep." The vast earth with all its busy enterprises of civilization could not exist and thrive without this great sea. It must have the warm currents to modify its temperature. The vapor arising from this mighty ocean is borne upon the wings of the wind and deposited as refreshing showers over nearly all the world, imparting moisture to the soil, and life and growth to vegetation. In certain localities no doubt the choicest flavor is imparted to fruits by the currents of air from the tropics. All this evinces the unbounded wisdom of our Creator, in the creation of the earth with all these things for the comfort, sustenance and preservation of its innumerable inhabitants. And as he has beautifully arranged his natural creation, so, in like manner, does he preserve order and system in the spiritual realm, and if we would share the benefits of the spiritual currents and tides we must comply with the laws which bring us in contact with this influence. If the laws, that regulate this natural creation are so amazing, which only tend to the preservation of the natural lives of God's innumerable creatures, what must be the magnitude and force and beauty of the spiritual regulations which renovate and save the soul and impart to it life eternal? Most human beings content themselves with the natural elements of God's creation, tax their ingenuity to effect more profound and extensive researches into the mysterious operations of it, and so fail to study and apply the spiritual laws for the purification and salvation of the soul.

O thou restless, and rolling deep, what a subject for thought are thy swelling waters and all the mysteries concealed in thy unexplored depths! No human power can repel thy proud, foaming waves when, like a mighty giant, thou art aroused to thy wild and furious spell. But thy angry surges, by furious tempests driven, direct the candid and believing mind to the Power that hath formed thy amazing depths and controls thy threatening waves. Thou art an evidence of his handiwork, of the unfathomable depths of his wisdom and power which no finite intelligence can ever explore. Thou, Oh my beneficent Creator, hast directed me, I believe, to study thy greatness and omnipotence in this watery world. It is my school of discipline. Thou, Oh Lord, wilt employ this raging element, with its abrupt transitions from mildness to severity, as a correcting influence, to wean me from the attractions of earth and the powers of hell, which have long prevented my soul from being united in humility and love to thee.

CHAPTER VIII.

The Cape Verde Islands. — Lessons at the Helm. — Bravo Island. — The Torrid Zone. — Our first Attempt at Whale Capture. — Disposing of the Blubber. — Some Facts about the Whale, its Size, General Appearance, etc. — Our Stormy Passage around Cape Horn. — My Lonely Watch on a Stormy Night. — Solemn Reflections and New Resolves.

CROSSING the great Atlantic we came to the Cape Verde Islands. On the voyage thither our experience in nautical labor was extended. It became our duty to box the compass and learn to steer the vessel. Each helmsman was obliged to take his position at the helm for the space of two hours at a time, at the expiration of which he tolled the bell suspended above the binnacle. The tolling of the bell was a signal for relief after the two hours had expired. The raw recruits or unskilled sailors had to accompany an experienced mariner to the wheel and take lessons in steering the ship. We watched him and thus obtained the theoretical part first. Then we tried the practical part while he stood by; and if the ship became unmanageable in our hands, he helped us out of the difficulty by seizing the helm and controlling it himself, thus affording us a better idea of its practicability both by precept and example.

Thus we were by degrees trained in this art, and were soon capable of controlling the helm. Good management at the helm greatly facilitates the passage of the ship through the contending waves. It is all easy and natural to the accomplished helmsman. Some, of course, have a greater adaptability to the art than others. A very slight movement of the helm will change the course of the vessel on her swift flight through the yielding element. The apostle James understood this when he drew his practical illustration from it, to impress the character of the human tongue. A ship in the wide, turbulent deep is much easier to control than the tongue of man. The tongue is a difficult member of the body to control in this world of iniquity, where the surges of sinful passion roll. Our nature is depraved and contaminated by sin, and the tongue, being " set on fire of hell," sets ablaze " the whole course of nature;" and in the storm of human passion and indignation the curses and imprecations roll from the polluted lips of man. When sinful passion is allayed and the storm is lulled, then the tongue may be induced to bless God and pour out the praises of the Creator's name. But the temptations of life and the sad reverses in this campaign of sin and strife, arouses its revengeful ire and leads it to curse man who is " made in the similitude of God."

True religion will enable the human creature to control the tongue and thus restrain the whole course of nature. " But he that seemeth to be religious and bridleth not his tongue, but deceiveth his own heart, that man's religion is vain." The proper controlling of the tongue, then, that little member, but the propelling power of the whole body, is an evidence of genuine religion. The true votary of the Christian religion will bless his enemies, not curse them. They are made after the similitude of God, and amid their bitter retorts, railings and abuses the power of redeeming love predominates in his heart and portrays to his renewed intelligence the worth and preciousness of the immortal soul, which to redeem and save Christ died.

> "We hate the sin with all our heart,
> But still the sinner love."

The Cape Verde Islands are a group of islands belonging to Portugal, lying in latitude 14-17 degrees north and longitude 22-25 degrees west, and distant about 320 miles west of the Cape from which they take their name. The principal islands are ten, viz.: Santiago, the largest and most important; Fogo, Bravo, Maio, Boavista, San Nicolao, San Antonio, San Vicenta, San Luzia and Sal. There are, besides, four islets, barren and uninhabited. The islands are all very mountainous and owe their origin to the action of submarine volcanoes. The highest elevation is reached in a volcanic peak 9,157 feet above the sea, on the island of Fogo, and is still active. The climate is unhealthy during the rainy season. Though water is deficient, vegetation is luxuriant, yielding African and Southern European products. Sugar, cotton, coffee, tobacco and indigo are grown. The inhabitants, who are mostly negroes, speak the Portuguese language. (Chamber's Encyclopedia, Vol. 2, page 247.)

We touched at Bravo Island in the Cape Verde group. The captain went ashore only for the purpose of engaging a few of the natives to serve in the capacity of whalemen. The Islands are inhabited by Portuguese. The captain employed two men; one a small and very black fellow, and the other a reasonably tall man of a yellowish brown color. They seemed somewhat at a loss for a time, and their separation from home and friends seemed to occasion a vacancy and loneliness in their hearts. I wanted to go ashore and explore these islands in the sea, but of course I could not. We soon left the islands far in the rear, and were ploughing the rolling deep again.

Our course was now directed toward Cape Horn, and we had a long, tedious and perilous voyage. It is, indeed, well for us that we do not know what kind of a future we must experience, or we should ever be filled with anxious fears. It was quite a novelty for us "green hands," as we were sometimes called, to get within the limits of the Torrid Zone. We found the weather very warm, although the almost constant breezes of the ocean break the intense heat and cool the atmosphere to quite an extent. Some days the sun would pour down its burning rays and so heat the deck that in passing over it bare-footed we did not feel inclined to tarry long in one spot, and the soles of our feet were well coated with tar. We needed but little clothing in the torrid regions. Within the belt of the trade winds, which always blow in the same direction, we did not have occasion to shift the sails as often as when we were in the Gulf Stream, or some other regions.

The starboard and larboard watches effected their changes with the same regularity as in other climes,—but the watchman and the helmsman were the only persons closely and constantly engaged. The rest of the crew would sometimes converse, sing, dance and engage in different plays for amusement until fatigued, when they would lie down on deck and sleep. My favorite position for repose was beside the bowsprit, where I was gently rocked to sleep by the vessel heaving with the swell of the sea; and when the wind filled the expanded foresail, the current of refreshing air would descend to fan me while calmly reposing during the nocturnal hours.

It was here that we made our first attempt to capture whales. This was to us, inexperienced sailors, a new and wonderful undertaking. I will give a description of the proceedings. In the first place there is a sailor stationed at the mast-head all the day long; the watchman is relieved every two hours. It is the duty of the mast-head's man to speak of every object of any note that he descries, whether it be a sail or a whale. He describes his object rather in the form of a song, with a kind of melodious exercise of the vocal organs, as, "There she b-l-o-w-s!" "Where away!" retorts the captain. "Four points on the lee-bow, sir!" responds the man at the mast-head. I give this to explain the mode of operation. Positions in the surrounding deep are designated by the points of the compass, which the sailor takes by the measurement of his eye. The captain then procures his telescope and, influenced by the mast-head man's directions, peers into the distance to explore the monster of the deep.

The vessel is now steered in the direction of the discovered whale. Everything on board the ship is aglow with life and energy. The lines that suspend the whale-boats from the davits are cleared away. Four boats are always in readiness. When yet a considerable distance from the whale, the men are in pursuit of, the four boats are lowered, two on the starboard, and two on the larboard side. Six men occupy each boat: one officer, one harpooner and four oarsmen. If there is sufficient breeze and adapted to the course to be pursued, they extend a sail and are thus propelled by the force of the wind over the bosom of the briny deep; but, if occasion demands, the oars are plied. The green hands were not very expert in handling the oars. There is a constant swell on the sea and the oars would

CAPTURING A WHALE.

have to be adjusted to correspond with the variation of the unstable element. Occasionally, in the wild exertion, one would miss his expected purchase altogether, not calculating for the depression when the swell was gone. The element above it, the air, not affording the expected resistance, the oarsman was completely unbalanced in the boat. The officer would frown upon him and curse him mercilessly. Any mishap on such an important occasion is denounced in the most cruel terms.

As we approached nearer and nearer to the huge monster we were apprehensive of great danger; and the severest trial seemed to be to approach our enemy with our backs toward him. The officer and harpooner had to be eyes for the entire crew. Everything is performed orderly and systematically. Before arriving within darting distance the officer repairs to the rear of the boat and plies the steering oar, so as to successfully guide the boat to the side of the prospective victim. When a reasonably good opportunity is afforded to begin the battle, the officer commands the harpooner to strike, and away goes the harpoon on its mission of death. Now the battle is begun. The whale, feeling the sharp iron pierce his huge body, begins a terrible uproar. He makes the deep boil with his rapid movements, and in the flurry and hurry he is apt to repel every obstacle in his reach. Then occurs the need of judicious maneuvering. The first command likely to be given after the whale is struck, is, "Stern all!" That indicates a retreating movement, lest, in the frightful struggle of the monster, the boat and crew be scattered in fragments in the deep.

Next the whale begins a rapid descent. The line, which is attached to the harpoon, inserted in the whale, is then rapidly taken out of the boat. The line is coiled nicely in a large tub in the center of the boat; thence it is conducted to the loggerhead, a round, short, upright post in the stern of the boat. Several turns are effected around the loggerhead and thence it proceeds on its swift course through the central part of the boat between the oarsmen who occupy their positions on either side. There is great danger of the crew coming in contact with the line as it proceeds posthaste into the chasm beneath. To fall foul of the line means sudden dispatch of life. All the movements are carried on by six men within a small space, and every one must retain his position and make every effort count.

The whale exists in the two elements,—air and water. It must have air to sustain its life while in the depths beneath, and when the air is exhausted it must rise to the surface to take in a fresh supply. This affords the whaleman a chance to resume the contest. I presume his hurried flight also, and the immense pressure of the water has a tendency to reduce his great strength and exhaust his powers. But like all created beings that have life imparted to them by God, the Source and Fountain of all life, this powerful monster of the ocean is extremely tenacious of that vital principle. He is troubled and plunges deep into one native element, and then rises to have the benefit of another; but notwithstanding all his efforts to preserve his life, he must succumb to the grim and resistless power of death. His pursuers are on the alert and seek every opportunity to dispatch him. They propel their boats to an advantageous position, plunge the long sharp lances into his heart, and the blood comes streaming from that organ until the dark blue sea is dyed with the crimson tide. His muscular powers are active in the convulsive throes of death, and his ponderous tail strikes the swelling waters in the painful ordeal; but at last life is extinct and the huge monster of fifty tons weight lies motionless on the briny waters.

The lifeless whale is now fastened to the side of the ship and a stage or platform is arranged along the bulwarks or upper side of the vessel and lashed fast to the ship, so as to afford the dissecting party a safe position while severing the oily blubber from the whale. They are supplied with sharp spades with long handles which enables them to make the proper incisions, and do good execution from the stage. The blubber is readily separated from the flesh; it is from ten to thirteen inches in thickness. It is raised on board the ship by a windlass around which a thick rope is turned; the rope is conducted aloft athwart the yard-arms, thence to the waist of the ship and down to the floating whale. There it is attached to a blanket-like piece of blubber, about four feet in width, which the dissecting party have partly severed from the carcass. A large iron eye attached to the tackle block is thrust through the blubber and secured by a round piece of wood which fills the eye, and thus toggled the crew are commanded to ply the windlass. They thus gradually turn the entire body of the whale in the water, while the men with their spades keep cutting the blubber loose from the flesh during the revolving process.

Heaving in the blubber is very hard work; the captain keeps urging the men at the windlass to greater activity. The large blanket pieces, as they are lifted aboard, are deposited in an apartment beneath the upper deck, called the blubber room. When the heaving process is completed, the trying works are put in operation. These are composed of a brick hearth with two large iron pots enclosed in the masonry. It is, of course, a stationary structure, and when not in use is covered with a board roof. When the blubber is ready to be rendered, the trying works are heated up and the scraps of the blubber, after the oil is extracted, become the fuel. These scraps still have enough oil in them to produce a very hot fire. Before throwing the blubber into the trying pots, it is cut in long, slender pieces and run through a mincing-machine, and thus cut in thin slices which lop over as they come from under the knife, but the entire piece remains connected at the bottom, so that it can be conveniently handled with forks and thrown into the trying pots. After the oil is rendered it is dipped into a copper cooler and then put into casks and stored away in the hold of the vessel.

The following are the dimensions of a large sperm whale that yielded ninety-five barrels of oil, as given by Captain Francis Post: "The whole length of the whale from the end of the head to the end of the tail, was sixty-two feet; circumference at the largest part of the body, thirty-two feet; head, twenty feet long, and jaw sixteen feet long, and contained two rows of teeth with twenty-two in each row (the upper jaw has seldom any teeth, and when it does they are very small). The tail was six feet long and sixteen broad. The head usually yields about one-third of the whole quantity of oil produced. The tail of the whale, like that of all the cetaceous tribe, is horizontal to the body; and wielded as it is by a great number of sinews, some of which are as large as a man's wrist, forces an irresistible blow, against which a cedar whale-boat forms a puny shield."

The whale is sometimes greatly exaggerated by men who have never ventured their lives to capture them. I have heard of whales measuring considerably more than a hundred feet in length, but at no time did any of such prodigious length come under my observation. But consider an animal as the one above described, and you have an enormous monster before your eyes. The one above described is a sperm whale. This whale, being supplied with teeth, masticates its food. It is remarkable for producing ambergris. The bowels of the whale are where this singular, fragrant substance is generated; but this is seldom found. Whales compare, in many respects, with land animals, having in common with them warm, red blood flowing through their system, though a certain noted philosopher declared they were cold-blooded; which goes to show that philosophers, too, have much to learn. They have a heart through which this fluid passes, and is propelled to the extremities of their huge body, and they are supplied with respiratory organs.

The head of a small sperm whale is heaved on deck entire, but that of a large one must be divided. The head contains what sailors call the "case," which in a large whale is supplied with twelve or fourteen barrels of fluid which is dipped out of the case. A large whale can be fried out in about thirty-six hours.

After all this experience in whale-capturing and procuring oil, we sailed through the warm waters of the tropical regions, and crossed that wonderful imaginary line called the equator. We had often studied about the different zones and geographical lines in our books at school, but now we were having a practical observation. He who passes through all these varied phases of the created world, and does not wonder at the wisdom and power of the great Creator and Designer of all must be very depraved. Every day brings its new experiences in this nautical school.

The next special place of interest in this watery world was Cape Horn, the lower extremity of South America. Here we had the most horrid experience of the entire voyage. About thirty-six days were spent in these lower dreary latitudes. The westerly winds sweep around the Cape in fearful puffs and gales. One dark and dismal night I was stationed as watchman in the ship's waist. I looked over the foaming sea, while the spray of the wild billows repeatedly dashed into my face and eyes, and blinded my vision for a time. The vessel was almost incessantly careening violently from the starboard to the larboard side. I said that I was stationed in the waist of the ship, but my position was not very stationary, for scarcely had one billow passed by, before another came rolling over the top of the bulwarks, submerging the entire bow of the ship beneath the raging floods. The ship had careened over and was lying on her side. She seemed to be creaking at every joint, and the towering billow that had reduced our precious Oriole to such a helpless condition had gone on its triumphant progress while our trembling ship was slowly righting herself again. Before she had gained her upright position I beheld, amid the darkness, a terrible wave approaching. I ran with all possible speed to the after part of the ship. This part of a vessel is the most steady in a storm.

On the starboard side was the cook's galley, and on the larboard side was a board enclosure in which was a door that admitted one to the flight of stairs leading to the cabin where the officers lived. The intervening space, including the cook's galley, and cabin gangway, was spanned by a water-tight roof. My purpose was to seek refuge under that roof. But though nimble on my feet, with every muscle strained to its utmost tension, my aim was defeated. The towering, foam-crested wave inundated our floating home, and the Oriole was violently precipitated into the cavity of the sea again. I was completely submerged by the billow and hurled against the board partition just where it rounded off from the cabin entrance and tended to the larboard bulwarks. Like the Irishman, at first I thought I was killed The violent collision of my head with the board partition caused the blood to stream from my nostrils, and the lee bulwarks were all that prevented me from being swept overboard. I recovered as soon as practicable and sought protection at the shaft of the helm, being faint and sick and cold and wet. O puny man, do you boast of your strength? Do you pride yourself in your wisdom, gaudy appearance, and worldly attainments? Such overwhelming manifestations of power, such horrid scenes amid the dismal darkness, would teach your proud heart for once in your life that you are poor and miserable and dependent upon the Being who controls the winds and the waves.

One dreadful squall followed another in gloomy succession. I never saw the elements in greater commotion. I never beheld anything that was so decidedly awful. The terrific pressure of the storm caused the billows to roll exceedingly high, and our helpless bark was continually tossed from the foaming crests of the successive waves down into the cavities of the restless sea. At times we feared that we should be buried beneath the overwhelming floods, and lie in the cold and mouldering sleep of death, till "the voice of the Archangel and the trump of God" would arouse us from the lone cavern of the deep.

I trust that I received here indelible impressions of God's unbounded power which may fill me with reverential awe whenever I revert to the scene. The orator may portray, with all the power of oratory, the terrific force of the winds and waves, but the sailor's practical conception is deeper and more vivid. Forlorn and dreary we were at our wits' end: we sometimes trembled with fear. We were at the mercy of our Creator by whose power the winds are lulled and the proud waves are stayed.

In this terrible crisis I resolved to yield to his sovereign control. O what a dreadful thing it would have been to be lost in that lone watery waste! It appeared like standing on the verge of time, ready to be hurled into the abyss of eternity. What is the world to us then with all its boasted honors? All earth's attractions vanish in the hour of gloom and death. I was determined, if God would rescue me from this state of jeopardy, that I would no longer be restrained from his humble service, by the world, the flesh and the devil, but that, amid frowns or smiles, sneers or ridicule, I would endeavor to serve him and obey his commandments. My heart was rendered contrite and penitent and my purpose was to consecrate myself wholly to the Lord.

May I ever remember this storm, whatever betide me, as Elijah, no doubt, remembered the earthquake and the storm as he stood in the cave with his mantle wrapped about him at Mount Horeb. But it is said, in that instance, that God was not in the earthquake or the storm, but in the still small voice that followed these commotions. Elijah had fled from the vile and wicked Jezebel, after God had shown his protecting might, and escaped to a secluded place. Here God asked his fugitive prophet, when the convulsions of the earth and atmosphere had subsided, "What doest thou here, Elijah?"

Ah, yes, we get sometimes where the Lord has not authorized us to go, and we must then make the best of our situation, with the humble hope that God in his great mercy will overrule our sorrows to our profit, and thus teach us submission to his will. God could say to me—and he did—amid the roaring elements at dreary Cape Horn, What doest thou here, George? I long sought for thee before the clouds of darkness and sorrow obscured thy vision, before thy heart was yet corrupted by sin, and while thy faculties were yet in their normal condition, but thou heardest not my voice of mercy. When the storm and thunder of battle were past, and thou hadst heard the shrieks and groans of the unfortunate victims, I spoke to thee again, and endeavored to save thee by the restraints of my love; but thy heart was disobedient and wayward. And now what doest thou here?

The storm, the earthquake, or the destructive billows on the sea, may awaken the goadings of a guilty conscience, but it is the still voice of mercy that instructs and saves. Oh how wonderful and mysterious is our internal being! Sin demoralizes our being, and renders our life boisterous, but the still and wooing voice of God reduces all to quietness and peace. "A meek and quiet spirit in the sight of God is of great price." The commotion produced by the elements at war were figurative of the woeful disturbances in my own soul. Oh what severe discipline it requires, and years of divine forbearance, to subdue our stubborn will and bring us to humble submission to God's moral and truthful government! I was conducted, as it were, down to the gates of death, and amid the roaring floods my heart was indelibly impressed with the final doom of the impenitent. May the Lord from henceforth keep me near his side and shelter me beneath his wings of mercy, when the infernal powers rage and the surges of human passion roll.

A STORM AT CAPE HORN.

CHAPTER IX.

In the Mighty Pacific Ocean. — Talca. — The Guano Islands. — Juan Fernandez, the Reputed Home of Robinson Crusoe. — A Poem, Composed by that Famous Hero of the Romancer's Pen. — A Visit to the Island. — Two Deserters left to their Fate. — Varied Experiences of my New, Spiritual Life.

AT last, the winds favoring us, we emerged from this gloomy and desolate region, and were ploughing the waters of the mighty Pacific Ocean. We touched at Talca, a port on the coast of Chili, but only the captain and a boat's crew went ashore while the vessel lay off along the coast. It was pleasant for our eyes to behold the elevated shore after such a long and dreary experience on the watery waste. How we longed to rest our feet upon the land! But we had to forego this ardent desire, and of course we could not learn much as to the condition and customs of the people in Talca.

We sailed along the coast of Peru and passed by the island where guano is procured. Shiploads of this are carried to the United States to invigorate the soil. It yields a stench which is very offensive. I am told that Chinamen are employed to load the vessels with this unpleasant cargo, their sense of smell not being as refined as that of the American people, and they being more pliable in this life of drudgery. It is said to be the excrement of numerous birds which inhabit these small islands along the coast of South America. The offensive odor filled our nostrils, when we were on the lee side of the islands, for a considerable distance at sea.

After cruising about in these latitudes, we steered for the island of Juan Fernandez, regarded as Robinson Crusoe's island. Juan Fernandez is a rocky island in the Pacific Ocean, about 400 miles off Valparaiso, on the coast of Chili, to which it belongs, latitude 33 degrees south, longitude about 79 degrees west. It is eighteen miles long, six miles broad, and is for the most part covered with rocky peaks, the highest of which, El Yunque, is about 4,000 feet above sea-level. There are also numerous and fertile valleys which yield oats, turnips, apples, strawberries, melons, peaches, figs, grapes, sandal wood, and other varieties of timber. Numbers of wild goats wander on the cliffs.—*Chambers' Encyclopedia, page 722, Vol. 4.*

Here our wishes, which were not gratified when at Talca, in South America, were met; we were allowed to go ashore. It seemed wonderful to explore with our eyes the mountain slopes that the famous Robinson Crusoe had looked upon and climbed. The following verses are supposed to have been written by Robinson Crusoe during his solitary abode on this island:

> I am monarch of all I survey,
>   My right there is none to dispute,
> From the center all round to the sea,
>   I am lord of the fowl and the brute.
>
> Oh solitude! where are thy charms,
>   That sages have seen in thy face,
> Better dwell in the midst of alarms
>   Than reign in this horrible place.

I am out of humanity's reach;
    I must finish my journey alone.
Never hear the sweet music of speech:
    I start at the sound of my own.

The beasts that roam over the plain,
    My form with indifference see.
They are so unacquainted with man,
    Their tameness is shocking to me.

Society, friendship, and love,
    Divinely bestowed upon man,
Oh, had I the wings of a dove,
    How soon would I taste you again!

My sorrows I then might assuage
    In the ways of religion and truth,
Might learn from the wisdom of age,
    And be cheered by the sallies of youth.

Religion! what treasure untold
    Resides in that heavenly word!
More precious than silver or gold,
    Or all that this earth can afford.

But the sound of the church-going bell
    These valleys and rocks never heard;
Ne'er sighed at the sound of a knell
    Or smiled when a Sabbath appeared.

Ye winds that have made me your sport,
    Convey to this desolate shore
Some cordial, endearing report
    Of a land I shall visit no more.

My friends, do they now and then send
    A wish or a thought after me?
O tell me I yet have a friend,
    Though a friend I am never to see.

How fleet is a glance of the mind!
    Compared with the speed of its flight
The tempest itself lags behind,
    And the swift-winged arrows of light.

> When I think of my own native land,
>   In a moment I seem to be there:
> But alas! recollection at hand
>   Soon hurries me back to despair.
>
> But the sea-fowl has gone to her nest,
>   The beast is laid down in his lair;
> Even here is a season of rest,
>   And I to my cabin repair.
>
> There's mercy in every place.
>   And mercy—encouraging thought,
> Gives even affliction a grace
>   And reconciles man to his lot.

This school of experience, this dreary and solitary dwelling-place, with all its dismal surroundings, drew out the pathetic yearnings of his heart. It was here that his heart, too, became penitent, especially when sickness assailed him in his lone and sad condition. Then he exclaimed, "Lord, what a miserable sinner am I!" Then he thought of his father's good counsel, hitherto unheeded, and the mercies of a kind Providence which never impressed his mind so deeply till now in his forlorn and isolated condition. He says: "Then I cried, Lord, save me, for I am in great distress;" which, he asserts, was the first prayer he had uttered for years. His conscience had been asleep. Had he not been brought into this lonely and afflicted condition, I presume his Bible would not become so sweet and precious to his fainting soul, and he would not have sought to find out God who, in his tender mercy, had no doubt before sought him. His Bible was stored away in his chest as a useless thing, but when the dark hours of adversity came, its pages were fondly perused and its inspired words brought life and peace to his soul.

So there are many Bibles at this time which are not examined by those who have them in their possession until the curtain of affliction falls upon their hilarity, and dark desertion comes. I am thankful that I can call upon the same God whom that penitent of old addressed in his lone and distressed condition, when he shed tears of penitence on this island, and implored God's saving power. May I not hope that the same God who restored Crusoe to his native land will also effect my restoration?

We had not time sufficient to explore very much of the island, but we ascended the mountain slopes and saw the wild goats leaping upon the tops of the mountains. A few Spaniards lived on the island, whose appearance was rude and untasty. They subsist upon fish, which are caught in great abundance here, and wild goat meat. I saw a number of donkeys grazing upon the mountain sides. The Spaniards used these beasts to draw their burdens and they also rode on their backs. The only fruit that I remember seeing was peaches and figs, neither of which was ripe, which gave us quite a disappointment. There was an English man-of-war there at the same time we were, and one of the marines tried to ride a donkey; but he jumped up on one side and fell off on the other. He could retain his balance better on the vessel than on the donkey.

I entered a cave which was dug out in the side of the mountain and saw the names of sailors, from various places of the wide world, cut in the rocks. We were told that they had a prisoner confined there for a long time. I did not engrave my name on the rocks within the cave on Crusoe's Island, but I trust that the scenes of sorrow and affliction in my wanderings may serve as an incentive to have it recorded in heaven. The Spaniards lived in uncouth huts constructed of timber and their habitations were not very inviting to refined persons.

Two of our men deserted the ship there and concealed themselves in the mountains till after our departure. They urged me to accompany them, which, I presume, I should have done had I been prepared as they were with three changes of apparel, but the announcement was made too late for me to prepare, it being our last opportunity to visit the shore and my clothes were all aboard the ship. The one was named Brown, a native of Maryland, and the other one was from Connecticut, whose name I have forgotten. We never heard of them afterwards and I have often wondered whether the Spaniards treated them kindly or not. They evidently assumed a great risk, but I presume at that time I would have hazarded my life also, had I been prepared, for we were all anxious to get rid of our severe discipline on the ship.

But I am glad to-day that I was kept from my purpose, for the language of the apostle to the sailors attempting to desert from the ship on which they had all been so severely tried, "Except these abide on the ship ye cannot be saved," may also have been applicable in our case. But another want would have been felt in Paul's disastrous voyage, I presume,—their lack of force to control the ship in the storm. The weakening of our force was at once noticed by our captain, and it threw him into a rage. He vehemently denounced their rash and daring act, and no doubt would have prescribed a penalty for their disobedience could they have been recovered. This ended our rovings on the island: he would not run the risk of having any more desertions, and we were commanded at once to heave anchor and put to sea. As usual, we gazed at the receding mountains till we could see them no more, and we were again launched on the watery waste.

Consecrating myself wholly to the service of the Lord became the full purpose of my heart. I desired to possess a religion that is permanent, that retains its identity as well in the time of storm as in the time of fair weather. The warring elements may have a tendency to arouse us to a realization of our perilous condition in sin, but the wondrous love of God must incite us to active obedience. I knew by my conceptions of the Bible that God required constant submission to his divine will. I humbly confessed my sins to God in secret and the manner of my life was materially changed. My sins had arisen like mountains before me, and especially the great sin of procrastination; but my penitence was real, my heart was humble before my Maker, and I devoutly prayed for his mercy.

But the work of grace would not be concealed in my own heart; its mysterious workings were demonstrated to the crew. My situation was among a mixed assembly of human beings whose hearts were steeped in sin and depravity; so I scarcely knew how to begin to act in a separate spiritual capacity, and thus be a witness for Christ on our floating home. "But God who commanded the light to shine out of darkness," began to shine in my heart, and he would now employ me as a light to those around me, however benighted the place. The crew and officers had all discovered the external indications of a terrible tempest in the heart, but there was no medium as yet by which they might learn the character of the contention within.

Everything appeared to be against me. I stood alone, and was not experienced in the work as was the heroic Paul who advocated Christ's cause in the presence of the officers and crew on his tempestuous voyage over the Mediterranean Sea. One great impediment which I had to contend against from my childhood was a spirit of diffidence. My readers may be ready to conclude that one who had roamed around the world as much as I had, should bravely overcome bashfulness; but I reply that we know how weak we are only when we are brought to the test; and especially is this manifested in the work of grace. It exhibits all the infirmities and defects in our constitution, and proves to us our helplessness before God. I had tried to inure myself to the bravery, characteristic of the military spirit, and I had cultured myself to be courageous as a sailor; but in the divine life the creature must sink to nothingness in himself, and wholly rely for strength and support upon his Creator. This is the most difficult lesson that we have to learn, but it is the best and most important.

One night I conversed with two of my shipmates about the Christian religion. The one was a Scotchman and the other an Englishman. The Scotchman said that he had once begun the religious life but made a failure of it; and he seemed to make his statement with some feelings of regret. This urged me to give vent to my suppressed feelings, and I expressed my sorrow for his failure in such an important work, a work that was occasioning me so much anxiety and worrying me more or less all through my life. I said that I considered the religion of Christ an honorable and commendable work, and that it had been my misfortune to delay my surrender to God until that time, but by his help I meant to consecrate my life to him, however unfavorable the situation which I occupied. This public confession opened the way. "With the heart man believeth unto righteousness, and with the mouth confession is made unto salvation." It is wonderful, indeed, how cowardly we are in acknowledging and vindicating the truth of God before we are fully sanctified by its power.

My auditors became the agents to announce this assertion to those who heard it not; and thus the tidings were soon circulated among the officers and crew. Some frowned, others laughed and joked about it and said that it would be folly to endeavor to execute such a work on board a ship. I could distinctly discern the storms of opposition arising, but by the help of God I meant to be firm in carrying out my resolution. Hell and earth had prevented me long enough; now the rolling deep was to hear my vows to God.

From that time on I lived distinct from the officers and crew of the Oriole, in a religious capacity, until the grace of God induced others to join me in the divine work. But while reproaches fell upon me because of my attachment to the cross, I felt that it was my wisdom to remain comparatively silent, for I could not expect them to have confidence in my sincerity until, by the grace of God, I had first established my character as a believer in the truth. I knew that God would accomplish his own work in me if I was called according to his purpose; and if I could be subject to his rule I need not consult consequences, for he could even "make the wrath of man subserve his purpose, and the remainder of wrath he was able to restrain."

I tried to conduct myself becomingly and to cultivate a "meek and quiet spirit." Though I must give this testimony relative to my own Christian life, yet I hope that I am giving it in a humble way. I am fully convinced that actions and life, controlled by the power and guided by the wisdom of God, have more to do in establishing Christian character and silencing the scoffer and gainsayer than the most fluent and pointed arguments without the life devoted to God.

The ocean speaks with more eloquence than ever I have heard from the tongue of the finest orator. Its storm-driven billows produce arguments that the most competent disputant in the world cannot refute. They show forth the power of God more vividly than anything else that has ever come under my observation. While they may strike terror to the heart of man and urge him in his fear and consternation to call upon the God who controls the waves, it requires divine love to melt the heart to penitence and keep the Christian in God's humble path of life and duty.

CHAPTER X.

The Marquesas Islands. — A Visit Ashore. — Getting Wood aboard under Difficulties. — Assisted in Manual Labor by a King and Queen. — Human Flesh still an Object of Strong Desire. — Our Experience in Eating Candle-Nuts. — Descending a Steep Mountain-Side. — Depravity of the Natives and the Ship's Crew, Necessitating a Bold Stand for the Right on my Part. — Novel Mode of Sleeping. — Reflections Suggested by the Scenes Around me. — Departure for the Sandwich Islands.

IN course of time the Marquesas Islands appeared to our anxious vision. "These are the southern group of the Mentana Archipelago in Polynesia, the northern group bearing the name of the Washington Islands; but the name is also applied to the whole Archipelago. The Marquesas Islands, in latitude 7° 30'-10° 30'; south longitude, 138°-140° 20' west, were discovered by Mentana de Neyra, a Spanish navigator, in 1596. They were named after the viceroy of Peru, Marquesas de Mendoza. In 1842 they submitted to the French, and they are now governed by independent chiefs under the protection of France."— *Chambers' Encyclopedia, Vol. 5, page 276.* We sailed along between the islands of Nucahiver and Whitchoo, and effected an anchorage in a bay at the latter island. The mountains, towering high, in some places approached the ocean in bold relief; then again they presented a comparatively gradual slope to where the ocean surf beat upon their base.

As we came in full sight of one of the fertile valleys, lined with tropical fruit trees, and decked with verdure and beauty, we fired a salute from our signal gun, which excited the natives and brought them hurriedly to the beach. An escort met us in their rude canoes, conducted by one of the chiefs. They boarded our vessel before we dropped anchor. Their appearance was so novel that we could scarcely desist from staring at them, which occasioned some cursing upon the part of our officers until we got the sails furled and the ship anchored. They bore a strange and savage mien and their yells were wild. Their bodies were almost nude, and they were tattooed all over. Their step was elastic and their movements were nimble and active. Their hair was straight and black, and they could swim almost as well as aquatic animals.

Their canoes were tied to the Oriole while lying at anchor, and they seemed for the time being to be more concerned about our stock of provisions than they were about complimenting us. We sailors took pleasure in giving them some of our hard-tack and meat, and they gorged it quite lively. One large, wild-looking creature stole some out of the forecastle, in addition to what we had given him. Some of the boys pursued him and yelled at him, and he leaped over the top of the ship's bulwarks, with eyes and mouth open, into the sea, which comical scene created much laughter among the officers and crew.

It was quite a treat to us sailors to have the privilege of again going ashore. The watches were alternately granted liberty. We climbed the mountain slopes and sat beneath the cocoa and orange trees and ate to our fill the delicious tropical fruits. I felt interested in the poor idolatrous heathens who worshiped wooden gods in their blindness and ignorance. One day I was standing near one of their idols, examining their helpless god who could neither see, hear nor defend himself, and in my reverie I was eating an orange, when a little heathen devotee approached me hastily with extended eyes, contorted features, and earnest gesticulations, saying, "Taboo." This meant that by casting my orange rinds on sacred ground I was violating one of their religious tenets, one of the laws of Whitehoo. Of course I desisted. I had been eating my delicious fruit in blissful ignorance of any intrusion whatever, and my conscience was perfectly at rest; but what is life and comfort and peace to one, is sorrow and gloom and death to another.

"From the selfsame quarter of the sky,
One saw a thousand angels smile,
Another saw as many devils frown."

It all depends on the training of that innate principle of our being—the conscience. How blessed is he whose conscience is enlightened and regulated by the divine criterion, the Bible. The heathens observed my peculiarities and my fondness for reading my Bible.

One day I was sitting beneath a shade tree near the beach and perusing the sacred pages of the Book of God, when presently I was surrounded by a number of the natives who seemed to look at me with intense interest. They occasionally addressed each other in their native tongue, and then gazed at me with seeming admiration. I pointed to the heavens above as being the handiwork of the God whom I adored. I also included in my signs and gesticulations the mountains and the sea, whose foaming surf was continually washing the shore. I found that I could speak with considerable force without using my tongue much, but I simply pointed earnestly to the works of nature to disclose nature's God.

I sometimes think that even preachers depend too much on their tongue. I believe that if the spirit of God animates the heart, our gestures and general appearance will preach. By pointing to God's wondrous works and having life in our motions even those who speak an unknown tongue will be interested and feel assured that something good is meant. Let us have life in our preaching if we want to keep our hearers alive.

> On the wings of thought I often go
> To that distant sunny clime,
> Where the fragrant breezes softly blow,
> And the warmest sunbeams shine.

I formed a special attachment for one of the little heathen boys who was amiable and kind, and always greeted me with a smile. Poor little nude fellow, I shall never forget him. He was not tattooed like the more mature of his race and was rather good looking; but had he even been homely his friendly disposition would have made him attractive. It is not persons' looks so much as their ways that render them attractive. He used to climb the cocoa trees and get cocoanuts for me. I wish the boys in America could have seen him go up the tree. The cocoa tree has a long trunk and is devoid of limbs till near the top of the tree where the fruit is. This little heathen boy would so adjust the palms of his hands and the soles of his feet to the tree that he could rapidly ascend and then he would sit up there and throw the cocoanuts down to me. The natives grease themselves all over with the oil of the fruit, which protects their nude forms from the sun and keeps their joints limber. They are about as nimble as show actors.

Sometimes the little naked heathen boys would come aboard our ship. It was quite amusing to see them climb the mast or ascend the rope ladder to the fore-yard, walk erect out to the end of the yard arm, which even few sailors would undertake, and then one after the other leap into the sea. They would always strike the water with their feet, their bodies being in an upright position, and the force of their rapid descent from the yard-arm would sink them deep into the water. After a little time their black heads would pop out of the sea here, there and all around, just like so many aquatic animals. The distance from the yard-arm to the water's edge was at least thirty feet. They can beat the boys in America in jumping, swimming and climbing trees.

We procured some wood on the island, and as the boats could not get close to the shore, on account of the breakers, each one of us had to take his piece of timber, lie on the top of it and swim it to the boats. Sometimes a wave would get the advantage of the navigator and his timber, and then he had to leave it or he would be carried more swiftly toward the shore than he had advanced from it.

Once I was advancing with a piece of wood toward the boats; a breaker got the better of me, and I and the log receded to the shore, the live freight being almost as passive as the dead. We were hurled upon a gradually-sloping, rocky shore. I felt quite faint for a while, but soon gathered up my piece of wood and tried it again, and the second time succeeded in reaching the boats. The king and queen assisted us in this somewhat dangerous employment. We do not often have the privilege of associating with a royal household in that kind of business. The natives appeared to appreciate our presence and were much inclined to traffic. We exchanged our edibles for some of their tropical fruits.

An old African negro lived here who claimed to have been in Dr. Kane's expedition to the Polar Sea, and he related to us many strange things about the natives. He said that sometimes the inhabitants of one island would wage war with the inhabitants of another. The captives taken would be sacrificed to their idols and the captors would feed upon their flesh. The French missionaries have succeeded in modifying their tendency to cannibalism, but still human life is not always secure in their hands, as the hankering for human flesh is strong.

One day two of my ship-mates and I started out to explore the island. A path led over the mountain to another fertile valley where dwelt another tribe. We entered the forest and lost our way. We were fatigued by our wearisome journey, rendered still more tiresome because we were lost. We sat down to rest under a candle-nut tree. This tree bears a fruit that is good to eat. The kernel is heart-shaped; the shell is hard and about the size of a walnut. They generally roast them before eating them, for in their raw state they are apt to purge and produce colic. The natives bore holes through the center, string them on rushes and hang them in their huts for lights; the oil in them feeds the flame. The lampblack, used for tattooing, is obtained from the candle-nut shell.

We were not posted as yet in regard to the effect that these nuts in their raw state would have upon our systems. We were hungry and tried eating them. They were pleasant to the taste, but one of the party said, " Maybe they are poisonous." And sure enough, we paid dearly for eating them, for they rendered us terribly sick and we were seriously impressed with the thought that they might contain poison in reality. This threw us into a state of stupidity, and for a time rendered our farther progress almost impracticable. We finally met a few of the natives and interrogated them with reference to the character of the nuts we had eaten. We did this by signs, imitating the process of mastication. We presented some of the fruit upon which we ourselves, by sad experience, were ready to place an interdict; they shook their heads, made many gestures in the negative and exclaimed, "No good."

After the terrible revolutions in our systems had somewhat subsided, we began to recruit a little in strength, and trudged on our weary way until we found ourselves standing high up the mountain-side, which position afforded us a prospect of the fertile and fruitful valley for which we had started in the morning. Our vision was met by an inlet of the sea. Our narrow way through the mountains was lost, and to reach our destination would be very difficult. Night was fast approaching, and there was no time to be lost. I planned a bold adventure, and expressed my willingness to lead off in the perilous undertaking. It was to descend the craggy steep in a zigzag course. We scanned, before proceeding, the possibly available places in the descent to the ocean strand. We started, not knowing what might befall us, and retained our equilibrium by holding to roots of trees, mountain grass, or anything that presented a show of security. We reached the base of the mountain in safety, and the natives conveyed us across an indentation of the sea with their canoes. They considered our descent on the steeps of the mountain perilous and said, "You *mocamania*" (you die).

We reached the valley of the cannibal tribes as the shades of night began to encircle us, and what our fate might be before the morning would come we knew not.

They were given to licentiousness, and the sad misfortune was that the entire crew were given to the same kind of life. I saw the crisis and that I must stand alone in the vindication of my purity in the trial now before me. They might be stirred with indignation at the position I sustained against their indulgence in this crime, which the Book of God denounces. I could say with Paul "that all men forsook me but the Lord stood by me" and blessed my feeble efforts to teach my wild and untutored auditors, and exemplify by a practical demonstration my disapprobation of their depraved and wicked actions. I pointed them to the stars in the heavens, and referred them to the waves of the sea and the mountain summits as manifestations of the great and mighty God whom I feared and worshiped, and tried to impress their minds with the idea that I dared not sin against this Great Being. I believe that God was in that little sermon, for they accepted my plea and appeared to take no offence at my remonstrations, but conducted me to their hut and bade me lie down between two stalwart men; the indications of their visages were that they meant me no harm.

I fell into a deep sleep, and was unconscious as to what portion of the world I was in, or whether I was surrounded by friends or foes. I did not awake till morning, and my sleep was sweet and refreshing. I thanked my God for preserving me, for how easily might those heathens have plunged a dagger into my heart! A mat was spread over the earth which only accommodated the upper portion of our bodies, and along the foot of our bed large round stones were placed to support the lower extremities of our bodies. These stones were worn round and smooth by the water. Although I did not comprehend the entire

NATIVES OF THE MARQUESAS ISLANDS.

philosophy of their method of sleeping, yet for once, I adopted the custom in the evening. I do not now remember whether my legs were suspended over the rocks all night or not. We had quite a soft pillow to rest our heads upon, and, in fact, there seemed to be an entire reversion of the Patriarch Jacob's method of sleeping in the desert: he selected a stone for his pillow, but the stone in this instance was used for our feet. They treated us hospitably in the morning, and supplied us with food to satisfy our appetites, after which they procured their canoes and conveyed us to the ship.

They all began to look upon me now as a pious man, and I strongly desired that I might be in every sense worthy of the name. It is true I was endeavoring to effect a change in my life, and the yearnings of my heart were to become wholly Christianized, but I felt as though much yet remained to be done. They gave me the appellation of missionary, which they pronounced, in their phraseology, "misinar." They seemed to respect my pious inclinations, and never essayed after my vindication of right and truth, to decoy me from the path of virtue. My total separation, in principle and practice, from the flagrant vices in which the ship's crew and the natives so freely engaged, had, to some extent, its beneficiary effect. They would all have felt more at ease had I indulged in their wicked practices; but true Christianity will counteract the power of sin, and the lives of pious men wield a sacred influence that wicked men cannot resist with impunity. The captain himself was a nominal professor; it would have been my glory and joy had he been a genuine Christian. He was an intelligent man and a competent navigator, but he evidently needed conversion to make him a Christian.

I have seen so much sham religion in the world that it makes my heart sick to think of it; to think of enlightened people, with highly-cultured intellects and a little superficial religion to conceal their immoral acts and recommend them in the refined and popular circles of society. Let me assure my friends that the heathens, in the day of judgment, will stand a far better chance of exemption from the fearful wrath of God than such people. I always knew that to live a Christian life in this wicked world was no small task, and that one fact long caused me to hesitate to espouse the cause. I have heard people say it is an easy matter to serve God. Well, there is only one way that renders this service easy, and that is restraining and subjecting the tongue and all the members of our body to his divine rule. Bringing ourselves into that humble attitude and remaining there, requires incessant vigilance and untiring effort. But merely to assume a religious profession that only effects a slight separation from the world in life, has little force or significance,—only has a tendency to harden the sensibilities of those who are under the controlling power of sin, and leads them to ignore the principle, and mock at the very name of Christianity.

But I had now avowed my determination to devote my life to the Lord, and, by the aid of his sovereign grace, I meant this sacred resolution, though earth and hell oppose. In severe tests and strong temptations is where the Lord is pleased. God can sustain his servants in the darkest places of the world, and all that he demands is our implicit trust in him. He can only use us to profit when we truly confide in him and are obedient to his sovereign will. I believe that our Christian character is mainly formed in God's furnace of temptation and affliction. At the very time that the officers were looking for me to drift into the current of vice, and forfeit my religion; yes, "when all men forsook me, the Lord stood by me, that by me his truth might be made known." I really felt the force of his presence and directing providence, and I felt willing to "suffer the loss of all things, that I might win Christ."

The old African negro invited us to visit him and share in a social repast. He roasted one of the wild swine of the island, and we steeped our pork in lime juice and relished our meal. The limes are still more acid than lemons, and we gathered them and squeezed out the juice in kegs that we might share their medicinal properties when out at sea. We also gathered cocoanuts, oranges and pine-apples, and procured two of the native hogs for fresh meat aboard the ship. We fed the hogs on the products of their native soil—cocoanuts. We generally had hogs on board the ship, but the officers consumed about all the fresh pork. We occasionally had a couple of wild hogs, and it was amusing to the sailors at times, to see them charge around the deck. They would usually secrete themselves under the bow-sprit until they were disturbed by some of the seamen, who would occasionally give them a kick and arouse them so as to have some sport. They would not stop for any one when they got started, officers not excepted; and their locomotion was post-haste, with bristles erect, elongated noses, lengthy tusks and eyes aglow. Whoever obstructed their passage was liable to be overthrown. We had a pen constructed abaft of the try-works for the tame hogs, with entrance and egress on the larboard side. They were terribly distressed in the time of a storm, when the ship would careen violently from one side to the other. I have seen them braced in single file at the egress of their unstable home; when the ship would make a sudden and unexpected lurch to the leeward, the entire dependence seemed to be placed upon the first hog; he occupied the most responsible position, as the entire pressure of the other hogs was upon him. But away went the leading hog and every last one after him, and all were precipitated in a confused pile against the larboard bulwarks.

This might illustrate the weakness and absurdity of persons leaning for support upon the weak and puny arm of man, which will be found to be a very unsafe support in the time of storm. We may fancy that we are secure when the elements are all at rest, but the time of storm will disclose the genuineness of our faith in God. Let not man with his usurped wisdom and power intercept the light between us and God, and boast in the day of prosperity of imparting the security which the strong arm of God alone can give, and which will be so seasonable in our woeful extremity. When we had procured our supplies of fruit and water, we were ready to depart and try our future on the rolling deep. We felt somewhat reluctant to leave the place,—

> Where the sun poured down his rays,
> And the fruits delicious grew,
> Where we learned the wild man's ways,
> And his country traveled through.

The natives lingered about the ship in their canoes while we were heaving the anchor and unbending the sails; but when our faithful Oriole began to move off before the breeze, the royal family and their subjects returned to their island home. The distance soon widened between us and the mountains towering above the sea, but for a long time their lofty summits could be seen.

Our next port was destined to be the Sandwich Islands, in the North Pacific Ocean. Our routine of nautical labor was again resumed, and our island roamings, beneath the luxuriant trees, freighted with their tropical fruits, was among the events of the past. So time speeds on its swift wings, and brings its changes, bright and drear. The earth with its attractions again disappeared from our vision. Naught met our view but the canopy of heaven above and the rolling deep beneath. The crew were degraded and vile, and their corrupt intercourse with the heathens seemed to have lowered them still deeper into sin and degradation. It was terrible to live in such strife and pollution, and have my peace annoyed with the filthy conversation of the wicked. However, patience must have its perfect work, for its virtue is evinced in temptation. So righteous Lot was vexed of old when he dwelt among those foul-mouthed and wicked inhabitants of the doomed cities. The perpetration of crime vitiates the criminal more and more, and sinks him deeper in the sloughs of iniquity, till "his throat becomes an open sepulcher, and the poison of asps is under his lips."

The Bible says they that "go down to the sea in ships, they see God's wonders in the deep." But the wonders of the deep fail to attract the attention of the hardened and depraved sailor. I have more than once stopped my ears when I was reading and meditating in God's Book, to exclude from my thoughts the hard speeches of the ungodly around me. But I had one great source of consolation, and that was to hold sweet communion with one who is pure and holy and separate from sinners, although he once lived among them and bore their insults.

We were all presented with Bibles soon after we departed from Bedford City, but mine was the only one used on board of the ship as far as I knew. That precious gift of heaven, so dearly purchased, was stored away perhaps in the bottom of the sailors' chests, as a thing of no value. Some of the Portuguese concluded, because I read mine regularly and tried to follow its instructions, that I was growing insane. A jet black Portuguese, of Cape Verde Islands, suggested that they throw my Bible over-board. I presume they would have done it had it not been for the captain's authority on board.

Righteousness and iniquity are as remotely severed as light and darkness. The Ephesians thought that the apostle Paul and his colleague were turning the world upside down, when they were really turning it right side up. Sin has rendered its votaries insane: the precious Bible will cure their insanity and impart to them the mind of God. I notice that wherever the apostles made a stir in the ranks of Satan, they generally were instrumental in bringing some out on the Lord's side. I hoped that this stir and opposition on board our craft might bring about good results.

In these dark hours of temptation faith in God's Word must be the regulating power. I cannot rely on feelings, for I sometimes experience very gloomy sensations, when the clouds obscure my spiritual horizon and I am tempted and tried severely. But we may sometimes be nearest to God in the darkest hours of life. Feelings alone can no more give assurance of our acceptance with God than the quiet or disturbed condition of the deep can designate our whereabouts on its expansive waste. The competent mariner has a more reliable system of pointing out his situation, and the Christian has an infallible criterion, which is the Word of God. The disciples were secure in the furious storm on Galilee because they were there by the directions of Christ, although their feelings were as much disturbed as the element through which they were trying in vain to row. They did what they could, and that was all their Master required of them. He did for them what they could not do for themselves, and he would not leave them alone in the woeful crisis. He came to rescue them, and their extremity evinced his power to save and his supreme control over the warring elements. He spake, and all was still. Christ's entire control of the winds and waves proves his ability to stay our fears and calm the commotions of the soul. Oh! if our faith in Jesus could always be unwavering, we should be just as secure on the sea as on land. It is just as easy for Christ to control the mighty Pacific Ocean as the Sea of Galilee, and if there are but few souls out upon its troubled bosom, doing what little they can, he will succor them as certainly as he saved his little toiling band of yore in the perilous hour.

If we were necessitated to stand entirely alone in this world, without an earthly friend to endorse our Christian sentiments or sympathize with us in the woes and sorrows of life, yet, having the assurance of the friendship of God and his Christ, would outweigh the force and favor of the whole world. When my faith can thus take hold upon God, my heart is composed in the midst of my calamities on this great and wide sea. When I lie down in my berth to sleep, I can remember that Christ too slept on the sea, and when I am roused from my slumber to perform my duty when the tempest is roaring, I know that Christ had the same experience and also left his slumber to perform his duty, and knowing his power to still the winds I believe and rest in him.

CHAPTER XI.

Arrival at Honolulu. — Becoming acquainted with Eld. Damon. — My First Attempt in Sermonizing a Failure. — Making some Pleasant Acquaintances. — Reluctant Departure from our Cheerful Surroundings.

THE Sandwich Islands appeared to our view in April, 1864. The steam tug came without the reefs and conducted us into the harbor. We saw ships lying at anchor here from various parts of the world, and especially did we meet quite a number of whale ships, as Honolulu is their principal resort when going to and coming from the Arctic Ocean. They take in supplies, and when partially laden with a cargo of oil they discharge it and forward it to America on vessels that are bound thither.

These islands, forming the kingdom of Hawaii, are so called from the chief island, Lord Sandwich being the first Lord of the Admiralty. They are a rich, beautiful and interesting chain, eight in number, exclusive of one or two small islets. The chain runs from south-east to north-west, and lies in the middle of the Pacific Ocean, in latitude 19-22 degrees north, longitude 155-160 degrees west. These islands form an oasis in the middle of a wide ocean waste and offer convenient stations for the refreshment and repair of merchantmen and whalers that traverse the Pacific. They are of volcanic origin, and contain the largest volcanoes, both active and quiescent, in the world. The most prominent physical features of the group are the two lofty peaks of Hawaii, Mauna Kea and Mauna Loa, each of which is 14,000 feet in height.—*Chambers' Encyclopedia, Vol. 7.*

We found several of the vessels here that left Bedford City, Mass., at the same time we did. We had been scattered on the broad ocean, though we were close to each other for some time after leaving Bedford. When vessels start out to try their chances on the deep, they, like persons, when exposed to dangers, feel a security in each other's presence. A vessel called the Congress was here. She was near us for some time after we left the United States, and afterwards had ill-success *en route* to this place. She came near burning up at one time, we were informed. It was thought the fire was kindled by some of the crew who, as they were not far from an island, expected to escape from their floating prison. The men who were supposed to have done this daring act were put off on one of the islands.

We were told also that the life of the mate of said vessel was endangered at the Marquesas Islands. He was seized by the natives on the island of Nucahiva, who were bent upon dispatching him, and would, I presume, have made a meal of him; but, assistance having been rendered, he was taken from the clutches of the cannibals. Thus, when vessels meet after long separation, they give an account of "thrilling incidents on sea and land."

Vessels starting out from port to encounter the perils of the deep, are in many respects like persons starting out to meet the ups and downs of life. It is uncertain what kind of a voyage they will experience in either case.

At the islands we obtained intelligence from the United States of America, which privilege we had been obliged to forego for a long time. We learned that the cruel war was still in progress which sad news darkened, like a cloud, our vision, and filled the heart with sadness. If we were ever so fortunate as to return to our native land, it was uncertain who of our friends would survive till we arrived. Doubtless many familiar ones would be seen by us no more in this world.

But there was no use borrowing trouble, for our worry could not effect any change. We had experienced our dark hours of trial on the voyage and desired to obtain all the consolation we could while here.

Honolulu was the attractive theme of every one on board the Oriole. We all yearned to walk along the shady streets and view the inhabitants from various countries pursuing their business. Merchant houses, dwelling houses, and church edifices arose to our view, all of which lent a sweeter charm than ever in life before. The gloom and monotony of ocean life fully qualified us to enjoy the enchantments of the shore. The mountains, towering high with their volcanic peaks, the verdant valleys far beneath and the luxuriant trees, laden with tropical fruits, presented a charming aspect to the sailor's eye.

These are the islands that we used to read and study about when attending school, but we did not think then that we should ever behold them with our eyes. They were discovered by the famous Captain Cook in the year 1778. History says that the natives received no favorable impression of Captain Cook. This great navigator, it is said, did not treat them respectfully, and hence excited their prejudice against him and his party, which subsequently resulted in his death. We learn from this event the propriety of being loyal to truth and exhibiting a spirit of kindness and friendship to all God's created beings. Vancouver, the famous navigator, also visited the islands and by his amiable disposition ingratiated himself with the natives and made

DEATH OF CAPTAIN COOK.

attempts to enlighten them. His instructions had a salutary bearing on their minds, and they were thereby led to destroy their idols.

The first missionaries, who visited the islands, came from America in the year 1820. On their arrival they met with a nation who had no religion and who, consequently, were in a pretty fair condition to be instructed. When once we have abolished our helpless gods, then there will be hope of drawing our attention to the only true and living

God and his worship. And when we find people so honest and susceptible of being taught the true worship, if we, of superior intelligence, impose upon their credulity and honesty, we may be sure there is a terrible doom awaiting us in eternity.

When our affairs aboard of the Oriole were properly adjusted, the officers and crew were granted liberty by the captain to go ashore; the starboard watch one day, and the larboard watch the following day, and so on alternately.

I went to see and form an acquaintance with Eld. Samuel Damon, one of the principal missionaries from the United States. I met him in the Bethel church, as it was called. He received me with courtesy and kindness and requested me to give an account of my religious experience on the deep. The abuses and ridicule endured from the crew and some of the officers had rather reduced me to silence. I had concluded that I had better cultivate "a meek and quiet spirit," and allow my actions to speak rather than my words. Having had but little experience in off-hand speaking, I was afraid, as the sailor says, of being struck by a head-wind and consequently declined to obey the elder. Had I been commanded to haul home the sheets or help hoist upon the top-sail halyards, I should not have hesitated, but to receive orders from an old, experienced missionary to speak before an intelligent audience made me feel inadequate to the task. Elder Damon, perceiving that I was even more mute than Balaam's ass, did not urge me.

After services he gave me a mild reproof for my diffidence and told me to be sure to give an account of myself at the next meeting. I used to write out my compositions in school, and I concluded that I had better give them a written discourse in the Sandwich Islands. I had a bright memory then, so I wrote my message and memorized it. The appointed time came and the inexperienced orator from the deep appeared. If I had taken the course which I afterwards saw the elder himself take, and many other preachers since, that is, if I had held on to my paper, I might have given a pretty fair report; but I put my paper in my pocket and relied solely on my memory. The intelligent-looking faces of my auditors threw me into confusion and my prepared sermon forsook me. It might have been said of me with more pertinency than it was of heroic Paul, that if my letter would have been judged to have some weight and power, yet my bodily presence was weak and my speech contemptible. Having had this sad experience in the commencement of my public efforts, I concluded that I would never have anything to do with paper sermons any more.

I was not upbraided, however, by my friends for my very imperfect attempt at speaking, but was cordially invited to meet them at their homes or at their meetings whenever I could. When Sunday came a number of the sailors, with myself, went to hear Eld. Damon preach. He made us feel welcome in the sailors' Bethel, as he called it, and said: "Boys, you can sit on the starboard or larboard side." This signified that any part of the audience room was free for the storm-driven mariner; the seats, not being graded, were common to all. He, however, stuck close to his paper when he preached and of course was not left at sea as I was.

I was then radically opposed to written sermons and imagined that the elder was setting a bad example. To this very day I am partial to off-hand speaking, and believe that the mind of the young speaker can be trained that way; and if by entreaty and prayer he gains the presence of the Divine Spirit to put life into his discourses and help his infirmities, I believe that he will be much better prepared for any and every occasion. Thus ran my first experience in speaking and hearing in Honolulu, the capital of the Sandwich Islands.

The next Sunday I repaired to quite a stylish church. The minister's discourse was on the reign of Ben-hadad, and his wars against Israel. I heard him at two different times, and both times his subject was Ben-hadad. He had oratorical attainments and ably presented the historical events connected with that dynasty of old; but I was much more interested in Jesus Christ and his mission into the world to save the lost than I was in the Ben-hadad dynasty. My chances were rare to hear preaching, and I desired to be instructed in things that were more in harmony with my practical life in the service of my God. Old Ben-hadad and his successors were always molesting Israel; but I was anxious to learn more of the love and humility of him who descended to earth to save the lost.

I next found a very kind and God-fearing old lady who was always ready to show hospitality to strangers. She had resided in Honolulu about thirteen years. Her native place was Maryland. Her husband was a naval officer and had died on the sea. Sailors were made welcome in her humble home, and we often gathered there to engage in Christian devotion. There were seamen from different countries who told of the perils through which they had passed, and how the Lord had delivered them out of their troubles. It appeared to be Mrs. Crabbe's whole delight to talk of God and heaven, and encourage us poor sailor boys to be steadfast in our trials and temptations on the deep. She stood like a beacon light to console the tossed and tempest-driven mariner.

One day she urged me to accompany her to the prison to visit the convicts. The jailer received us kindly. Our visit seemed opportune. He conducted the prisoners to a special room and granted us license to speak to them about their salvation. Mrs. Crabbe addressed them very tenderly. At first the prisoners seemed to feel ashamed to appear before us, but as the aged lady continued her remarks upon the love of God, they were attracted by the words of life presented with so much pathos. Their feelings were wrought upon and the tears of penitence flowed freely. We looked with pity upon these poor unfortunate beings, who perhaps were once cared for by affectionate mothers. If those mothers were still in existence, how much would they be comforted to know that their sons were cared for by others in a foreign land. The prison is designed to punish criminals and reform their lives, and though men and women have fallen into criminal acts, yet Christians should have a concern for them in their gloomy condition and urge them to reform. The heart, even in prison, may be prepared for the good seed.

The Catholic religion has been introduced on these islands, as well as many others in Polynesia, and the natives seem to be very zealous in that worship. How many sects and isms do we find in this broad sea and land, all of which are claiming the power divine! I saw them bowing and ejaculating their prayers in their native tongue and following the choir with flute and song. The original heathen worship is abolished, but other forms of idolatry are introduced. The blind lead the blind till all fall in the ditch together.

The patriarch Job says, "Oh that I knew where I might find him." He means God, and it surely requires quite an effort amid all this confusion in the world to find God and his authorized plan of worship. But the truth of God must be the Christian's guide through life, and we are allowed to endorse the teachings of men only so far as their instructions harmonize with God's unsullied truth. If we sacrifice our honest conceptions of truth to please men, we forfeit the friendship of God. The advocates of God and his Word will find sympathizing hearts wherever they rove on land or sea.

This is my conclusion, and with my divinely-enlightened eyes I cannot see anything in this world more beautiful and sublime than God's precious Word, and its noble advocates. How consoling to realize that we may be doing a little work for the Blessed Master who has done and is doing so much for us! Just as soon as we are ready to espouse his sacred cause and confess his name, many opportunities arise for our service to him, no matter in what portion of the earth or sea we chance to be. Our light should shine all the time, that the world in darkness may be enlightened. Those who are brought to the light of truth by our weak agency and God's power will rejoice for our pious influence.

I formed the acquaintance of a very amiable English family. My remembrance of them will always be pleasant. I gathered them some pearly shells on Lower California strand as a memento of their kindness. I also enjoyed very pleasant religious intercourse with a German shepherd, who was herding sheep on the islands. He was humble and zealous, and reminded me of the shepherds of old. I distinctly recollect Mr. Ingram, too, the president of the College at Honolulu. His learning did not elevate him above the common people, for he took much interest in my welfare. May God bless all those dear people for their care for one who was far away from home and friends. I was treated very kindly by a family from Sacramento, Cal. The wife and mother professed sinless perfection, and we disagree to this day on that subject; but apart from that I cherish their kindness and hospitality, and hope that she has discovered her mistake.

Upon the whole, my first visit to the Sandwich Islands served as an incentive to my religious life. Most of the pious friends whom I met on the Island of Oahu seemed to appreciate my circumstances and congratulated me on my consecration to the service of God. They endeavored to stay my somewhat disconsolate heart against the oppositions of the depraved crew, and assured me that God would give me strength as my days of trial and adversity would require. The mountain scenery and verdant aspect of the islands of Polynesia, and the tropical trees, laden with delicious fruits, in connection with the spiritual comforts and Biblical instructions, I never can forget while my mind is normal and active.

As the magnificent scenes of the creation attracted my anxious vision, as I measured their exquisite beauty and consummate design I could, to some extent, grasp the unutterable power and infinite wisdom of the Great Designer. If the external creation on land and sea so reveals the Creator's wisdom and power, what must the spiritual vision of the redeemed and purified reveal! Under the withering blight of sin our sensibilities are hardened and stupefied, but the light of heaven illuminates the dismal chambers of the soul, resurrects us from the grave of sin, and we are led into a spiritual world to develop and mature; and according to our several capacities we shall advance to the full stature of manhood in Christ Jesus. Then shall we be qualified for the superior glory of the celestial world. John, the inspired writer, says: "It doth not yet appear what we shall be, but we know that when he shall appear we shall be like him, for we shall see him as he is." That is, when Christ appears in his glory we shall see him in his glorious attitude, and we shall experience a transition which will be the sequel or consummation of the spiritual growth in this life. This completion of our transformed condition will prepare us for the vision of Christ's personal glory and the existence in the immortal state.

The Scriptures first teach a resurrection to newness of life; and, secondly, a resurrection from the physical death and the mouldering grave to a state of immortality and blessedness forever. The God who hath planted the beautiful islands in the sea, clothed them with the charming robe of nature, and caused the tropical trees, arrayed in their grand foliage, to spring out of the earth laden with their luscious fruits, to comfort his creatures, is able to bring from the mouldering domains of death the forms of life and beauty to inhabit the celestial realm where the scenes that appear to our immortal vision shall be transcendentally fair.

Coming from the troubled ocean, where the elements are often at war and the ship, the home of the sailor, is tossed on the foaming crests of the rolling billows, and buried beneath the floods, the towering mountains and the green and fertile valleys are much more impressive than to the landsman who is gazing upon such scenes, or has the privilege of doing so continually; hence the illustrations drawn from such scenery may be deeper and more permanently fixed upon the mind. In this light, then, I regard the Sandwich Islands as a precious memento in the early stage of my religious career. Their beautiful aspect was attractive as it disclosed the Creator's wisdom and power and bore my mind to the splendor of the heavenly world. Even now, while writing this book, I soar on mental wings to those sunny islands, and am impressed with the reality of my rovings on their surf-beaten shores and the charms of their scenery.

We reluctantly left the dear friends and their comfortable homes on the island to experience again the hardships of ocean life. We were now bound for the frigid regions of the north, a lone and untried locality to myself and a number of the crew. About eleven months had passed since we left our cherished homes in America, and many weary days and nights of toil and woe must come and go before our course would be again directed toward our native land. But hope is a wonderful support amid the dismal storms of life. The Apostle defines it as " an anchor to the soul both sure and steadfast, and that entereth into that within the veil." As our natural anchor stays the vessel in the fury of the storm, so the spiritual anchor within the veil holds the storm-tested spiritual mariner, till the furious elements on the ocean of life shall be lulled to peace. Mariners cannot often consult that which is congenial to taste or feeling, and Christians may be frequently deprived of this privilege also.

CHAPTER XII.

To the Frigid North. — Escape of a Part of the Crew. — A Tedious Voyage North. — The Portuguese, and their Music and Dancing. — Christ, a Perfect Musician.

WE sailed from the Sandwich Islands in the month of May, 1864, *en route* for the Arctic Ocean. I felt reluctant to start on what seemed to me a dreary voyage. I would much rather have remained on the islands and found a ship bound to the United States, but that was out of the question. I had signed the ship's articles which bound me for the voyage, and however loath to see the cold and frigid north and experience hardships among the icebergs, I was bound to go,

Some of our men had tried to escape, but were captured and brought back. Among them was a large negro from the Island of Jamaica, in the West Indies, and a native of Austria. These two were captured, but three made their escape: the one was an Englishman, entirely too delicate to be a whaleman; one was a native of Pennsylvania, and the other was a native of the Tahiti Islands. This vacancy made it necessary for the Captain to ship three of the natives of the Sandwich Islands, in order to complete the number requisite to capture the huge monsters of the deep, and care for the oil.

The voyage north was long and tedious. There were no changes to break the monotony; our vision was forever bounded by the expansive deep and the vast canopy of heaven. The only deviation from sameness was the changing of the skies and the variations of the sea from its ordinary swell to its furious agitation by the force of the winds. I had learned at the Sandwich Islands that the war was still raging in the United States, but I was left in suspense as to the existence of my friends, having had no word from them.

Just at that juncture everything appeared to be wrapped in gloom and uncertainty. My separation from the dear friends on the islands, caused a deep vacancy in my heart, for on board the ship I had no one whose sentiments coincided with my own, and all things just then bore an aspect as gloomy as the domains of death. Oh, could I have had just one Christian brother who could have entered into full sympathy in the divine work! But there was no one, and I was doomed to stand alone. My feelings were deeper and sadder than I can describe.

Every duty in my maritime life seemed to be a burden, and I scaled the masts many a day and night with a heavy heart. But, after all, the activity requisite to perform our duties on board the ship was beneficial to me; for had there been time for me to brood over my lone condition and seemingly unfavorable situation, the burden might have been greater than I could bear. Labor is a great modifier of sorrow, and God's injunction, "Thou shalt earn thy bread by the sweat of thy face," shows his wisdom. This command of the Almighty was given after the fall of our first parents in Eden, and indicates that, since sin has contaminated our being and imposed upon the race of Adam the sorrows and woes of our mortal life, if it were not for the counteracting force of labor, we would sometimes sink in despair. And we notice that in proportion as this principle is ignored and despised, vice and crime, insanity and suicide increase.

>This world, it is a world of woe,
>And let us humbly through it go.
>Our course is marked for the frigid zone,
>Where winter reigns on his icy throne;
>Again our home is the rolling deep,
>Where storms and billows in fury sweep.
>Our daily duties we perform
>In rain or shine, in calm or storm.
>How can the billows overwhelm,
>While a kind Father holds the helm?
>The ship that bore heroic Paul,
>For whose dear sake were rescued all;
>Though the ship was broken by the waves,
>Yet all were saved from watery graves.
>Amid the perils of the deep,
>May the God of Paul, us safely keep,
>Until the tedious years expire,
>And then fulfill our fond desire,
>To reach our native land in peace.
>There furious storms no more shall sweep,
>Nor surges fill the mind with dread,
>Nor horrid visions of the deep.
>There, sailor, rest thy weary head.

The Portuguese tried to while away the time in dancing. Nearly every evening when leisure time was afforded them they were on deck. Their movements were not very elastic and the music was not very charming, but I presume it was with them as with some speakers to whom I have listened: they were more interested in their own discourse than in their audience. A very black native of the Cape Verde Islands, played the guitar. He, like his music, was homely; he had an exceedingly long nose, and his busy manipulations on the strings of his instrument presented a comical aspect. The dancers responded very energetically at least, if their movements were not so graceful. They seemed to throw all their spirit into the work, and thus interested themselves, whether others were interested or not.

The Savior makes a forcible comparison from musicians, Matt. 17: "We have piped unto you, and ye have not danced; we have mourned unto you and ye have not lamented." The children in the market failed to attract the passers-by. I would conclude that a market would be a poor place to charm with music, for the minds of the people are absorbed in their traffic. But the performers were interested in their music, as they generally are. I presume the children in the market played some lively airs, but their music did not thrill the passers-by sufficiently to excite the responsive dance. And then they would change to a mournful tune, and throw all their energy into that. The performers on instruments were, in those days, employed on funeral occasions to excite the spirit of mourning: and there was, no doubt, a close imitation of the real spirit of sorrow.

Christ played the true celestial strains in the presence of the people. There was no affectation in the music which he produced; it emanated from the depth of his infinite heart, but comparatively few were attracted by the harmonious strains. It was the purest and sweetest music that ever was played in this world, but the hearts of the people did not vibrate at the joyful and mournful accents that fell from the lips of the heavenly performer. The soul must be tuned in order to be thrilled by the divine music. Sin has demoralized our being, and our faculties are all out of tune; consequently the celestial music lends no charm. Men are too much engaged in earthly pursuits. In the midst of their confused noise and bustle they criticise spiritual performers and condemn the music because it does not harmonize with their business enterprises, or with their creeds and modes of worship.

So we observe that Christ himself, a perfect musician, who never threw out one discord in all his strains, whether of a joyful or mournful character, could not attract the people in general, because their hearts were not prepared for the music divine. Their hearts being untuned, their criticisms were rash and indiscreet; they threw reflections on the pure and spotless character of Jesus, and also discarded the holy and devoted life of his authorized servant, John the Baptist. So the music from the world above lends but little enchantment to the world at large and to self-righteous people, who are absorbed in the music composed and performed by their own skill.

But I know that the music of heaven has a sweet sound for me, and whether the strains be mournful or joyful, I hope my poor heart will ever beat responsive to the sound. Perhaps I was only learning the scale while on the dark blue sea, but I want to learn it correctly, so as to give no uncertain sound. I was once interested in martial music, and I practiced vigorously, so as to be able to perform my part well in concert with my fellow-musicians; and I am just as earnest now, if not more so, to be expert in playing on the divine instrument. I want to charm as many people as I possibly can with the music of heaven. But I have learned by experience that we must not become weary in playing.

The Portuguese dancers were not weary of their amusement, and their actions proved that they threw all their energies into the sport. They paused not to inquire whether it interested others or not. Their playing only gave present relief to the tedium of ocean life and excited their carnal passions. But the music of heaven, that vibrates through the spiritual senses of my soul, will ever fill me with comfort; and the charming influence will not be transient; the strains will never die. The music will ever interest the ears of Christ and the angels, whether the performers play in sunny or frigid climes.

Sailors in the Forecastle.

CHAPTER XIII.

Kamtschatka. — The Natives and their Dogs. — At Behring Strait, a Distance of 20,000 Miles away from Home. — Blockaded in the Ice for three Weeks. — The Scenes Around us. — A Dreadful Experience during a Collision with a Floe of Ice.

ON our voyage north, arriving in the Kamtschatka Sea, we met the Kamtschadales, natives of those northern shores. "The Peninsula of Kamtschatka forms the South-east extremity of Siberia, from which it stretches southward, extended between 51 and 60 degrees north latitude, and in longitude 155–165 degrees east. It is 725 miles long, and averages 190 miles in breadth. It is of volcanic origin. Agriculture is much hindered by untimely frosts, periodical rains, and sometimes by multitudes of mice and rats. The most valuable domestic animal is a peculiar kind of dog which never barks. The Kamtschadales are small in stature, with a large head, black hair, small eyes and broad shoulders." They are dressed in skin suits, and their features are not attractive. They are filthy and rude in their habits, but they appear to be full of energy, and seem happy. After the tediousness and gloom of our voyage from the Sandwich Islands to this place, it was a pleasure, to me at least, to meet them and be in their company. They came to our ship in their skin canoes and seemed to appreciate our arrival.

I had met a son of one of these women in the Torrid Zone. A sea captain who had admired this Kamtschatka boy took him to America with the view of educating him; but the youth, in the ruddy glow of health, longed to return to his own country, thus showing his attachment to the land of his nativity. When I told the mother of her son whom I had met in the sunny clime, she burst into tears and bemoaned his absence.

> O the beauty of maternal love,
> That follows us where'er we rove,
> No frigid clime can chill its power,
> It lives, however dark the hour.

The natives were amiable and full of vigor, and they were humorous and sociable. One day I was ascending the stairway which led from the forecastle to the deck, and hailed a Kamtschadale who stood at the top of the stairs. He seemed to be brimful of good humor, and was singing an English song, which he, no doubt, had learned of some of the sailors. I do not know who was most amused, the singer or his auditor. It was not the melody that lured me, but the sanguine exertions of the vocalist in delivering his favorite air. I concluded that Christians might learn of this inhabitant of the North, and sing the songs of Zion with more spirit and energy than they are sometimes wont to do.

The dogs appeared to be just as lively and ready for business as their masters, and seemed to attach just as much importance to their respective vocations as we do in the more refined pursuits of life. The dogs consumed a large amount of whale meat, and it was laughable to see them gorge it. Their masters were not far behind them in taking in nourishment, as to bulk and hurried mastication. What they did they seemed to do with their might; and to observe the eating process, one would be ready to conclude that there would be no danger of starvation, as long as they had recourse to sea and land for provisions, and were blessed with good appetites.

Well, it is pleasant to behold the smiles of contentment and love, and as indicated by the old adage, " Home is home, be it ever so homely." It is better to live in the rudest cot, and in an out-of-the-way part of the world, than to dwell where strife, scandal and slander are rife. But it would require some training and patient endurance for a citizen of the civilized world to become accustomed to this climate and mode of life.

In June, 1864, we passed through Behring Strait, and were then twenty thousand miles from home, by way of Cape Horn. We had experienced one year's changes in our floating home. We had twice crossed the equator and had felt the burning rays of a vertical sun, but were now merging into the regions of frost and chill, where it was best to meet hardships with a resolute will.

Extensive floes of ice were encountered on our passage through the Arctic Ocean. We entered a large field of ice and were blockaded for three weeks. It seemed strange to take up our abode in a world of ice. Everywhere as far as the eye could explore, there was ice, with open spaces or channels winding through the extensive body. Several vessels, composing the whaling fleet, were enclosed in the same field. This afforded us sailors much recreation. We would leave our circumscribed home and make use of more territory. Some of the boys, I presume, wandered at least a mile from the ship.

It seemed wonderful to 'walk over the ocean. Sometimes we were necessitated to step across the small open spaces, and once a Portuguese slipped into the sea.

Had he been alone he might have drowned, but he soon obtained assistance and was rescued. It was sport for the boys to roam about, and the exercise and novelty of the experience were good for our health. When the children of Israel crossed the Red Sea, the Lord opened the passage to the bottom and congealed the waters, or at least piled them up, on either side of the channel; but in this instance our passage was on top of the sea, and we did not feel like venturing too far away from our faithful Oriole, our only place of security in many a threatening gale. The ice might break away and the return be prevented.

A ship is a fair representation of the church of Christ: it is the only place of safety in this world of sin. It is best not to venture outside of its limits as we have no promise of safety. The awful depth of eternity is beneath us, and we know not how soon the brittle thread that holds this flickering life will give way and let us sink into the awful chasm of eternity. I have known people to wander away from the church and never again return. They floated awhile upon a flimsy support that was in reality no safer than the floating ice in the Arctic Ocean, and they kept drifting and drifting, till at last they were lost in the element of the world, the flesh and the devil.

Amid all our terrible experience our only safe place was the ship. We did all we could to control and regulate her amid the pressure of the storm, so that our lives might be preserved; and I trust that I shall ever have grace and wisdom from above to help control the Gospel ship in furious storms, so that the spiritual lives of God's dear children may be preserved. We cannot think of quitting the natural ship till she has conveyed us through the element for which she is constructed; neither should we think of leaving the church of Christ in her militant state, for Christ has built the church to save his people out of the world that lies in wickedness and under the condemnation of God. We have no license from God to leave her until he himself shall effect the transfer to the church triumphant.

The ice kept separating more and more, and afforded our Oriole more room to float in her native element. Whales were seen in the open spaces in the expansive field of floating ice, but the obstructions were too great to capture them. I believe one or two were procured by the fleet. They were killed almost instantaneously by shooting, from a short, heavy gun, a lance filled with explosive material. We were finally freed from the ice and began our pursuit of the sea-monsters in good earnest.

I was now exercising in a new department of my practical school. I was taken up higher, at least so far as proximity to the North Pole is concerned, but I trust it did occasion a descent in point of Christian humility. I felt glad that my constitution, which had been injured through exposure in military life, was rapidly regaining its normal condition, so that I was able to endure the hardships of the North. Change of climate, regularity in coarse, wholesome diet, and climbing and exercising on the ropes facilitated a cure of my diseased lungs. My ocean school, I trust, has afforded me a life-time lesson, and given me the incentive to stem the storms of life, to gain the country where the extremes of heat and cold are unknown.

One of the wonders of this Arctic Region is the appearance of the natural sun above the horizon for weeks. I never before lived in a country where there was no night. We read that in the heavenly country there will be no night, and even the sun that gives light by day will not be needed in the other world. But here the sun appears to pass around the horizon and keeps above it for a long time. It rises toward the zenith, then lowers toward the sea. It descends more and more till at last it dips its golden disk beneath the deep, but does not leave us without its presence long. Each time it descends, it remains longer, and the nights keep increasing to the time of the equinox, when the days and nights are equal all over the world. Then the light of day decreases, and the nights increase until the light of the sun disappears entirely from the Arctic world and darkness reigns supreme.

We see great structures of ice with turrets towering high, and to our curious eyes, they present a very imposing aspect. It is wonderful to see a city of ice in a frozen world. The crystallized fabrics rise above the sea with varied forms of beauty, surpassing the works of art, all of which are devised by the skillful hand of nature. O how grand it is to know and love the God of nature, and thus be able to see him and admire his wisdom in all his wondrous works! But after viewing these scenes of grandeur in the Arctic world I would prefer living where night regularly follows the setting sun. Being where the light of day was constant, our physical powers were often taxed to excess.

Our ship was often endangered by the floating ice. We met with solitary pieces and were frequently in danger of a collision. Even fragments of ice that had no formidable appearance gave the ship a heavy jar, as ice sinks deep beneath the surface of the water. An officer sometimes took his position on the bow and motioned to the helmsman to turn the ship from the approaching ice. The helmsman held a responsible position. This should teach us a spiritual lesson.

During midsummer here the sun has quite an influence; though its rays fall obliquely. In the middle of the day it melts the ice considerably. There are cold, frozen hearts that can be melted by the Gospel sun. Its rays may seem to fall long upon those hearts, and we may think that we discover no yielding; but at length the heat becomes too great, the frigidness is overcome, and that once frozen heart is melted to penitence.

We sometimes exchanged visits with officers and crews of other vessels, and we thus became acquainted with persons from every quarter of the globe. There were always quite a number of whale ships in the Arctic during the summer season; and they seemed to all be doing their best to kill the sea monsters and gather the oil and bone.

There is a pureness in the atmosphere in this Arctic Region which produces health and vitality. The air is bracing, and we possessed more energy than we did in the Torrid Zone. The clearness of the air renders objects at a distance perceptible; and the vessel that bore us over the water, was at times reflected beneath the transparent bosom of the deep. Sound is heard at a great distance, it having free course in this pure atmosphere.

Every living thing is aglow with energy and life. Seals and walruses are visible, with their curious forms ranged along the floating ice, and ready to plunge and hide beneath the clear, yielding element, at some startling sound or appearance of a human form. Numerous aquatic birds are either soaring on the wing, or skillfully plying their webbed feet, which comprise the motive power in the unstable element beneath. Thus everything seems to lend its influence to cheer and beautify this frozen world, that through a great part of the year is excluded from the light of day. To listen to the many voices of animals and birds, and to view the many scenes of beauty that greet the vision on a clear calm day in the Arctic world, is admirable, and cannot fail to cheer even a disconsolate mind.

But physical labor scarcely knows any respite in this region of constant day. Whales are numerous here, and we are nearly always chasing them, if we do not always succeed in their capture. It is similar to the huntsman in quest of game; he is ever upon the alert and in pursuit of his favorite prey, though his expectations are not always realized. Sometimes we would have quite a streak of good luck, and the valuable oil is kept flowing for quite a while. I have labored for thirty hours without any respite, and my physical energies would be so much reduced from the constant strain and loss of sleep, that if I would stand still, I would almost fall asleep upon my feet. At such times all the beauties of nature would lose their charms, and all the faculties of my being were suing for rest in sleep. I presume when we pass through the throes of death, and our powers become exhausted in the final ordeal, "and desire fails" we shall long for the last sleep.

The poor sailors, I often pity them. There are no human creatures in existence, I presume, that toil harder, and endure greater hardships than they; at least during some periods of their lives. Often they are hurled instantly out of life, without any one to care for their souls. But I was deeply interested in their welfare, and was glad that some of them began to realize it. They sometimes, when we experienced a little leisure, interrogated me on Scriptural topics.

The wise man of old said, "Cast thy bread upon the waters, and thou shalt find it again after many days."

Doubtless his figure was drawn from the scattering of seeds in the river Nile, while its waters had overflowed its banks. The product of their labor was realized after the floods had abated, and the rich soil had grown and matured the seed. But I was trying to disseminate the seeds of Gospel truth, amid toil and adversities, sunshine and shadow, in human hearts, upon the waters of the dark blue sea.

Some of our sailor boys had not seen their homes for many years. The ship carpenter (an Englishman) had not seen his parents and home for sixteen years. A very active and expert seaman, whose native place was Austria, deserted his home when he was about twelve years of age, and had been sailing over the deep ever since that time. He told me that he had forgotten how to converse in his original language. He could speak the English, Spanish and Portuguese languages, but could not speak his own mother tongue. He had strayed afar in the wilds of sin, but deep down in his depraved heart there appeared to be a tender spot, and he might yet be susceptible of religious teaching and influence. How sad to think of the wandering and the lost for whom Christ died! We may think, in our periods of sorrow and gloom, that our peculiar and old-fashioned religion has no bearing upon human hearts, but truth in its native simplicity, exemplified in the lives of its votaries, gradually penetrates, as do the oblique rays of the Arctic on the congealed icebergs.

The long Arctic day at length was interrupted by the shadows of night, and then the moon furnished us light. That wonderful orb reflected beautifully its borrowed light, and appeared like a great body suspended in the heavens. All these varied scenes and new phases lent their charm to us sailors in our practical Arctic school.

KAMTSCHADALES.

The Aurora Borealis shone in its beauty. The heavens were brightened with a flickering light. This luminous phenomenon dispels the darkness of the Polar night. How dismal would be the winter's gloom, without its streams of light, when the bright orb of day has disappeared. In these high latitudes the Aurora makes a grand display. It appears in the north above the horizon in the form of an arch, and spreads its brightness to the east and west. It has a fluttering motion, and rises and lowers, and its bright rays occasionally dart toward the zenith like the lightning's glare. It sometimes separates at one place, and concentrates at another, and upon the whole presents an imposing aspect. It displays its beauties, and performs its wonders above the horizon for several hours, and then gradually declines. It greatly diverted the minds of the sailors, and reminded me of the light and glory that shall burst upon this world of sin and darkness when our Savior shall appear. The prophet Daniel says that "a fiery stream issued and came from before him." And the Apostle Paul says that he shall exterminate sin with the breath of his mouth and the brightness of his coming. May every phenomenon in God's created universe teach us his divine wisdom and power, and urge our preparation for the great and notable day of his coming.

Many thoughts revolved in the mind when in the frigid region of the north. We thought of the exploring parties who had encountered the perils of this frozen sea, many of whom had sacrificed their precious lives. Some of them wintered amid these weird and desolate scenes where the stern and piercing winds of winter moan. O, how dreary must have been this howling waste where the empire of night holds sway, and the golden disk of the sun is not visible for months! In this bleak and gloomy region Dr. Franklin and his men were lost. He and his hardy crew no doubt sank into the lone and ghastly sleep, where the stupendous icebergs bind and cover their wasting bodies that, perchance, were with anguish riven before they were forced to yield to the grim and fatal grasp of death.

What sanguine efforts have been made by brave and renowned men to learn the mysteries of the Arctic world, and yet but comparatively little is known. Even these caverns of the deep shall give up their dead when the Archangel's voice and the trump of God shall sound. And while great adventures have been made in this frigid world we must ask ourselves the question, Who is willing to suffer loss and bear the Cross to gain a world of immortal beauty, where the extremes of heat and cold are unknown?

> No winds of winter there shall moan,
> Nor anguish-riven hearts shall groan;
> No shades of night shall there prevail,
> Death cannot come within the veil.

During our first visit to the Arctic we had a dreadful experience, one night, in a gale. During the dense fog and darkness we ran into a floe of ice, and suddenly huge masses of broken ice were charging upon our helpless ship. The alarm was given, but too late to escape the shock. The Oriole had plunged, as it were, into the jaws of death, and was quivering from bow to stern. We were left in awful suspense, and were obliged to surrender to the congealed masses colliding against our ship. Oh, what a dreadful hour when fluctuating between life and death!

We awaited, in trembling attitude and with pale faces, the result of the strife. Every human effort to relieve ourselves was in vain. We looked over the bulwarks on accumulated heaps of ice, that were threatening the total destruction of all on board. The captain moved hurriedly, with visage pale, upon the quarter-deck. His voice and mien showed that he feared our bark would founder. Had the ship been crushed, our lives could not have been saved. The boats could not have been lowered, and broken pieces of the ship would not have benefited us, as did those of the ship upon which Paul sailed when it stuck fast in the sand bar. I had witnessed the direful contest in the shock of battle, but when the weaker force was overwhelmed the retreating movement could be effected; not so in this terrible disaster,—from the congealed masses we could not fly. If death was to be our fate we must stand and die.

But at last the congealed body slackened its frigid grip and our gallant Oriole was again released, and like a bird liberated from the cage spread her white wings and moved along in her native element. We were graciously favored with an open space and the precious light of day. This was a wonderful salvation, but it only faintly represents our rescue from outer darkness and the regions of despair. Let sinners think of the hour of dissolution when their soul must be agonizing in the grim and dismal darkness of death, when the horrible phantoms of death will confront them, and there will be no escape. Let them try to train their obdurate hearts to appreciate the means of grace and salvation in time. For that purpose I draw illustrations from these horrid and thrilling incidents on the deep.

CHAPTER XIV.

Return to the Sandwich Islands. — Pleasant Greetings. — A Letter to my Mother. — Our Departure for the Torrid Zone. — Lessons from the Scenes around us. — At Lower California.

AT length the time came for us to leave the Polar Sea and return to the Sandwich Islands. But some of the whaling vessels were bound for San Francisco, Cal. Quite a number of the whaling fleet had spent the summer in the Irkootsk Sea, north of the Empire of Japan. We left near the autumnal equinox. If we had left later than that time we should have run the risk of meeting blockades of ice. We were all glad when the time arrived to leave the frigid clime where the long night of gloom was coming on.

Time brings on the changes of life, from heat to cold, and from cold to heat. Now we are under the cloud of adversity and gloom, and again we are allowed to bask in the sunny clime of prosperity. It will be a blessed exit at last from this cold, dreary world of sin to the immortal clime, that will need no sun, or moon, or sea. But the crystal river shall spring from the throne, and the luxuriant trees shall yield their monthly fruit.

We arrived at the Sandwich Islands again about the last of October, 1864. It was an entertaining sight to see the many vessels at rest again within the coral reefs at Honolulu, Oahu Island. Our bark Oriole was drawn by the steam tug into the pleasant harbor, to be moored and relieved of her cargo of oil which had been procured in the Arctic region. The towering mountains, the tropical trees, and the fertile landscape showed their charming aspects to our eyes again. Quite a contrast between these and the congealed masses in the Frigid Zone. Pleasant greetings were given us by our friends, whose amiable presence the hardships of our voyage had made doubly dear.

We had now had nearly seventeen months experience in the marine life, and during the greater portion of that time I had endeavored, in my weakness, to devote myself as best I could to the Christian cause. It was pleasant to remember that I had tried to reverence and adore my Creator in every Zone; however, that would have but little significance, if my heart did not have the proper temperature. I trust that God's wisdom and power may ever inspire me to activity in his blessed cause of truth.

Elijah of old was preserved at the brook Cherith till his appointed time. Moses was held in seclusion before he was sent to Pharaoh. John the Baptist was in the wilderness till the day of his showing unto Israel. The Apostle Paul dwelt in seclusion in Arabia after his apprehension by Christ. And so I trusted that God would preserve and discipline me in my isolated floating prison, and prepare me for usefulness in the sphere and capacity for which he designed me. A college course may place men before the world in a more polished and refined attitude, but to be corrected and disciplined in seclusion, amid the woes and hardships of life, is perhaps better designed to mould our character for endurance. But if we could have the two elements combined, and then be controlled by the Divine Spirit, we would no doubt be better adapted for the service of God.

Well, we were at the islands once more enjoying the society of our friends, who feared the Lord and kindly received us into their houses to worship around their family altars. They informed us that the cruel war in America was still raging. We had fondly hoped that, by this time, hostilities would have ceased; and to have received the intelligence of their cessation, would have afforded us much consolation indeed. But in these islands we heard not the booming of cannon, nor gazed upon the desolations of war. We realized the force and propriety of God's command to his people, "To pray for kings and rulers, that they may lead a quiet and peaceable life."

These islands were once unsafe on account of the barbarous condition of their inhabitants. But the wild man's nature has been modified, and his cannibal tendencies subdued by the sway of civilization and the Bible. Could we have had a church of our choice in this place, we would have greatly enjoyed being taken into church relationship, but, as this was not the case, we were necessitated to forego this fond desire till our return to our native home. We were ready to acquiesce in all which the Bible enjoins, as observed by the kind and God-fearing people on the islands, but there were other requirements that we wished to observe in order to receive a clear title, and "the answer of a good conscience toward God."

I will here insert my first letter, written to my dear mother, after my departure from home.

HONOLULU, Sandwich Islands, Nov. 5, 1864.

Dear Affectionate Mother:

I am addressing these lines to you, but as to whether you are alive to receive them or not, I have no means of knowing at this time; but I hope and pray that you are still in existence. More than seventeen months have elapsed since I took my leave of you and brothers and sisters and friends in America. You have been left in suspense so long as to my whereabouts, that I presume, by this time, you have wellnigh despaired of ever hearing from me again. But if your life is prolonged to receive this intelligence from your roving son, it will no doubt, afford you comfort to learn that he is still alive.

I learn, since I have arrived at the Sandwich Islands, that the cruel war is still continued in the United States, without any indications of its cessation in the near future, at least. How I would like to know as to whether my brother Daniel is alive, who experienced, like myself, many ups and downs in the hostile movements of the army. But until I obtain intelligence from home, I am destined to live in uncertainty, in reference to these anxieties of my mind. But my fervent wish and prayer is, that God may preserve us all to meet again.

Dear mother, the best news that I have to communicate to you is, that my heart has become penitent and humble, and that I am endeavoring, in my weakness, to serve the Lord. My submission to Christ has afforded me much consolation, and the longings of my heart are that we may all be united in the bonds of Christian peace. The Lord has been my preserver in all my temptations and perils on the rolling deep.

If John Detwiler and Isaac Kulp, our dear Christian neighbors, are still alive, tell them that I thank them for the religious instructions, which they imparted to me, near the time of my departure. Their timely advice has had a salutary bearing upon my mind. May the Lord make them instrumental in doing much good!

I presume you will be interested to learn our course of sailing on the great oceans. After leaving Bedford,

Mass., we sailed across the Atlantic to Cape Verde Islands, near the coast of Africa; thence our course was directed toward the eastern coast of South America. We cruised for some time nearly opposite the mouth of the great Rio de la Plata. From there we steered to Cape Horn, where we were held in dread suspense for thirty-six days, being baffled by furious storms. After doubling Cape Horn we sailed off the coast of Patagonia, Chili and Peru. We touched at Talca, a port in Chili. Thence we sailed to the Island of Juan Fernandez, in the Pacific Ocean; thence to the Marquesas Islands; thence to the Sandwich Islands. From the Sandwich Islands we sailed to the Arctic Ocean and have now returned to the Sandwich Islands again. In a few days we expect to sail to the coast of Lower California, and, after a cruise of about three months, we will return to the Sandwich Islands again, *en route* for the Polar Sea. So you observe that I have sailed many thousand miles over the rolling deep since I left home.

I must now conclude my letter with the anxious prospect of a reply, when we return to Honolulu from the coast of California. Address me, Whaling Bark Oriole, of New Bedford, Mass., Honolulu, Sandwich Islands.

Give my love to my friends and neighbors, and inform them that I have begun to serve the Lord, and that my humble prayer is, that we may all serve him in his appointed way. May God in his mercy preserve us all to meet again, is the wish and prayer of your absent and wandering son. Affectionately,
GEORGE D. ZOLLERS.

The time came again, when the course of recreation and personal associations with our island friends had to be broken; and we were necessitated to nerve ourselves for the turmoils and hardships of the rolling deep. Sailors are destined to be on the move, and their pleasant visits in the quiet haven are of short duration. We hove anchor and were drawn by the steam tugboat without the Coral Reefs, on the broad, heaving bosom of the great Pacific Ocean. Our sails were unfurled and spread to the winds, and we watched the dim, receding shore, until the mountain peaks entirely disappeared from our vision.

We were now left to cope with the rising floods again, and, amid the reverses of ocean life, reflect on the consolations that attended our brief visit on the Islands. Our dismal separation may, in some sense, be compared to the gloomy hour of dissolution, when we shall all have to cross the turbid waters of death. How sad may be the last farewells, and how lonely, for many, at least, will be the entrance into the dark shadows and the voyage across the troubled deep, to lie with the mouldering dead, away from earth and time and all the business under the sun. Let these impressive incidents, of our mortal life, fix indelibly upon our minds the gloomy event of death and our final separation from all that we hold dear on earth.

We resumed the active toils of ocean life as we ploughed the tepid waters in the Torrid Zone. The breezes, heated by the vertical rays of the sun, wafted us over the foaming waters and we flew through space without any visible motive power. "The wind bloweth where it listeth, and thou hearest the sound thereof, but canst not tell whence it cometh, and whither it goeth: so is every one that is born of the Spirit." The treasures of the Spirit are similar to the treasures of the wind, so far as their profound depth and quantity are concerned. They are alike immeasurable and are hidden in the depth of infinitude. We cannot comprehend the mystery of their source or ending, but there are overt manifestations of their respective powers.

Our flying ship evinced the force of the wind, and nautical science utilized this hidden force. Without a system reduced to practical use there could be no benefit derived from this powerful element, the wind. Though navigation has been made a matter of profound research by those who are especially interested in that department of science, yet there is still much room for improvement. A more perfect knowledge of the currents of air is now acquired, and the fixed reliable winds, called the "trade winds," are used to a decided advantage in navigation. This is the outgrowth of human investigation of this wonderful, mystical element, the wind.

May we not, then, reason by comparison, and illustrate from the wind the wonderful manifestations of that Divine Power called in the Bible, the Spirit? Faith discloses the power of the Spirit and reduces it to practical use. God's Word opens the way for discovery, and conveys a knowledge of its influence and bearings. The individual who is born of the water and of the Spirit is completely controlled by its influence, just as the vessel is under the controlling power of the wind. But shall the child of faith or spiritual mariner sail at random? Nay, we reply, the science of Christianity teaches us to employ the perfect system which God through Christ, who is at the head of spiritual navigation, has transmitted to the human family. He must take daily observations of his spiritual sun—Christ—and thus define his course in the spiritual realm, gain a knowledge of the favorable breezes and use them to advantage, to bear his valuable freight to the haven of unending rest. His aptness in utilizing the power of the Spirit, and his success in spiritual navigation are what will recommend him to all candid thinkers and honest hearts. It is the good, systematic control of a vessel, and her steady and successful voyages, bearing her valuable freight to remote portions of the world, and enriching and consoling the recipients of her commodities that afford her worthy captain and crew a wide-spread influence and a reward of merit. So I remark that the spiritual navigator is rewarded for his diligent application in the spiritual life, the good control of his character by the divine system of faith, which is designed to regulate and balance him. The spirit in this divinely-regulated character manifests its fruits in "love, joy, peace, long-suffering, gentleness, goodness, faith, meekness, temperance," and bears these richest of all treasures to thousands of the human race. Thus, as we sail over life's tempestuous seas, may we draw many lessons from the Book of Nature to impress indelibly upon our hearts the more refined and superior lessons of Divine Revelation, or the spiritual Book of God.

In the latter part of December, 1864, we arrived at the coast of Lower California, our destined whaling ground, and began active operations in pursuit of the great sea monsters. The captains of the different whaling vessels selected the quiet bays for safe anchorage and the security of their ships. This refuge from the storms on the open sea we held as a safe retreat, and when the winds were sufficiently allayed, we effected our exit from the bays to the open bosom of the Pacific to secure the valuable prize of our pursuits—the whale. Along these barren shores we must now take up our residence for quite a period of time, where our energies must be applied.

I kept a diary of the daily proceedings. By reading this the reader may contemplate the many unpleasant things attending a seaman's life. I will commence Jan. 1, 1865; that year is memorable for the close of the civil war in the United States of America. While the American people were rejoicing over the cessation of hostilities which, for four successive years, had thrown the country into a commotion I, with others of her citizens, was confined in this lone part of her extreme borders, where the acclamations of her victorious sons could not be heard. Already had the shouts of victory measurably abated before the intelligence of the discontinuance of the war was borne to us in these isolated and barren shores of the Republic. We had experienced her storms of battle, but we saw not the homeward march of her surviving troops.

A Bay in Lower California.

CHAPTER XV.

My Diary. — New Year's Day and Its Experiences. — The Disgrace of a Harpooner. — The Drudgery of a Seaman's Life. — A Portugese Finds a Grave beneath the Foamy Waters. — Abusive Officers, Etc.

Sunday, Jan. 1, 1865.

NEW YEAR'S DAY, 1865, found us anchored along the coast of Lower California, in Margarita Bay. I awoke as day began to dawn. A dense vapor obscured the morning sun and we could not view the glory of its rising beams. Our watch below were wrapt in slumber; I awoke them from their sleep, and wished them all a happy New Year. Solemn sensations stirred our bosoms when we again heard that old familiar sentence, freighted with sweet memories of the past, so often uttered in our homes beyond the rolling deep. But here no children's voices rang, though it would cheer our hearts to hear them sing a pleasant New Year's song. Anchored in this lone dreary bay we are far from home and friends across the rolling sea.

My guest that day was once a Virginian slave, who experienced much ill treatment, and fled to the sea for refuge. He, of course, became inured to another form of slavery. I tried to teach him the divine law of liberty, which frees the soul, though the body be bound. Paul was bound with a chain, but his soul, impregnable to human force, was concealed in Christ and could not be bound.

Ships from the frigid North to the sunny South, propelled by gales across the rolling deep, find a retreat in this quiet bay, where no tempests rage and no waves of desolation beat. Shall we view them coming from life's stormy sea, and finding a safe retreat in the celestial country? The light of New Year's Day is waning; the shadows of the night appear. The old eventful year is gone—a thought that is serious, solemn and significant. Our mortal years are borne on the wings of time, which with the rolling tide moves ever on. Let us work for God ere our period of probation is forever past.

Monday, Jan. 2, 1865.

All hands were signaled at four o'clock A. M. Breakfast was served, the boats were lowered and launched. The sailors impelled them hurriedly from the vessel's side, and were beyond the bounds of vision before the break of day. We paused and hearkened to the splashing of the oars as the whaling fleet advanced to engage in the ocean contest. Poor sailors! their lives are in jeopardy. Perchance before night some of the toiling crew may be enclosed in death's cold arms beneath the sea.

An Austrian seaman and I remained aboard when the boats had departed, and the curtains of night were still suspended. The time till dawn, when we took up the cares and burdens of the day, I spent in reading the Bible. I read the Patriarch Jacob's blessings upon his twelve sons before he died. O may the counsels of the just direct my spirit! Many centuries have fled since that ancient worthy passed away; but his words of wisdom still retain force, and are much admired. They yield sweetest consolation on land and sea. His prophetic vision of Shiloh is dear to me.

That day I toiled on board with busy hands and aching heart. My feelings were pierced with many a pang. The Austrian's imposition fully tested my submission. While his angry passions like the billows rolled, I could scarcely keep my temper. The boats returned at four o'clock P. M. The fourth mate's harpooner was deposed from his position and the poor, unfortunate man is held in derision. He poised and darted his harpoon but missed the whale, and here they forfeit honor who come short of their duty. He leaves his post of honor under the captain's frown, and another gains his title. So moves the world; so many rise and fall; they toil for wealth and fame then lose them both. But I would find my pleasure in religion's lowly path and secure a lasting treasure beyond this waning world.

> O may I not behold my Captain's frown,
> And see another take my heavenly crown.

Tuesday, Jan. 3, 1865.

All hands were wakened from slumber before dawn. The boats were launched and made their exit from the bay. I searched the Book, given by Inspiration, to guide the Christian on his way to heaven. Its living counsels are food to my spirit, and yield sweet comfort when the waves of sorrow roll. I peruse its pages with eagerness while the light is breaking in the morning skies. Two sailors wrangled in a fit of rage; the whole course of nature was set on fire. Anathemas were hurled in their frantic wrath, .their tongues seemed set on fire of hell.

The captain with a boat and crew boarded the ship Fabius. I washed the forecastle, and cleansed seashells for myself and the sailor boys. We were collecting them for our distant friends. We hoped to cheer them in the future with these trophies of the deep.

> A cloud of darkness veils my heart,
> O may the truth its light impart,
> And anon repel the gloom.
> I am a wanderer far from home,
> This floating prison is my home:
> When will my freedom come?

A whale was captured by the larboard crew. It was midnight ere they came with their ponderous victim to the vessel's side. When the prize was thus secured, and the enthusiasm was over, then all was quiet save the constant swelling of the deep. The harpooners were chosen to keep the watch while the rest were ordered to their berths to sleep.

Wednesday, Jan. 4, 1865.

The beams of the morning broke over the sea; the watchman's voice addressed us, and each obeyed the call though against his will. The monotonous meal was served: meagre coffee, hard-tack and pork. The usual stir and bustle prevailed upon the deck. Profanity knows no limit among sailors; it sears the conscience and destroys the soul.

The fire is lighted and the flames arise in the early dawn. The blubber is put in the pots and the oil extracted. The larboard boat's crew furnish the help needed to cut and hoist the blubber on board. Their task achieved, they steer for the rolling main to meet the other crews. Across the swelling sea they swiftly go, nor do they heed the motion of the foaming tide. So we are rowing on the sea of life; we are swiftly going to the eternal shores.

What a graphic picture of our course through this world is ocean navigation with its cares and strife!

The weary scenes of the day are ended and night brightens the blazing fire. Humility is gained in affliction's school. May I be inured to heaven's discipline! I want a truth-molded and divinely-tested character.

Thursday, Jan. 5, 1865.

The watchman's call was made at 5 A. M., and aroused the wearied men from quiet sleep. Our rest was short and we were still fatigued and worried. In an evil mood we were hurried from our sleep. Surely the strong man armed maintains his infernal sway, and any balanced mind would call this the devil's school.

Contrast this infernal scene of wild commotion with the calm of a Christian home. This is a whaleman's life,— a life of wretched labor, his hands, face, and garments steeped in oil; a life of frowns, curses, and abuse, where all man's vilest passions are set free. Some manned the boats, some toiled at the furnace. All grave and sacred thoughts seemed for the moment crushed. I cut myself with the blubber knife, and oil and blood were mingled. There was no pause to bind the bleeding wound, no relaxation. Within the bay the tide is in commotion, evincing that the ocean without is disturbed.

The ship Fabius' crew towed in a whale. The boats were two days absent from the ship, exposed to damp and chill upon their perilous trip. Three whales were to-day captured by the fleet. We greet their return with a nocturnal fire blazing in the furnace. The crew on the Oriole have ceased their noise and for the present we enjoy a more modified life. It is like the calm when ocean tempests and the furious waves are lulled to rest.

> O blest domain where sin shall ne'er molest,
> "Where the wicked cease from troubling
> And the weary are at rest."

The Bible says there will be no sea in the new world, and hence no confinements on ships or nautical adversity. But I see here alternate storms and calms; daily ups and downs among the crew. This is a floating prison, this dreary home where thunders roar and winds of desolation sweep. May I know again the freedom of my native land, beyond the rolling sea! I will cherish its liberty more than ever till I quit its bounds to dwell in bliss.

Friday, Jan. 6, 1865.

All hands were early summoned on the deck. The coarse meal was served without any dainties. The fact is, we eat to live, we do not live to eat. The boats betimes were impelled athwart the bay, to chase spouting monsters.

The captain gave us tidings relating to our country's civil war. Still hostilities were raging and battle fields were being stained with human blood. It brings to memory scenes of blood once viewed when we stood amid the slaughtered hosts. When shall human strife and carnage and all those hostile storms be lulled to peace? We hope the cruel warfare will be over when we reach our native shore again.

To-day a pig was killed but the official board monopolized it all. I essayed to advocate the cause of truth while opposition and error confronted me. It is difficult to aid the blind who think they see, or conduct the flesh-indulgent into true liberty. I read the blessed Bible with thrills of joy but ribald jokes annoyed my peaceful hours.

Saturday, Jan. 7, 1865.

The crews proceeded early to their dismal labors. We helped the German cooper to hoop the casks. The captain's carnal passions were all at liberty and the wisdom from beneath controlled his tongue. "The tongue," says the inspired James, "no man can tame." It hurls its anathemas along life's way and stirs its thousands to relentless wrath. Pure religion will restrain the tongue as the horse is governed by his bit and rein, or as the ship is guided by the helm.

It is sad, indeed, when he who has control loses his balance and acts the fool. He murmured at our ill success and vented on us his rage because the deep would not yield up more of its treasure and grant him rivers of oil. Anon his eyes look athwart the ocean, and, lo, the boats are all approaching near, with a black sea monster floating behind them. The welcome scene dispersed the captain's anger and gave his agitated soul relief. He truly paid his homage to the whale. We launched our boat and helped the crews to draw the ponderous victim to the vessel. A lifeless cow and calf were floating side by side; the pangs of death could not separate them.

The ship Onward left the bay for the open sea, to be more convenient to the chase. The Fabius' crew fastened to two whales, but one, with bleeding wounds, escaped. With harpoon inserted it darted through the water, leaving its foaming wake all stained with blood. It headed toward the breakers; they should have cut the line, but still they braved the danger and hoped to gain their prize. "Cut the line," shouted the mate while the boat was flying in the very jaws of death. Soon the rash and reckless crew were struggling in the spray. A Portuguese from the Cape Verde Islands sank beneath the foaming waters and rose no more; the others of the crew were saved from death, but the boat was lost. Rashness and impetuosity made all that trouble. Man, in the height of frenzy, loses control of himself and often destroys both his body and his soul.

I would learn a lesson from this rash and reckless crew: let calmness rule me when I am in dangerous places. May faith in God be my support whatever happens; amid the raging seas and stormy skies the Lord will guide my boat. When thunders peal and breakers roar, his word can still the storm and bring my tempest-driven boat safe to land.

Sunday, Jan. 8, 1865.

We are without the Bay sailing before the wind. We encountered a strong breeze and rough sea, which drove us back into the quiet bay for shelter from the storm. Again the ship is anchored and the furnace started. The crew are hard at work as in other dreary days. The captain is rejoicing over the returns; he is always in a pleasant mood when we have a copious yield of oil.

Over my heart hangs a dismal cloud. My external appearance is that of a greasy slave, but my heart is not much attached to whale oil. I would much prefer worshiping in God's church to being left in this unpleasant place while saints are bowing round the altar. I hope the day will come when I can mingle with kindred spirits and pay my homage to God with the pure in heart on the Sabbath day.

Monday, Jan. 9, 1865.

The boats were lowered early to cruise for whales; one boat's crew was left to care for the rendered oil. The captain exercised his muscles in the toil and scolded vehemently. He imprecated me in his frantic spell, but I answered softly and tried to overcome his rage. My passions though, were somewhat stirred, for he acted unwisely. A sorry specimen is the life of a Christian, involved in such strife. Such sham religion is by the mariner abhorred, his heart cannot be right in the sight of God. A man in the full blaze of carnal passion, rolling polluted language from his lips; surely I pity his soul and desire the grace of God may control my captain. He was a man of highly-cultured intellect in nautical science and astronomy, who could define his position in the sea from the sun and stars, and yet disregarded the God who rules these mighty orbs. Men may boast of their birth, genius or fame, yet their actions disclose them for just what they are worth. We performed our unpleasant duty till noon; it was rendered more unpleasant by the actions of the captain. Nothing else worthy to record occurred, save that the fourth mate fell overboard.

Tuesday, Jan. 10, 1865.

The boats were launched early: The crews must take their daily trip. We laboriously lowered through the main hatch-way, cask after cask of rendered oil. But my heart was tuned by grace divine, and sweetly communed with its Author. May he direct our bark across the sea and moor us again in Columbia's port. There shall my ocean thralldom cease, and this life of turmoil, pain and sorrow end.

The captain of the Governor Troop came on board the Oriole, to interview our captain in regard to the whaling enterprise. Ned, the colored boy, was one among the crew who was proficient in witticisms, but tender-hearted too. He sang his comic airs, showed his quaint antics and danced to amuse the boys. I talked with him on religion, and struck a sympathetic chord that lay buried beneath the animal propensities, but should be drawn out and utilized. The few words uttered seemed to find fruitful soil, and were seemingly employed by the Divine Spirit to awaken the latent sensibilities, the development of which will be mentioned farther on in this work.

. Wednesday, Jan. 11, 1865.

The boats departed as usual. I had a little time for Bible research. I swept the deck, adjusted casks in the hold, and ballasted with salt water. The captain clamored in revengeful mood. He stirred my wrath but I quenched it, for a Christian's anger should soon expire. We went ashore in the evening to procure some sand for ballasting the ship. It awakens joyful sensations to gain even this barren strand. No wonder Christopher Columbus kissed the earth, when released from ocean toil. The land was never more dear to me than when I stood on the soil of Lower California. My eyes were weary of the agitated ocean.

In the evening we discovered a steamer bound from Panama to San Francisco. We exercised our skill and muscular power in rowing to come up with her, but urged by two invisible forces—steam and wind—she was going too swiftly, so we desisted from the chase. We longed for tidings from our native country, which was highly cherished in our isolated home upon the sea. As we returned to our floating craft, the moon was sending her silvery beams over the bosom of the swelling deep. How grand was the scene! As we plied our oars, we mused on the power and wisdom of him who created the sun, moon and stars, the earth and sea, whose presence fills immensity, all of whose judgments are unsearchable, and whose ways are past finding out. The boats were all safe aboard at night. The chief mate hailed the steamer and procured news from our native land. Thus ended the occurrences of one more fleeting day.

Thursday, Jan. 12, 1865.

The boats, at early dawn, pulled from the vessel's side. A brief period remained for Bible reading before we began the toils and turmoils of the day. We scrubbed the deck with lye and cinders, it being saturated with oil. The crew were furnished with molasses to-day, and though but a common grade, it was esteemed a luxury.

We rowed the captain to the Governor Troop. Nicholas, the Austrian, was commanded to accompany us, but remonstrated against the captain's order; the captain heard his murmuring tones, and for once allowed his subject to have his way. The boats and crews of the Governor Troop were absent in the open sea after whales. Only the ship-keepers were left to associate with. We found them eating their noonday repast, prepared and served in sailor style, without distinction to rank or nationality. I spent most of the time in the forecastle, reading, as I could not affiliate with the boys in their wild career. "The world knoweth us not, for it knew him not." A little rain fell this evening which is rather unusual, I am told.

Friday, Jan. 13, 1865.

Cloudy this morning. Ere yet the watch was called, I rose. I had slept in sweet repose beneath my Father's guardian eye. When I awoke my thoughts were in a Scriptural channel. I welcome the Bible day and night, for it yields the sweetest comforts in my distant, lone retreat. I ascended to the deck to survey my Creator's handiwork, but the clouds obscured the beauty of the sky. I retired to my berth till signaled by the watchman, then we ate our morning meal and the boats proceeded on their daily errand. Nicholas, the German cooper, and I hoisted shucks from the fore-peak to set up whale-oil casks.

I washed clothes for myself, the cook (an African), St. George (Portuguese), and the cabin boy, for accommodation. The cook rewarded me with a piece of pumpkin pie, and the cabin boy gave me a piece of wheat bread, which kind of diet was a rarity with sailors before the mast, but nothing unusual for the officers. I simply say that I relished the food. And this day will be remembered as one bringing gifts and comforts on the sea, which may afford a pleasant reminiscence in the future.

Saturday, Jan. 14, 1865.

At an early hour I was awakened by severe physical pain. A tortured body stupefies the brain. In weal or woe it is best to serve the Lord in the glow of health. I retired to my berth to rest my wearied frame, for I must needs try to regain my precious health. The crew were hurried to their labor early, beneath official frowns and curses. The captain scolded constantly; our lives were worried and spent unpleasantly. But soon the boats appeared with an oily monster. The captain hurried over the deck with nervous rapidity, yelled, and hurried up the boys. The bloodstained corpses were a mother and her offspring, over which floating victims the sailors cursed and sang. A fatal lance had pierced the vital parts and side by side they lay in death's convulsive throes. Two boats' crews remained to cut and hoist the whale, the rest steered for the open sea.

A jet black Portuguese poised and darted his iron but it failed to fulfill its mission. They branded him as a dupe, deprived of skill. Hence the poor, colored Portuguese, of Bravo Island, forfeited his fame as a harpooner. I wish that I could convince him of a more honorable life than whaling, urge him to employ his talents in the service of more judicious and merciful officers, and depict before his spiritual vision the prospect of gaining a more valuable prize. I would gladly console him in his dishonored plight, and do him good for injuries already done to me. I remember his hatred of my religion, because of his attachment to Catholicism. He once wreaked his revenge on me and, like a ferocious beast sank his devouring teeth in my flesh. I had done him no injury, but he did me an injury. But the grace of God supported me and disclosed to me, through this act of suffering, the calm submission of the blessed Christ. It was he, too, who encouraged the crew to deposit my Bible in the sea, signifying that it would drive me to insanity, for the reason that it was in opposition to his own Catholic teaching. But the Lord has preserved my Bible and me, and is teaching me from its sacred pages love instead of hatred and revenge. Reverses in life sometimes bring about a humble spirit in proud and obstinate

FLYING FISH, AS SEEN ON THE ROLLING DEEP.

men, and I still hope they may have had this tendency on the native of the Cape Verde Islands.

Sunday, Jan. 15, 1865.

We were signaled early by the loud, shrill call of the third mate. Physical toil they never underrate, nor call the men too late from sweet repose. Well, our eyes from sleep unsealed; no use to worry. We are doomed to hardships and must arise and hasten. Within the heated pots we hear the blubber boil, the compensation for our labor; for a whaleman's wealth all emanates from oil. I long to be where Brethren meet and bow around the mercy-seat. But far away in this lone place, I must spend in sorrow this precious Sabbath.

The captain's heart swells with glad emotion; it is firmly fixed on these treasures of the sea, and he never speaks of a treasure in the other world. It is quite difficult to procure his treasures from the sea, and I presume he concludes that it is more difficult to procure it in the other country; and it cannot be procured by carnal means. But I respect him in his responsible position as captain of our ship, and I pray God to make me instrumental in enlightening him and his crew spiritually. He rescued me from the vengeance of his officers, I believe, by God's directing power. Having been raised to strictly abstain from Sunday labor, I refused, from a conscientious standpoint, to work. The Mates and part of the crew were ready to brand me for stubbornness; but the captain was more judicious in his decision, and protested against rashness and abuse, averring that a little forbearance would induce me without punishment to submit to the rules of nautical government. The captain, in this instance, was made God's agent of mercy to me.

I confess it was an erroneous design, considering my situation. Had they demanded a recantation of my simple service to God, a discontinuance of prayer and the study of the Bible, then my refusal to obey might have been persevered in; but merely to protest against their method of procuring their prey on the Sabbath day, when no binding rule is disclosed in the New Testament, did not seem to me, after due deliberation, to be demanded by the Lord. Were the day and its attending duties specified as they were under the Jewish economy, then I would have been justified in my non-continuance in nautical labor on that day; but as I can see no such restrictions in the New Testament imposed on one in my condition, I gave the captain credit for his prudent course in setting me right. Though I am giving an unbiased account of the daily occurrences on board of our craft, I do it with merciful feelings to the officers and crew, and can pray God all the while to save them from their lost estate.

The starboard boat dispatched a whale, but they had to see him sink to the bottom of the sea. They taxed their brain, and plied their strength to keep their prize, but despite of all it sank. They cursed and almost wept. So sink all earthly treasures from our grasp, and leave us to groan at death and gasp for life's most cherished breath. Vain man, release your fond desires from earth and sea whose glory soon passes away.

Strong breeze this morning but toward noon it decreased in power. Though darkness veil the skies and tempests roar, we will trust in the God who rules the winds and waves.

Monday, Jan. 16, 1865.

We were early signaled to resume our tasks. The boats sailed off to their ocean labor and we were left to render out the oil. We hailed the J. L. Stephens and obtained intelligence from our native country. Such news is cherished on the lonely sea. The waist boat was stove by a whale, but the crew escaped unhurt, and were rescued by the other boats. The larboard boat's crew fastened to the monster first; he was dispatched and then sank in the sea.

Friday, Jan. 20, 1865.

Roused from slumber we viewed the beautiful, bright morning. The boats again went away. A light breeze was blowing. I spent my watch last night in musing. The sea, illumined by the moon, is truly grand. Our God is great and good and wise; we view his power and wisdom on sea and land. His power controls this vast expansive sea, and the rolling planets in their swift motion. O what delicate balancing of forces, as these worlds revolve in their distant orbits! It humbles any soul to view His majesty.

The boats with their white sails appeared at twilight. The officers reported the recovery of the sunken whales doubtful. Even putrid whales are sought with eager eyes. Their prize procured they are merry, and use their muscles to extract the oil. But Jesus sought those lost in sin, and bore their sins and sorrows on that woeful day. No one can know His burdens when He crossed the deep to ransom fallen man, condemned and lost. He raised him out of the horrible pit and consumes the dross by his refining fire. O that men would contemplate the love disclosed by his condescension!

A tumult among the boys in the forecastle troubled my peace.

Saturday, Jan. 21, 1865.

The moon shed its silvery light, adorning both the azure sky and the dark blue sea. After launching the boats on the troubled waters I retired to the forecastle and read the pathetic narrative of the meeting of Moses and Jethro, his father-in-law. Blessed tidings to cheer the Christian amid ocean tumults where waves of sorrow roll. That meek Prophet, Moses, saw much woe and strife, and bore great burdens till he stood on Mt. Pisgah's height, exempt from toil, and viewed old Canaan's shore. There he who was the type of Christ expired and left this world of sin and strife to share a purer, sweeter rest than Canaan's shore.

The ship Martha's Vineyard left the bay to go on a sperm whale cruise. While adjusting the blubber machine, the captain and an Austrian sailor wrangled in a fit of wrath. No latitude excludes the bane of sin. Its hellish power intrudes on earth and sea. I told the Austrian to quell his wrath and save his polluted soul. The boats towed in a fish, portending sorrow, as the devil means to make us violate the Sabbath. However well disposed to hallow it, I must toil in this abominable grease. I am confined to this prison, a drudge and a slave; I must brave the hardships and waves of the sea. Again I view the twinkling stars peering down to solace my poor, broken heart. My God, remember me.

Sunday, Jan. 22, 1865.

All hands were aroused ere the break of day, not with thrills of gladness but forlorn. To hear cursing instead of praise and idle stories, pursuing whales instead of meeting with the saints. Gospel privileges once slighted are now fondly cherished while out on the sea. So they of first choice are oft doomed to be last, to wail when the season of harvest is past. The impenitent sinner feels no anxiety till he quails in the shock of the avenging storm.

Well, we started betimes with more clamor than rhymes, more darkness than light, and more care than prayer. But with my humble appeal to my Creator I will submit to the scourge of his chastening rod till he plants my feet on the earth that my feet trod in childhood. I assisted the carpenter this forenoon, and then the cooper in the blubber room. Though toiling against my will, my heart is fixed in heaven. The Austrian is more docile since the reprimand. Love's reproofs are effectual to my friend. God bless him! Clamorous voices and ribald jokes annoy my soul, and swearing is so prevalent among the boys. Poor mortals! They brave the terrors of the sea but know not Christ who died on Calvary. The pain our blessed Savior felt should melt the hearts of the seamen. O, could these tongues that curse and swear, be used to tell his sufferings! O could our songs in concert ascend to God who rules the sea and skies. A New Hampshire sailor had vowed to live a Christian life; but vows are soon made and broken by an unstable mind, and the profession is soon forgotten. I like to see the child of God stand fast, as the anchor holds in the storm. Before I retired to my berth I gazed and wondered at the works of God.

Monday, Jan. 23, 1865.

The boats were launched to stem the swelling flood. The fourth mate's crew was kept on board to help extract the oil. I filled my greasy station and by hurrying we finished our task by noon. While my hands were active, my thoughts were also busy, and I had a grand review of God's saving mercy. We dissected and rendered the hump-back whale. Fifteen barrels our victim of the deep supplied.

The Governor Troop came sailing in to-day. The Onward hove her anchor, spread her sails, and is now exposed to ocean gales. So vessels meet and sever on the ocean; some are foundered and appear no more. A world of changes on land and sea—all moving onward to eternity. No rest for mortals until the final repose; in the earth we moulder or in the restless deep.

My misdemeanor now troubles my heart. Ah my foolish jesting with the boys! Our carnal propensities are hard to overcome, and their indulgence produces sorrow. The Book of Inspiration ascribes no wrong to the man who rightly regulates his tongue. Exempt from condemnation is he who fully yields himself to God's control. But when bound to this sin-indulgent crew, it is hard to meet the Scriptural model. Grace is our cherished theme, no Sinai's gloom or thunder. Grace does not crush its subjects for each defect. It hears the voice of penitence, respects the mourner's tears, forgives his failures and quells his fears. Grace wields its benign influence over earth and sea, hence in my isolated state there is grace for me. Thus end the proceedings of another day. One truth is learned by me, that time is passing away.

Tuesday, Jan. 24, 1865.

There is hurrying, the usual noise to lower the whale-boats and dismiss the sailors. Each one seizes his accustomed oar and dextrously impels the boat. The sailor's life is one of toil and woe, and they must meet great hardships and perils. No landsman knows the burden of a seaman's life. John, the Portuguese, and I are in the blubber room. A landsman would be diverted at our costume when scooping up the oil collected in the hold. The try-works are blazing, the boys must toil to fill the pots with blubber. Nicholas is on the sick-list, retired from duty; a mild form of sickness affords relief.

The Cammilla anchored and abides with the fleet. This is a safe shelter from ocean storms. We hailed her as she passed our stern and the Captain and a boat's crew went aboard. The chief mate and boat's crew of said ship boarded us to exchange compliments and discuss nautical themes. Two seamen trod the barren coast in sorrow. They proved to be deserters from the ship Nimrod. The ship Cammilla now affords them a home. They had starved and perished had they been left to wander. The boats came early from their cruising expedition and we raised them to the davits of our gallant ship. I was grieved at the surly and petulant crews. So hard are their hearts and polluted their mouths that they pour out disgraceful torrents of oaths.

The sky at sunset wears a crimson hue and reflects its tints on the ocean. The grand display fills my soul with awe. How majestic the scenes of God's nature! I greatly admire his wonders on the sea, and wonder at man's future destiny. We boast of the splendors of human art and man's device, but God can eclipse all human displays of grandeur. And if the beauties of his eternal creation so much exceed man's imperfect efforts, what will personal appearance and the manifestation of the celestial world be? Let us not go through this world blind, and think we see.

Wednesday, Jan. 25, 1865.

All hands signaled at break of day. The Cammilla and Oriole have weighed anchor and sailed out, heading S.

S. East. We hailed the steamer "Golden Age," moving post-haste. She gave us tidings from our native country to cheer us in our solitary state. I would gladly scale her as she glides over the sea and, with the pleasant passengers aboard, be restored to my native land. I would embrace my Christian friends, speak with rapture face to face, and all these gloomy hours forget. But it cannot be. Be patient till the appointed time and thou shalt reach thy native shore.

We espied a hump-back whale along the coast, but it is best to count the cost before a battle. The breaking surges and the flying spray warn us to let the monster be. The men to-day are not so ill-disposed, and our nautical government is more tranquil. We are standing our regular sea-watches again. Oft, when billows overwhelm, the helmsman must still hold his post. It is one o'clock A. M. The relief is designated by the bell. The winds are lulled, the waters gently beat, and the stars above greet our yearning vision. Two hours more to keep our watch this night, and we shall have access to our berths to sleep. When toil is over, it is sweet to rest, where no pain intrudes nor sorrow heaves the breast. Let the weary sweetly sleep; let naught disturb.

Thursday, Jan. 26, 1865.

Dead calm this morning. Heading S. E. by south. To-day I hope to place a guard before my mouth. On duty on the larboard from 7 to 11 A. M., adjusting casks, ballasting,—ship-work for every man. A large shoal of black fish were seen; they were chased, and one captured by the Cammilla's crew. A whale or fish cannot escape the whaleman's sight, and if at all available, it must die.

It is past meridian; our watch is retired from duty. Relief from toil is ever much desired. So when the toils and woes of life are past, may we enjoy the calm repose where no cares annoy, no sorrows pierce the breast,

> "Where the wicked cease from troubling,
> And the weary are at rest."

I conversed with my shipmates upon my private theme, salvation, that unspeakable gift of God. Steering south-east; propelled by noble breezes, with towering masts and sails unfurled, we plowed the foaming seas. Now on the starboard then on the larboard side see her careen. Lo, see her bravely stem the rising surge! A ship with extended sails is a grand sight. When tossed and driven through the restless, foaming deep, agitation animates the crew. We retain our equilibrium as the ship rolls in the sea, and we are repeatedly drenched by the flying spray.

Friday, Jan. 27, 1865.

Our watch was called at 3 o'clock, A. M. I arose, and till break of day controlled the helm. The usual deck ablution then became our duty, more for health and cleanliness than for beauty. The sun appears crimson and tinges the swelling element of blue. No mountain tops, or forest trees obstruct our view. Again, O brilliant orb, thy beauty is revealed, thy pure, celestial light awakens and animates the world. Thy swift daily race is now begun, thou dost run thy course with great precision. Shining orb, disclosing thy Creator's might, and teaching his unbounded wisdom every hour. Thou dost guide the mariner across the main, whose position is uncertain when thy beams fail.

The cooper was irritable, the crew were profane; sometimes I reason to have them cease. I try to appease their anger and get them calm, but they are like the troubled sea which cannot have peace, while sin, the fire of hell, disturbs their breasts. The night is fair, and beautiful and bright; the numerous stars are shedding forth their light. It is no great task to keep our watch at night when all is tranquil on the swelling deep; but we tremble in the furious storm. The dreadful aspect fills us with alarm, when clouds of darkness veil the light, and foaming billows are rolling high. A sailor's life is a life of trouble when surges beat and angry tempests blow.

> O home eternal, fair and serene,
> Where no tempests sweep, no clouds shall intervene;
> All sinful passions shall forever cease;
> Naught in that heavenly clime shall mar our peace.

Saturday, Jan. 28, 1865.

I plied the helm in the middle watch last night. With my eyes upon the compass I knew my course was right. So with my eye of faith fixed on the Book of God, I shall be guided to his divine abode. When our four hours on duty had expired, I read the sacred volume of truth till I went to rest. I laid aside my ocean cares, consigned my all to God, and sought repose. At 5 P. M. my refreshing slumber came to an end, and I heard the murmuring deep as I awoke; a sound that startles not, for all is well, only the vessel's rise and fall. But my sleep was broken by the winds at war, when I heard the waves and tempest roar; and a scene terrific burst on our waking eyes—a foaming ocean and sable skies, with forked lightning playing through the air, and sharp thunder. If the final judgment portrays a deeper darkness, then only God can know the sinner's doom. Our changes at sea are from weal to woe, from a charming sunset to a furious storm, from a view of the stars to thunder peals and a sable night. Can we rest secure in this changing world, when we may be hurled from the summit of pleasure into endless deeps amid the darkness of death?

Steering south-east by east, with noble breeze, our bark glides swiftly on. The Cammilla, with sails extended, is left quite a distance behind. Of Christ's second advent I am reading now, and commenting thereon to my shipmates. The same Christ who walked on the sea and stilled the proud waves, shall come; the dead shall arise from their graves, and the saints shall meet and repair to the haven which is eternally fair.

> Perchance far down in the briny deep
> Some have mouldered away in their ghastly sleep,
> But shall arise when he comes, their reward to reap.

Sunday, Jan. 29, 1865.

The sun arose in beauty this morning, and shed his golden beams upon the sea. We have no special duty to perform to-day, only to control the ship upon her course. I spent my leisure time in the perusal of the Bible. The weather was pleasant, and a light breeze prevailed. The sun set in splendor; it was truly the emblem of peace. The moon and stars shine in beauty. O that my exit from the shores of time may be as lovely and serene as the setting sun to-night! It prefigured to me the peace of God in the soul, the light of the Christian displayed in his course of life, and his final, peaceful retirement in the shadows of death.

Monday, Jan. 30, 1865.

A lovely morning, so calm that our vision is cheered with the beautiful sight. The captain himself ascended to the masthead and performed the duty of a watchman; the chief mate is regulating the work on deck, mending sails, etc. The captain discovered a shoal of black fish. A boat was lowered and went in pursuit of them. Four times the harpooner darted but failed to secure any. Again he strikes, and the harpoon penetrates the heart, and the victim is secured. Three more boats were sent to their assistance, and they towed the fish alongside the ship. I read to J. Nolan from a pious book. I was ridiculed by Wallace, who, when I rebuked him, acknowledged his wrong. The night is beautiful and I am steering east south-east.

Tuesday, Jan. 31, 1865.

The larboard watch, ten in number, were aroused at 3 A. M. From then till 5 A. M. I stood on guard, peering through the darkness, over the rising flood, till the night was lost in the dawn of day, and the sun arose on the dark blue sea, and another bright day was begun. I gazed with cheerful vision on the scene, and thought of God who rules the darkness and the light. So shall this night of sin depart, and a golden day be ushered in; sorrow, vigilance and care will be past, and the saints shall rest in endless light. I am steering south-east by east, before a gentle breeze. The weather is warm; we lie on deck and sleep at night.

CHAPTER XVI.

Our Departure from Lower California. — Our Meetings in the Forecastle. — Our Invitation to the Captain and Officers, to Share in the Benefits of the Meeting. — Crossing the Equator. — Thoughts of Home.

ENOUGH, I presume, has been recorded in the form of a diary, giving an account of the daily occurrences on shipboard, and I now proceed with the general characteristics of my maritime life. As the close of my diary indicates, we had left the coast of Lower California, and were steering in the direction of the Marquesas Islands. On our voyage to the latter place, I was wielding my influence under the divine direction, to inculcate the principles of religion among my shipmates. I had now been with them a sufficient length of time to demonstrate my sincerity in the divine life, and my anxiety for their salvation, as well as my own.

George Wallace, the New Hampshire boy, and John Nolan, of New York City, began to be my warm adherents, and were apparently candid and earnest inquirers after truth. John Nolan was reared in the Catholic faith, but my fervency and untiring perseverance in the Christian cause, which I, by God's help, maintained, proved an incentive to farther investigation of the Scriptures. They appeared to sincerely and humbly confess their sinful depravity, and solicited my prayers in their behalf; and Nolan, being very sanguine in his penitential ordeal, opened the way to effect our religious exercises more publicly than I had before been accustomed to hold them. I was naturally inclined to be reserved, but he, being of a more impulsive and forward disposition, urged me to advance and publicly advocate such a pure and holy religion.

Our meetings were conducted in the forecastle, mostly during dog-watch, which is a broken watch between the regular day and night watches, during which time the two watches eat the last meal of the day. Our method of conducting our meetings was plain and simple, but God moved upon our hearts, and our little, unassuming service was interesting and attractive. The sailors before the mast especially attended, and one of the Portuguese from the Azores Islands—a Catholic by profession—was wrought upon, and could not resist the divine influence. He seemed to see more beauty and sacredness in our humble method of worshiping God than in anything he had ever witnessed before. He appeared to appreciate our devotional exercises, and his demeanor portended a penitent heart; but, of course, the Catholic element protested against his acceptance of such a religion, and ultimately succeeded in suppressing his honest convictions and quieting his mind by making him contented with his parental training.

Nicholas, the Austrian, to whom I referred earlier in this work, was also much disturbed. He had deserted the parental roof in his youthful career, and lost the use of his native language. He spoke the Spanish, Portuguese and English languages. He was an expert in marine duty and possessed a strong constitution, and was much esteemed by the officers and sailors. O how we yearned and prayed for a breaking down of the tempter's power, and a thorough conversion, if possible, of the entire crew.

We had now merged into the shock of battle, and we endeavored to hold up the ensign of the cross. The cabin boy, who was a pet of the officers for his humorous antics, witticisms, and aptness in nautical duties, became deeply impressed, and experienced, perhaps, the first wooings of the Divine Spirit. It was a rule on board our ship, that cabin and steerage boys should not mingle too much with the seamen before the mast; but the cabin boy was under the convicting power of God, and knowing the restrictions of nautical rules, he pleaded with the captain, with tears, for permission to attend our little meetings in the forecastle. And the captain, who was a professor himself, would not withstand the earnest entreaties of his youthful servant. The result, then, was that he came, by the consent of the captain, to our meetings and appeared to enjoy our Bible reading, prayer, singing, and plain and simple talks of the Savior's love and condescension to redeem and save the lost.

Thus, while some laughed and made sport of our humble, religious proceedings, others became seriously concerned about the salvation of their souls. The captain would not permit any disturbance of our peace. O how I longed for the captain's full consecration to God! He who rules the heavens and earth and sea, knows the yearnings of my heart. But though I was not privileged to see his humble surrender to God then, yet I sincerely hope that he may reap some of the benefits of the seed sown on the floating bark under his command. His heart was bent, at least, to ratify our humble and heaven-approved course. I struggled one whole night to overcome my own diffidence to solicit him and the officials to attend our meetings in the forecastle. My new associates in religious ties urged me to muster up fortitude. But the infernal adversary argued that if I obtained the consent of the officers to attend, we should be too puny and weak to entertain them. I presume that was about their reason for not coming.

It is quite a condescension on the part of the great and eminent to affiliate with the common and lowly persons on land or sea; but this is God's rule and order, the ignored and downtrodden shall be raised up, and the famous and exalted must be lowered to the plane of the Gospel. The humble Jesus, when in the meek and lowly walks of human life, could not, by his exemplary life, and pure and wise teachings, influence the proud and exalted inhabitants of Capernaum to condescend to the humble plane which he occupied. But their non-acceptance of his proposals was no reason that he should not offer them mercy on his own divine and equitable terms. God uses us as his agents to offer salvation to the low and high, but we are not licensed to accommodate the unsullied and blood-purchased religion of Christ to the carnal inclinations of depraved humanity.

The divine power seemed to urge me to appear before the captain and officers, and invite them to worship with us; and I was impressed with the idea that it was the appropriate time for me to clear myself of their blood, at least, if I could not accomplish any more. And after much hesitation and prayer to God to prepare me for the event, I braced myself up for the occasion and started on my errand, perhaps with feelings somewhat similar to Jonah's, on his way to Nineveh. I was soon ushered into the presence of those who had authority and superior intelligence. The shades of night were beginning to gather, and the captain and chief mate were walking back and forth on the quarter-deck, conversing together as they were often wont to do. I approached them with affability and Christian courtesy, removing my sailor's cap from my head,—as nautical discipline in the presence of an officer required,—and in a humble, solemn manner, presented my request. I asserted to them my prayerful anxiety for their religious welfare and that of the entire crew; that I was pressed to humbly solicit the presence of the captain and his officers to unite with us in our devotions to God, and lend their influence to a work so momentous and divine.

The captain replied with courtesy and kindness, and said: " George, go on with your religious work, and no one shall interrupt your services, and if we see proper to attend, we will do so." I politely thanked him, and returned to my place before the mast, with the consciousness that I had performed my duty, and that the Lord would take care of the little message I had communicated with meekness and godly fear. Whatever the result of my labors might be, I was happy in the thought that I was doing all to the glory of God, and for the good of my officers and crew. I had long with patience borne the insolence and abuses of some of the officers and crew, but now the Lord was affording me spiritual influence, and the fact that the opposing influence was, to a considerable extent, overcome, corroborated the evidence in my soul that the Lord, who controlled the sea, was blessing the work. And if those who began the Christian work with me, according to God's Word, failed to continue, still the work would be valid. The ten lepers were healed by the power of Christ, but only one of the number returned to give him glory. So many devils may be driven out of the human heart by the power of God in repentance, and yet afterwards it may not continue in his service till it reaches the full stature of manhood in Christ.

I wish that I, with all who have repented and believed on Christ, might now pass through the baptismal grave and experience the divine relationship in full, and fellowship with the people of God. But I can proceed no farther at present, neither can I lead those any farther, who are under my spiritual guidance. Yet the Lord will open the way for all things, if we trust him. We held our meetings regularly, save when our marine labors interfered with our appointments, and I truly felt much encouraged that I had sympathizers and helpers in the divine work. Withal I realized that my responsibilities were increasing, and that I must needs exercise a vigilant care over those who had less experience in the work, and be ready to impart to them seasonable instruction, so as to keep them fortified against the wiles of the devil and the baneful babblings of skeptics and infidels, who were swayed and prompted by infernal spirits, to quell our influence and destroy our peace in Christ.

It is one thing to prepare the human heart for the reception of the incorruptible seed, and another thing to nourish and cultivate it after it has been deposited. We learn in Divine Revelation of churches having been established by apostolic authority, that promised a vital, spiritual growth, but were hindered in their advancement and rendered abortive by Satanic influence. Thus the commands in the Scriptures, to watch and pray, are very significant; and though we be ever so vigilant ourselves, it is even then difficult to keep those governed and regulated under our care and supervision. We must bear in mind that while our religious efforts were being put forth we met with many rebuffs, scoffs and sneers by some of the depraved skeptics and infidels among the officers and crew; but physical violence the captain would have prohibited.

The devil frowns and sneers when the cause of Christ advances, and this frowning and sneering is accomplished by merging his infernal spirit into his agents. The more men are calloused in sin, the more effectually do they carry out the work of the devil. They become despisers of them that are good, high-minded, lovers of pleasure more than lovers of God. It is still worse when they come with the form of godliness, but deny the power.

One of our officers, who was very vile and abusive, molested me often, and I patiently endured his curses, sneers and abuses for a long time; but one evening I was passing from the after-part of the ship,—from duty, I presume,—to my proper place before the mast. When I reached the main hatchway, where he and the second mate were standing, he addressed me with insolence and cast reflections on my Christian profession, and, as a certain poet declares, "The Lord's appointment is the servant's hour," I felt that it was God's time for me to reply. I did, and God gave me the power. I vindicated the religion I had espoused, and apprised him of the fact that I was fervently attached to it, that all the impositions and abuses to which my adherence to it had subjected me, had not lessened my love for it; and that he could not deny that I suffered much abuse from him, but, to my knowledge, I had never given him an unkind word.

This was about the tenor of my reply, but not all of it. The second mate, who had more respect for religion, sanctioned my reply and gave me credit for the life I was living right in presence of the mate who was opposing me. The latter colored and held his peace, and from that time on, to the end of the voyage, I am pleased to say that he treated me with more respect. May God have mercy upon him, is my prayer.

I asserted in the closing of my diary that we steered in a south-easterly direction soon after leaving Margarita Bay, and yet I said we were bound to the Marquesas Islands. This would seem to be contradictory, as we were steering in the wrong direction. But I would reconcile the matter by stating that we were still cruising for whales after leaving the coast, and hence sailed in a south-easterly direction at times, and sometimes we adjusted our ship to the wind and were not regulated by the compass at all.

Steering as close as practicable to the wind is more difficult for the helmsman than to steer by a given point of the compass. I have often controlled the helm with much displeasure under the frowns and curses of an officer who was watching every defect, to criticise the helmsman. I have been so discouraged under such circumstances that I was almost ready to despair. With an agitated sea it was with great difficulty that we kept the ship either from coming too close, or suddenly escaping too far from the wind. Each digression would bring forth rash and unmerciful criticism. It is much easier to criticise than to perform. We often rashly condemn others, when, under like circumstances, we should do no better, and perhaps not as well. Christians are often criticised for their mistakes in life, when, if those, who are ever ready to find fault, would know by experience the temptations which they coped with and the trials to which they were subjected, they would be more slow and ruthful in their criticism. How often, in this checkered life, must critics bear the weight of their own severe criticisms! Christ himself declares that the judgment dealt out to others shall be meted back. It is lawful and proper to judge, providing we make use of righteous judgment.

On the twentieth day of February, 1865, we crossed the equator *en route* for the Marquesas Islands. Here the greatest heat of the sun is experienced. It is difficult to realize that we are just mid-way between the North and South poles, where the rays of the sun are vertical and the days and nights are equal. Here the ocean and the atmosphere are incessantly heated by the fiery sun. The heat is very oppressive, and there is a dense, close air which occasions a feeling of dullness and lassitude. I would not like to take up my abode in this region of intense heat, and frequent calms. This seems to impress one with the idea that it is the vast reservoir of the world. No doubt the heat is generated in such copiousness as to influence and modify the conditions of all other zones on earth and sea.

It is a great region for water supplies. The peculiar and stupendous work of evaporation is amazingly carried on, occasioned by the co-operation of the burning sun, the ocean and the atmosphere. What an intimacy and harmony exists in the mystical workings of these different elements and forces! The clouds above are the receivers of the immense volumes of water thus elevated from the sea, and the strong winds become the propelling power to urge them onward with their waters above the firmament, which are precipitated in the form of rain drops, and thus utilized to moisten the earth, and produce her timely vegetation for the sustenance of her millions of inhabitants. The mighty rivers whose courses are inclined to the sea are formed on the earth and though they are constantly depositing their vast volumes of water in this expansive reservoir, yet it is never full to overflowing. "All the rivers run into the sea; yet the sea is not full; unto the place from whence the rivers come, thither they return again."—Eccl. 1:7.

The trade winds digress from their regular course over the surface of the deep, and are upward inclined, to constitute another current in the upper regions of the atmosphere. God has most wonderfully balanced these forces in the universe, and controls them in their mystical operations with the greatest regularity. In the beginning he reduced all things from a state of chaos to order and harmony. He separated the land and water, and arranged the firmament above to divide the waters from the waters; that is "to divide the waters which were under the firmament from the waters which were above the firmament: and it was so." Thus all things are wonderfully made and the exquisite design discloses the infinite wisdom and power of the Designer.

That heart must be steeped in sin, darkness and ignorance that cannot see the beauty and propriety of fearing and serving such a wonderful Being, whose presence fills immensity and whose power and wisdom are displayed in the handiwork of his creation. It can be observed that everything in the great universe of God fulfills its purpose and design with the greatest accuracy; but man is an exception to the rule. He is also "fearfully and wonderfully made" and we are not obliged to wend our way over foaming billows to the equatorial regions to study the wonders of the creation of God; we can discover them right in the complicated machinery and intricate structure of man. But sin has demoralized his being and wrenched him out of his assigned place in the creation, and the redemptive process is far more difficult than the creative.

Since man's will power was consulted in the fall, it must be consulted in his restoration; and he being rendered abnormal by sin—that poison in Adam's posterity—the blindness of his vision prevents his admission into the spiritual atmosphere, to recognize and appreciate the force and beauty of the Redeemer's sacrifice. God's spiritual laws are organized and established with as much symmetry and harmony as the natural laws which govern the universe; and the change from our polluted condition in sin to the new element or spiritual sphere, is so vast that we must actually be "born again." And what then will the resurrection from the physical death be, when body and soul shall be fitted for the new heavens and the new earth? when this great sea shall give up her dead? And how many millions have been received with anguish into her amazing depths whose forms have wasted and vanished from human vision, and are now concealed in the deeps of eternity! But the power of his resurrection shall bring them forth, to bask in the sunshine of celestial bliss forever, or to wail in the infernal regions of woe. O may the contemplation of God's wisdom and majesty, and our accountability to him "for all the deeds done in the body" have the salutary tendency to keep us humble on land and sea! Let us diligently study the disclosures of his great wisdom and power in the books of revelation and nature; and may the knowledge we obtain be controlled and regulated by divine wisdom, so as to reveal our insignificance and entire dependence upon God for even the breath of life which we breathe.

I am perusing, in my leisure hours, a book on the sea, entitled, "Disca Mori,"—learn to die. It aims to impress the mind with a constant preparation for the event of death and our exit to the other world. Death should evidently impress a seaman's mind, for his yawning grave is ever visible. I recently was wrapped in slumber on the deep, and in dreams I soared to Columbia's land. I saw my sister Mary's pallid form in death's cold sleep. How lonely and dismal and sad was the scene, and how anxious I was to know whether it was only a dream. The tidings that she had landed in the deeps of eternity would sadden my heart on the sea. In the cherished home circle I would greet her once more. If the Lord will restore this prodigal I'd rejoice like the Biblical wanderer who from poverty's wreck was restored to the fold.

Bread-fruit.

CHAPTER XVII.

How I Lost my Wearing Apparel. — Replacing the Lost Goods at a Disadvantage. — An Interruption in our Repast. — Reflections Suggested by our Duties at the Helm. — An Imperative Command. — Our Arrival at the Marquesas Islands. — Depravity of the Natives. — The Abundant Supply of Fresh, Pure Water. — The Folly of Idol Worship, Contrasted with the Beauties of True Religion. — Deplorable Laxity of Matrimonial Life among the Natives. — Some Reflections.

ON February 21, 1865, while floating in the torrid region near the equator, provisions and clothing were distributed on our craft. I had recently lost several pieces of wearable goods and blankets, and consequently stood in need of another supply. After I had given them a thorough ablution, I attached a rope to them and fastened them to the ship and towed them in the sea to completely cleanse and rinse them. A defective place in the copper lining of the ship's exterior cut the strands of my tow-line and deposited my entire washing in the ocean. The proprietors hold the vantage ground; their trade is not extensive, but quite expensive. There is no competition, and in the emergency the consumer is obliged to purchase at any price. Patch upon patch is usually characteristic of a sailor's garb, until the original goods are barely discernible. So you discover that the loss of my clothing was quite a reduction on the income of my voyage.

To give my readers a sample of some of our ups and downs in the dining process, I will relate a circumstance.

We had a native of New York State, who had been reared and cultured on the Erie Canal. He was clumsy and ill-starred, and was incessantly meeting with misfortunes. One day some of us were eating our meal, which consisted of hash, hard-tack and coffee, in the forecastle. Presently we descried large bare feet descending the stair-way with a heavy coat of tar on the soles. It being in the Torrid Zone, we nearly all worked barefooted. Some one suggested that the hash-dish had better be removed, as the unfortunate New Yorker was descending; but we were all too busy taking in our coarse diet, and we paid little attention to the precaution. Finally he landed from the stair-way in the forecastle, and charged with one of his tar-coated feet right square into our hash-kit. Of course we were stuck on that meal. At another time it became the New Yorker's duty to return the hash-kit to the cook's galley, and when he reached the waist of the ship he essayed to deposit in the ocean a few crumbs that remained in the kit, and, in the attempt, threw the whole outfit into the sea. Having dispensed with more freight than he had designed, he was left with a feeling of dread suspense. The captain and mate, who were walking on the quarter-deck, got a glimpse of his startled mien, and were enabled by their quickness of perception to take in the bearings without any verbal explanation. The entire proceeding, in connection with the startled look, occasioned loud laughter.

On Feb. 22 we were in south latitude four degrees and thirty-five minutes, with a strong breeze all day, heading west south-west. On Feb. 23 my diary describes us as flying before the wind, still steering in the same direction. We had now come under the influence of the south-east trade winds, and the atmosphere was more bracing and exhilarating again. Our dullness and stupidness of feeling had vanished, and we were buoyant with life and cheerfulness. The nights were bright and starlight. Our Oriole flew before the wind, now raised on a billow's foaming crest, then down in the cavity of the deep. With her white sails extended, how grand the scene, as the gale wafts her over the ocean at night!

> Impel, ye winds, the Oriole,
> And o'er the billows let her roll,
> While thrills of joy pervade my soul!

So occur the changes of life on the dark blue sea. Sometimes I am stationed at the helm to guide our flying bark, as she raises and lowers over the foaming surges, and at other times I retain my responsible position as watchman, to discover and signalize any object that may chance to appear on the agitated deep. The watchman's position is truly responsible. On him, to a large extent, is dependent the safety of the ship and all on board. It is his duty, therefore, to be on the alert. For two hours he must cast his watchful eyes over the troubled ocean, and at the expiration of that time, he is relieved by another watchman. So I remark that the old ship Zion must ever be supplied with watchmen. She, too, is sailing over a troubled ocean. God supplies her with officers and crews, who succeed each other in the order of their generations. The very competent and experienced Captain has the whole affair under his supervision. The voyage is one of the highest moment. Terrific storms are encountered. Pirates are sailing over this tempestuous sea of life to perpetrate their cruel deeds of plunder and death. We must look out. Our safety depends upon our vigilance and prayerful mood. If we indulge in ease and comfort on our responsible posts of duty, our interests in this wonderful cause will be lost. We must shake off dull sloth and arise to action. We will have this care and responsibility as long as life endures. When death ends our career, another will relieve us. So the ship Zion must be guarded and supplied with trusty seamen, who will have fortitude to brave the perils of the deep, and whose fidelity to the Great Captain will never waver.

Often when we were relieved from our responsible stations on the Oriole, we were so fatigued that we heard with pleasure the relief signal, and soon were wrapt in deep sleep. So, when the woes and burdens of life are ended, we may gladly await the summons from the world above, to break the spell of care and sorrow, and hurry us away to lone and quiet repose in the domains of death.

One night, as I was plying the helm, a storm arose, and the rain was precipitated from the dark clouds in torrents (for in this torrid region the rain descends in torrents), the order from the mate was given to shorten sail. About all, save the watchman, were asleep on deck, it being more pleasant to repose on deck than below in this warm belt of the world. The officer was necessitated to repeat the command. It was thundered the second time with a severely imperative tone, accompanied by the most violent oaths. The sailors sprang to their feet and ascended the masts with hurried flight. They slipped along the yard-arms with dextrous movements, and soon the order given in wrath and harshness, was carried out by the boys.

I was relieved from my station at the helm in the midst of the storm, my two hours having expired. Everything moves on with regularity there, in storm or shine. Being relieved of my responsible task, I divested myself of my thin garments and bathed in the floods that were descending from the clouds. This was a refreshing bath in this ever-heated clime; sailors are regular water ducks at any rate.

We still have our religious meetings as we are sailing on the wings of the wind over the rolling billows. We read the Bible and talk of its saving power. Sometimes we peruse the Old Testament and at other times the New. We read recently of the Syrians' defeat under the power of Elisha's God. They went with an army to secure one man, and he, by the wisdom given him from above, deceived and conquered the entire host. How easily he controlled them! He would not allow them to be abused either, when the king of Israel came out and requested his decision in the matter of life or death. If we would ever keep before us the blindness and helplessness of our adversaries under the Gospel economy, we would not use rashness either. Their defeat is often shameful enough without submitting them to the secular power. "If they hunger, feed them, and if they thirst give them drink, for by so doing thou shalt heap coals of fire on their heads." Rom. 12: 20. The Syrians ate that meal in a very unexpected and critical place. I presume they were astonished. They certainly must have been at their wits' end. I would rather be a sailor on a pent-up floating craft than a Syrian fooled that way. Men of God are not always to be trifled with. When their time comes to gain the conquest, they are backed up by a host of re-inforcements. Take courage, my soul, Elisha's God controls the sea. No one knows what he may do for thee.

On Feb. 28, about 11 o'clock A. M., we dropped our anchor in Whitehoo Bay at the Marquesas Islands. As we entered the bay we fired two salutes from our signal gun and two canoe loads of the natives came aboard before we anchored. A number of the native women are aboard this evening for licentious purposes. I can measure the force and pertinency of that old missionary hymn we were wont to sing in our youthful glee in Sunday-school:

> "What though the spicy breezes
> Blow soft o'er Ceylon's isle;
> Though every prospect pleases,
> And only man is vile."

O the joy and blessedness that will follow the renovation of this sin-polluted earth. Every nook and corner of it is contaminated by the destructive bane. Our eyes must continually view with abhorrence its ravages on sea and land. The mild and persuasive methods of the Gospel can never quell its withering blights which are so universal. It will require the personal presence of a conquering Christ to stay its baleful power and wipe it out of his own created world. "He will destroy it with the spirit of his mouth and the brightness of his coming."

We take in a supply of fresh water at these islands. It flows in a perennial stream out of the crevices of the huge, solid rocks, reminding one of Israel's supply of old in a weary land. The lofty summits of these mountains attract the dense clouds, freighted with water, secured by evaporation on the deep; it is deposited in the form of rain upon the mountain tops, and thence penetrates the earth and the crevices of the rocks and becomes cooled and purified and fitted to slake the thirst of man and beast in this torrid region where the intense heat creates a burning thirst. So wonderful are the provisions of our beneficent Creator. But notwithstanding all his goodness and mercy in supplying all the needs of his creatures, man is ungrateful for his benefits and disregards his guardian care and love.

A SCENE ON THE MARQUESAS ISLANDS.

We presented the chief of the tribe with some of our edibles and were permitted in return to partake of the delicious fruits of the islands. These islands in the sea are similar, I presume, to the oases on the bleak and barren deserts, where the weary caravans are refreshed on their long and tedious marches. It is, indeed, refreshing to eat of the fruits of these fertile valleys, where the wild man roams and where the sun pours down his intense heat, to be sheltered beneath the cocoa's shade and lave at pleasure in the rolling waves of the sea that break in these safe retreats on a mild and gently-sloping shore.

We read the Bible and worship the universal God in a country where the inferior gods of wood are adored. The words of the prophets of the Lord, spoken long ago, deeply impress us when they earnestly remonstrated against idolatry. Isaiah declared that they cut down a tree and burned part of the tree in the fire to prepare a roast, and warm themselves when fire is required for that purpose, and from the stalk or trunk they manufactured their gods. Isa. 44. Poor Israel of old had become the devotee of such wooden gods; and after utilizing the tree for the various purposes alluded to by the prophet, they still imagined that the trunk of the same tree which they had carved into the shape and figure of a man, was a god. Their hearts were woefully deceived; and notwithstanding these plain disclosures of their sins and follies they would still adhere to their foolish, senseless, dead idols.

Any fool ought to note the deficiency of such a god, particularly when it is pointed out by a person of such sacred mien and profound intelligence as the inspired Isaiah of old. If the life, virtue and attributes of a god were in the trunk of a tree to deliver the mechanics who carved and polished it, as well as the king and all the subjects of his dominion, the remainder of the tree would undoubtedly recoil, and, with the force of a god, resist such unmerciful treatment. But consider, too, the ignorance of the Dagon worshippers of yore. That god, who had neither life nor brains, confronted the ark of God and fell over on his face. When his devotees came early in the morning (they had much more respect for him than he had for them) they found him in a helpless condition: he could fall, but he could not get up alone. They helped old Dagon up again. Perhaps they thought that he was in rather a sad predicament; but then they had always been educated to believe that he was really a god. It is difficult to change the mind that has always been trained in idolatrous worship, and likely the Philistines concluded that Dagon was a god and they would make him stand. But he fell over the second time before the ark of the Lord. The last time he must have been precipitated with more violence than the first, for the shock knocked his hands and head off. As a judgment from the Lord they were smitten with emerods, and their decision, amid judgment and pain, was to replace the ark of God where it belonged, with the conviction that it was hard on them and their god.

The Philistines should have discovered that Dagon was not able to help himself, let alone the people. But there are religious worshipers in this enlightened age of the world who, perhaps, are as badly deceived as the Pagan worshipers and the transgressing Israelites were.

We are born of the will of the flesh, and of blood and of man, and we may hold fast to the respective beliefs as tenaciously as they of old did. Our conscience may be at times reproved and the god of our affections be injured, but yet, because the heart has been fortified by early religious training in that course, we are reluctant to discard it. Some eminent, intelligent man may steal the affections of our hearts as the learned Jewish rabbis deceived the people, even in the days of Christ's personal teachings and display of miraculous power, and thus we may be born of the will of man. And if thousands of human beings were mistaught and deceived by men with the advantage of Christ's personal teachings and disclosures of power, may we not, with good reason, conclude that many will be misled now by human teaching and influence, even though they have access to his Written Word?

Men of intellect and culture will become a power for good or evil in this world, therefore each for himself should study and examine the living words of Christ and his inspired apostles. They are the only safe-guard against deception, and the detective power to discriminate between truth and error. Blood relationship has a prominent bearing on our profession, especially if we have not experienced the genuine new birth, or birth of God. Christ says, "He that loveth father and mother more than me, is not worthy of me: and he that loveth son or daughter more than me, is not worthy of me. And he that taketh not up his cross and followeth after me, is not worthy of me," Father and mother have a deep seat in our affections, and it is right that they should have, but not to the extent that should mislead in the doctrines of Christianity. By virtue of the ties of natural relationship we should always respect them, but we should not allow an influence as close as theirs to warp our judgment with regard to Christ and his superior teachings.

The spiritual ties of relationship, experienced by virtue of our union with Christ, are far above the natural.

The newly-born child of God is completely controlled by this new bond of union; and we can only love father and mother, son and daughter in a superior sense, in the sense in which Christ has loved us all, and laid down his life for us. There has been many a family thrown into a commotion because of a separation of carnal fellowship and union with Christ; but unless this separation is effected in its Scriptural significance, we can never exert the pure Christian influence, in its purity, over our blood relatives. By accepting Christ by the faith of the Gospel, we may be made the instruments in his hands, of bringing our own relations to the light; and if they have been erroneously taught, and have misconceptions of the Word of God, the Lord will enable us, in the home circle and among our relations, to counteract their spurious teachings. By being living examples of the truth, as it is in Jesus, we may become the agents in God's hand of leading them into the divine relationship, whose bonds of union shall endure forever.

To be "born of the will of the flesh," is to be flesh-indulgent and pursue all the avenues of carnal interest. It may be under the guise of religion, but the gratification of the carnal propensities is the leading characteristic. How many religious entertainments come under this head, where the love of money is the ruling element, and pomp and ostentation, style and gaudy attire follow in the course of sacrilege? This kind of religious worship, I am fully persuaded, is quite prevalent all over the civilized world. It is not prejudice, but a love for Christ and his pure, unsullied religion that induces me to protest against it. It will evidently be found connected with the spiritual Babylon, whose terrible downfall is depicted in the Apocalypse.

They who are bent upon flesh indulgence, will have it, possibly to the full; but their climax of pleasure will be reached at perhaps no very great distance in the future; Babylon, with all her wealth, fame and ostentation, will go down with a fearful crash. Her opulence, including all the

APPROACHING ONE OF THE ISLANDS.

varied costly commodities, enumerated by John the Revelator, extends over and enriches the greater portion of the world, and the sudden and unexpected decline of her glory will be lamented over land and sea.

Paul told the wise but perverted Athenians of old, after they had reached their extremity in manufacturing gods, as signified by their own inscription, "To the Unknown God," "whom yon ignorantly worship, him declare

I unto you." He told them that in this God, whom he declared, we live, move, and have our being, and that he had made of one blood all nations, and had fixed the bounds of their habitations. Paul's God is the great omniscient, omnipresent and omnipotent God; his foreknowledge took in the situations and locations of all nationalities, and I can conceive, as I look upon these heathen people, bowing down to stocks and stones, that God has fixed the bounds of their habitation in these remote islands of the great ocean, and I am convinced that they greatly err in their judgment of the living and true God. But the Athenians, with all their refinement and proficiency in the arts and sciences, knew no more about him, and I must conclude that many of the popular and intelligent in this nineteenth century, arrayed in the popular garb of religion, have but little more knowledge, practically, of the crucified life and the vital power of the cross than the Athenians or these islanders.

Pandering to the flesh wars against the soul, finally extinguishes the spiritual life of the once live believer, and he recedes into the formal life, devoid of spiritual power. The Jews, who were instructed in their code of laws, enacted and transmitted to them by the God of heaven, ceased to be guided by them, and apostatized into the popular religion of their day, which was idolatry. The prophets of the Lord disclosed the foolishness and utter impropriety of their service; but, animated by heathen fame and popularity, and wholly given up to such a service, they recoiled at the representations of the true God and his service; the great chasm of separation became wider and deeper between them and God's faithful prophets, and their words of truth and power became to them as idle tales. Like the

Sodomites of old, they were ripe for destruction; and the wrath of him, whose supreme delight it was to bless, was poured out upon them.

The apostle John says, "Little children, keep yourselves from idols." He evidently does not have reference alone to the gods constructed of wood and stone, which these South Sea islanders adore. There are other idols which are more likely to steal the affections of a refined and cultured heart, such as the idol of wealth, or the idol of fame, or of pomp and show, pride, love of self. All these indulged and pandered to are included in tne idolatrous channel alluded to by the inspired writer, and it requires close examination and scrutinizing care to escape the pollutions of these baneful influences. We are too apt to locate idolatry among the heathen people and overlook the fact that our own civilized world is rife with it.

The Bible is a very close reckoner and Christendom itself, I fear, is too superficial in her observations. It reminds me of the story I used to hear about a faithful preacher. His preaching was too strict and searching for his congregation. He preached against pride, and they took exceptions to it. He preached against covetousness, and they did not like it. He condemned their union with the world and its customs and maxims, and they were offended. Feeling somewhat disheartened, he said, "What shall I preach?" They said, "Preach about the Jews." So, I remark, when the minister is loyal to his divine appointment, and discloses the restrictive discipline of God's Word, which discards and severs all the fashionable idolatry in the civilized world, the people are ready to shift the entire responsibility on to the untutored heathen; and if he preaches about idolatry at all, they would rather have him confine it to the heathen world where the devotees bow down to stocks and stones.

Let me relate some more about the natives of the Marquesas Islands. They appear to remember us distinctly, from our acquaintance at the first arrival, when we experienced some trials and adventures among them, as already recorded. They still recognize me as the missionary, because of my adherence to the Great God of the heavens and earth and sea, to whom I had, by gestures and signs, cited them before. I feel rejoiced at the thought that I am leaving impressions on the minds of these poor, deluded idolaters that I will not have occasion to regret when I appear before God in the other world. We are responsible for our lives and actions, wherever we go in this world; and although I cannot, through the medium of their own tongue, communicate to them a knowledge of the condescending Christ and his dying love for the whole world, yet my demeanor, as a follower of that humble, self-sacrificing and loving Jesus, should be known and read of all men, the wild man not excepted.

Their customs and modes of life are singular. There does not appear to be much tenacity in wedlock, or matrimonial life. The marriage ceremony is of a very crude and eccentric order. I am told that the parents of the bridegroom secure one of the hogs that run wild over the island, of slender form, long, with long bristles, elongated noses, and large tusks. It is dispatched and roasted, and the friends of the groom and bride, including the parties engaged to be married, share the repast, and marriage is consummated. But from what information I could gather, the bond of union simply connected is often disconnected, perchance without any ceremony at all.

Some of the civilized nations also have a bad record on the marriage question. It is surprising to notice the dissolutions of the matrimonial bonds in the United States. There is commonly much style and ostentation in the nuptial ceremony and feast, but perhaps the cohesiveness, as to duration of time, is nearly similar to that of the wild, untutored parties of the islands in the sea. Let me tell the young people of America, that the marriage union is one of grave solemnity. In hundreds of instances it is too loosely entered into by the giddy, light and gay. God, in the beginning, instituted wedlock, and rendered it legitimate by giving it his own divine sanction. It was regarded as a grave subject by our ancient worthies, and they were cautious in making selections for their sons and daughters. If more precaution and sober thought were exercised in this age of the world, we might show a better example to the heathens.

In proportion as the religious world relaxes its moral restraints, in about the same proportion, I conclude, will be the declension of virtue and fidelity in marriage. Everything will be known by its own fruits at last, and the censure will be located by the righteous Judge where it justly belongs. Lightness and frivolity in religion begets the same spirit in marriage. Cheerfulness, fidelity, honesty, sincerity, gravity and humility will wield their salutary influences over connubial ties. If this spirit of laxity and license to the flesh continues in the churches and the world, what will be the magnitude of their atrocities in the avenging day?

"Let him that nameth the name of Christ, depart from iniquity." That is one of the seals of the genuine Christian; and the other is, "The Lord knoweth them that are his. Christ never countenanced or ratified sin in any of its phases, neither can the Christian; and his separation from it will evince to all his integrity and attachment to Christ. "The Lord knoweth them that are his," and it matters not whether those whose consciences are defiled by sin know it or not, the Lord is the great and just Being with whom we will have to deal at last, and it will be worth more than all the fame and wealth of the world to be known and identified as his. Let us descend low into the vale of humility that we may learn the real mind and character of Christ, so as to obtain his mercy in the great day of final accounts.

CHAPTER XVIII.

Habits of the Marquesas Natives. — Intoxicants and Tobacco, their Great Curse. — How I got rid of the Tobacco Habit. — Serious Thoughts. — A Native Dinner. — Eating in Primitive Simplicity. — Music among the Natives. — My Experience with a Bamboo Fife. — The Bread-Fruit Tree. — The Restraining Power of a Godly Life.

IN our island roamings in nearly any direction we can see the almost nude forms of the dark-skinned natives. Some are stretched in lazy attitude beneath the cocoa shade; others, with rapid gesticulations and quaint antics, are conversing in their strange tongue, unknown to us; some are sitting composedly in a cross-legged posture in their rude and uncouth huts, while others are at intervals bathing in the sea.

They have their social entertainments and drunken revels. Even in these remote islands intoxicants are manufactured. The traffic is not so extensive, nor is it systematized as in the civilized world. They have no signs suspended designating saloons where the special traffic in the abominable poison is carried on, and thousands are hurried along the drunkard's path to ruin. They indulge in an intoxicating drink, manufactured from the juice of the kava root. I am informed that they chew it and spit the juice in a wooden bowl, and then, after diluting it with water, strain and drink it. Their brain is uncultured when in its normal condition, but who would wish to risk his life among them when intoxicants have crazed it? Oh, ye tipplers and inebriates of the civilized world, will you imitate the heathen in their drunkenness and debauchery? Ye, who have all the facilities for the culture of brain and intellect, and modesty and decency of character, will you allow the destructive intoxicants and the demon alcohol to dethrone your

METHOD OF THE NATIVES IN KINDLING FIRE.

reason and deprave and waste your God-given faculties until you become forlorn and desolate wrecks, reeling and tottering on the verge of grim death, with the dark forebodings of the drunkard's doom in hell?

Tobacco is also voraciously devoured. Their systems must be entirely saturated with this narcotic. They even swallow the juice, and their whole organism must be affected by its excessive use. They smoke vigorously, and it does not seem to concern them where it enters the system or finds its egress, or whether it escapes the precincts of the body at all. They apparently swallow an occasional whiff, and a portion of the smoke is forced out through their nostrils, part of it through their large mouths, and some, I presume, descends into the interior of the demoralized system. That we may call heathenish. But the civilized man furnishes the wild, uncultured men with the tobacco. That looks bad. He chews and smokes with him too. So far as the traffic and habit are concerned, you might take them all to be heathens; and in many other bad traits besides, you would be driven to the same conclusion.

I was once a tobacco-chewer myself. I still continued the habit in the commencement of my religious career. My eyes had not been opened yet to observe that it was an unbecoming habit for me, who professed godliness. A vile officer with a Jehu spirit, was the agent for my reproof. One day the crew were encircling the booby hatchway. The captain had a tobacco cask opened, and was issuing the large, black plugs to the officers and crew. I stood in the class of receivers. Plug after plug was handed out, and finally a long, broad and thick navy-plug was presented to me by the captain. I good-humoredly received it, intending to chew it as I had been wont to do. Presently the officer in the Jehu lineage looked into my eyes with a taunting smile, and said, "That looks nice for a Christian." He had evidently hailed me in the very act, and reproved me before all, not that others might fear, but that I might be made a gazing-stock, a reproach and by-word.

It was an unexpected reprimand, and it came from a source unlooked for; yet there was a bearing of propriety in it. There was a sarcastical smile accompanying the ironical remark, and I was left before that laughing assembly in an awkward position, with the heaviest plug of tobacco that I ever before handled. I studied the tobacco question and the propriety of a Christian using it. I was habituated to its use, and to break the fleshly charm would require a resolute will; but I did not want the use of it to reflect upon my Christian character, and so I vowed before God and my shipmates that I would discontinue its use.

One of my shipmates rejoined, "If you quit it, George, I will quit it too." And we together hurled our plugs overboard, into the great Pacific Ocean. My colleague in this self-sacrifice was afterwards overcome by his hankering appetite and resumed its use again, but, by God's help, I have not used tobacco since the year 1864. I am glad this day for the mate's reproof, and my abandonment of the unbecoming habit, I hope, has convinced him of my sincerity in the Christian cause and my full desire to deny myself of anything that might prevent the free course of God's Word.

An aged minister of the Gospel once said: "A Christian ought to retain his balance, for God watches him; he should watch himself; the world watches him, and the devil watches him. They all watch for their respective purposes; but though the watching is prompted by various motives, it should keep the Christian straight."

Some of the civilians and unbalanced professors may conclude that my illustrations, drawn from heathen practices to reprove them, are uncharitable; but I remark that Christian reproof, received and given, is a means appointed of God to reform and save us, and we should have love enough and stamina enough to correct each other. "An open rebuke is better than secret love."

> "Sin is sin where'er 'tis found,
> On Christian or on heathen ground."

I am in the school of discipline myself, and I am daily being bettered by the buffetings of the devil, and the re-

A CABIN BOY ATTACKED BY NATIVES.

straints and wooings of divine love; and I will not admit to any one that I am a peculiar creature for nothing,—it is the correcting influence of God that makes me so. I have quit the pursuit of worldly pleasure, and must remain in the crucible to reflect the image of the refiner. The refining process to myself is often painful to the flesh, and you flesh-indulgers need not look for ease and comfort from me, for I can impart only the kind of treatment to you that I get myself. The smelting furnace of God's Word has extracted some of my preconceived ideas, and it continues to cast off the dross and alloy each day.

This renovating ordeal induces me to endorse all the good qualities of my parents, and blood relatives, and discard the bad. Truth is a wonderful balancer, and Christ must be honored above father and mother. Whatever principles have been instilled into our being, by their influences, that do not harmonize with God's perfect criterion, must be consumed in the purifying furnace.

I never had a more tender feeling for my mother than during my long and dismal absence on the deep; and I often portrayed to my vision her lonely attitude, her sighs and prayers and tears, but, notwithstanding all these maternal qualities, my mother was not prepared, in my youthful career, to teach us the system of faith, in full, which effects our separation from the world, and moulds our will-power to a full consecration to the divine service. Hence, in these things, I was constrained, by divine love, to take issue with mother.

One day, while I was roaming leisurely over the island, I accosted about four of the natives in the act of dining. They were sitting cross-legged on the ground in a circle, around a large wooden dish, which was filled with boiled tara roots, of about the consistency of boiled mush. It reminded me, somewhat, of the mush-pots of America; but the eating process was altogether different. They were not supplied with spoons, but each thrust his fingers into the nutritious substance, and there appeared to be no time lost. They gave me a cordial invitation to participate in their uncouth repast. I did not hesitate to seat myself in the circle, and, if one had judged from my method of taking in nourishment, he might have concluded just then that I had been raised on the islands. But while dipping my finger into the dish, I endeavored to keep to my own side, and if I did not eat heartily, I went through the motions at any rate.

It is good, in some things, when we are in Rome, to do as Rome does; but that rule will not hold out in every particular. Paul said that when he was among the Jews, he became a Jew. I presume that feature, in any of their customs, did not militate against the Gospel. And we will find, if we travel much, that it is not best to be too radical in our own peculiar customs, unless we have direct Scripture authority. If we have, we need not consult consequences.

The inhabitants of the Marquesas Islands, like nearly all other human beings, are fond of music; but their musical instruments are not very finely graded, and their science of music is not in a high state of culture. All the instrument that I saw was a rudely-carved, oblong, flat box, hollow, with a string spanned tightly over it. At the end they would place their mouth over the string, and then manipulate, with their finger, over the hollow place. Different sounds would thus be produced by the action of their mouths, something on the principle of performing on a Jew's harp. They seemed to be quite elated at their proficiency in the uncouth art, and charmed themselves more than they did us. We thought, "When ignorance is bliss, 'tis folly to be wise." I felt just then that, if I had my cornet, upon which I used to discourse some sweet music, I would summon them together with the accents of my horn, and afford them some idea of America's culture in the science of music. Perhaps there was a little pride lurking somewhere in me.

I went and procured me a nice, straight piece of bamboo, and manufactured a fife, which instrument I also played in my military career. It was indeed amusing to see the attraction. They came together from all directions, and regarded me as some supernatural being, and even the sailors themselves wondered that I had kept my musical talent a secret. I was repeatedly called upon to perform, and I found, eventually, that it lent a greater charm than my religion. Seeing that it began to disturb the sailors' feet, and fearing that it might grant license to the flesh, and intrude upon the sacredness and solemnity of my Christian profession, I treated my instrument as I did my tobacco, I threw it overboard.

I would not say, on account of this circumstance, that any and all musical instruments are forbidden to a professor of religion, but I would say, at least, that whenever we see that they are detracting from our spiritual influence, we should evidently abandon the use of them. The Bible affords many incidents, of the performers on instruments, in olden times, and some excellent musicians were found among God's own people. But Christ, who could have played all instruments to perfection, as far as we know, never gave us one example, and never said that his disciples should use this awakening method to inculcate the divine music of the Gospel. All the Christian's license in the science of music must be sought for in the performers of old.

The bread fruit tree bears very valuable fruit and comprises one of the staple articles of food. The inner bark is tough and pliable, and is manufactured into clothing. But little clothing, however, is required, as the natives go almost nude. The cloth is produced by pounding the bark, with a round piece of wood, on a large, smooth stone. The tree is of fair size, about forty to fifty feet high, and devoid of branches till quite a distance up the tree. The leaves are from twelve to fifteen inches long, and are dark green in color. The fruit is roundish, and rough on the exterior. When it is fully ripe it is yellow, but it is gathered for use before it is fully ripe. The pulp is then white, and nearly of the consistency of fresh bread. The natives dig a hole in the earth, and place therein heated stones. These are covered with green leaves, then a layer of fruit, then stones again, next leaves, and so on alternately until the hole is nearly full; after which the hole is filled with leaves and earth. In less than an hour the bread fruit is baked. It is very nutritious, and answers for bread.

The time is drawing near, when we must again leave these islands, and take our chances on the unstable ocean. We have enjoyed this pleaasnt recreation, and cannot help but feel a degree of reluctance to effect our departure. Truly we could not think of settling permanently with these wild inhabitants of the islands; but to reflect on our many days of gloom, in the past, on the troubled ocean, and then of the enjoyment of this respite, and the great comfort, afforded by the delicious fruits, makes it seem hard to shape ourselves to the old channel of hardships again. I have tried to deduce all the instruction I could with my limited conception of things, and ability to make an application of the knowledge, and I desire to utilize my experience for the benefit of others, religiously, since I have been benefited myself.

Our grave decorum and pious mien was a restraint upon the sinful indulgences of officers and crew. They could not sin with as much ease and freedom as they could have done, had there been no moral and religious counter-action. Hence they would demur against us, and we would defend our position from the Bible, and reprove their wickedness.

CHAPTER XIX.

Departure from the Marquesas Islands. — Thoughts Suggested by our Onward Movement. — Difference between Paul and Jonah. — The Power of a Godly Life. — Arrival at Hawaii Island. — Value of Good Anchorage. — Bro. Robert Jones' Recital of his Experience in the English Channel. — Some Incidents while in the Bay of Hawaii Island. — Departure for Honolulu.

MARCH 14 we took our leave of the natives, hove the anchor, and set sail for the bosom of the ever-rolling deep. We took our lingering look at the natives and their island home in the sea, believing that we should never see their brown faces any more in this world. We watched the lofty mountain peaks, until, in the dim distance, they were lost from our vision. So we had merged again into the old element of the sea-faring life.

But the spell of gloom was, in a great measure, broken by the religious meetings which continued. O how much religious exercises break and modify the irksomeness of life's hardships and woes! We can have no greater pleasure in this world than these exercises, and we should apply our Christian energies to influence others to have the same pleasure in them. The love of God is very pure and unselfish; and when the child of grace is controlled by this divine principle—love—he cannot seek to enhance his interests alone, but the interests of others. It is, in reality, by forwarding the interests of his fellow-men that he advances his own. Hence, the way to be happy ourselves, is to make others happy. I endeavored to carry out this principle to the best of my ability, and I sincerely hope that not one of the officers and crew can arise in the judgment and say that I did not free myself of their precious blood, if they are so unfortunate as not to be rescued and saved after all these evidences and entreaties of the Divine Spirit.

We are all performing our respective parts in the great arena of time, and we are operating either for weal or for woe. Eternity alone will disclose the full magnitude and responsibility of our existence in this world. God holds our destinies and will mete out the judgments for our disobedience, and reward us for our compliance with the instructions his Son has given us. So great is the contrast between time and eternity and so terrible will be the wailings of the lost and doomed that the crosses and oppositions, encountered by the Christian, will be so little in comparison with the misery of the damned, that the Christian, who is enlightened in God's Word, should stand for the right though all the world oppose and men forsake him.

Paul, when a prisoner on the Mediterranean Sea, on his way to Rome to appear before Cæsar, admonished the seamen, but they did not heed, at least not all his admonitions. They might have saved themselves much sorrow and hard experience, had they heeded his words of wisdom, influenced and suggested by the Divine Spirit. But because they refused his instructions, Paul did not say, " Do as you please, then, and I will not try to instruct you any more." He pitied them still, though he knew that he must suffer adversity with them. That hero of the cross was so accustomed to opposition that it seemed immaterial to him whether he endured it on sea or land. He prayed that God would preserve their lives and obtained the assurance that he would, though the ship was doomed to be lost.

I imagine I can see that ship of yore "driven up and down in Adria," with the disheartened seamen aboard, save the renowned prisoner who was undaunted by the roar of the tempest and the dashing of the foaming waves. He knew more than the captain did about their fate, and so the children of God could often forewarn people how to escape danger and sorrow in this life, but their judicious admonitions are regarded as being insignificant, and they are left to suffer for their own disrespect and heedlessness. They must have been in great distress, as they had not eaten for fourteen days, and Paul broke the long-continued fast by blessing the bread and meat which they ate. This serves as a remarkable instance to give an idea of what sailors endure when struggling between life and death. The needed comforts of life are all forgotten in the spell of gloom and sorrow. How those comparatively small ships in that age of time must have been overwhelmed in the cavities of the furious sea! The seamen must have been continually drenched, and in terror and jeopardy day and night.

O could they but have realized what a jewel they had on board. He was no fugitive Jonah, soliciting them to plunge him in the deep for his misdemeanor; but it was heroic Paul absorbed in the element of divine "love that casteth out fear." Let the reader think of the difference between fleeing from the presence of the Lord and being bound with a chain for adherence to his cause,—in the line of duty and out of it. Let him look at the serenity on the one hand and the terror and dread on the other. Jonah conceals himself from the mariners in the hold of the ship; and, loaded down with the burden of his guilt, he tries to forget his sorrows and woes in sleep. Ah, what an insecure sleep! The seamen are astonished at his drowsiness in such a perilous hour. The black clouds lowering, the tempest in fury sweeping, and the destructive billows beating mercilessly upon the helpless ship, and the prophet of the Lord asleep! The captain himself was obliged to awaken him out of his stupid, guilty slumber. Hear his memorable words in that woeful night: "What meanest thou, O sleeper? arise, call

A SHIP IN THE STORM!—CHRISTIAN MARINER ON LIFE'S TROUBLED OCEAN, HOW IS IT WITH THEE?

upon thy God, if so be that God will think upon us, that we perish not." Jonah 1: 6.

Let the careless, drowsy professor remember fugitive Jonah. Is he evading duty? Is he trying to escape the restrictions of the Lord? Is he evading the cross of Christ? Has he relapsed into dull, heedless and guilty slumber? Can he sleep while the storms of sin are raging and thousands are perishing around him? Even the unconverted are startled at his stupidity and wonder at his lethargy, while the winds of desolation sweep.

The two disasters occurred on the Mediterranean Sea. But observe the vigilant eye of Paul. The captain does not need to arouse him; he is wide awake. No occasion for an unbeliever to tell him to call upon his God; he made a business of that in gloom or shine, in storm or calm. He had already consulted the Lord as to their fate and destiny, and the Lord assured him that not a man should be lost. He was in the line of his duty, he needed not to fear the sea or be ashamed of his chain, for he was a prisoner for Christ's sake. Let them extend the main-sail and let the ship drive before the wind, there was no danger of foundering on the rocks in the dark night. The wreck must take place where the seamen can make their escape. Paul prayed for the safety of the crew.

Let reckless sons and daughters of pious fathers and mothers think how many prayers are offered for them, when storms are raging and dangers are threatening on every hand, when they are in danger of the physical death, but much more of the horrors of the second death. Perhaps, in many disasters of life, their lives are spared through the earnest pleadings for mercy of their pious parents. God loves them for their obedience to him, and hence hears their prayers in their children's behalf. Let them think of it solemnly before they reach a disastrous scene that will prove fatal and they are hurled into eternity beyond the reach of prayer. Pious parents are a great blessing; let their children think of their value and heed their precious counsels.

God's people should be greatly admired and esteemed. They are the salt of the earth and their prayers and religious influence have a preserving quality. They save the erring when they are not aware of it. I conclude that it is a precious thing that God places here and there a grain of salt among the demoralized seamen on the rolling deep. But for the salt there would be a mass of corruption. I presume that all on board the ill-fated ship on the Mediterranean would have been lost, had it not been for that one man whom God honored. Because he had influence with the God of the sea and the storm, and pleaded for the safety of the rest, God had mercy and saved them. I meet now and then a man on the sea who fears God. They are few and far between, but God raises up some in whom he has delight, and makes them a preserving power to others; I mean in the sense already alluded to, through their prayers and Christian influence.

Abraham prayed for the preservation of Sodom and Gomorrah. He began with forty and ended with ten; and God promised to save the cities if ten righteous were found in them; but those cities did not contain the specified number, and consequently could not be saved from the burning flames. That faithful man of God went to the full extent with his pleadings. He knew that his God was terrible in judgment when once his vengeance was aroused. He dreaded the impending gloom, the sable cloud that hung over the doomed cities. There was not a sufficiency of salt, and the storm of wrath could not be stayed. But not one grain of the precious material will God permit to be lost in the fatal disaster.

When the time of probation is over, then will all men know how God discriminates between the righteous and the wicked. When the wicked are intoxicated with the pleasures of this world, they may regard the righteous as the offscouring of the world; but when their cup of iniquity is full and the wrath of God is poured out without mixture into the cup of his indignation, then shall the wicked know that the righteous people, whom they often ignored and despised, were the preserving power of the earth. The saving of the righteous will even be a sacred work. So precious and costly was the blood that was shed to save us, so pure and unsullied was the sin-atoning victim that was sacrificed on the cross, so terrible is the counteracting force of sin and so adhesive to this corrupt flesh is sin that even the impurities that remain in God's people must be eradicated ere they can be rendered meet for the pure and spotless clime.

"Lot's wife looked back and became a pillar of salt." In a fleshly sense there were attractions. They had hurriedly left their home in the city, where they had often been grieved, it is true, because of the gross crimes perpetrated by those wicked inhabitants, and the baleful influence that was exerted by them over their own sons-in-law. They had borne their insults and had been vexed for years in succession; but still fleshly ties had a strong hold upon them, and it was a moment of deepest trial when the hour of their anguish was near and the revengeful storm was threatening. We must set our faces straight forward and flee from the spot we have so long occupied and from the faces that were so familiar to us. But when God withdraws his help, we can do no more for our friends or kindred. All communication may as well be cut off then, and our presence be speedily withdrawn, for the day of his wrath is here, and the time of their wailing in anguish has come.

I never realized the force of this command so much as when in the hazardous contest with the monsters of the deep. The oarsmen who impelled the boat were obliged to enter the battle with their backs toward the enemy; and it required the strictest vigilance and the most cautious restraint to keep from turning our heads to survey our dangerous plight. But the harpooner in the bow of the boat, and mate in the rear, or stern, had to be eyes for us, and our vision had to be thrown directly opposite to the scene of slaughter and death. And when the whale was quivering beneath the harpooner's blows, and striking his ponderous tail on the surface of the deep, and the vehement and imperative command was uttered by the Mate, "Stern all," every instinctive impulse of nature had to be counteracted to prevent our heads from turning and looking back.

This only serves to illustrate how difficult it sometimes is to overcome our natural sinful propensities and the surrounding pressure of the world, brought to bear upon us, and fulfill the command of God. We are too apt to take hold of the Gospel plough and look back to the world, and so render ourselves unfit for the kingdom of God. The contest between the flesh and the spirit is so strong that it is very difficult sometimes to perform the things that we would.

In navigation we have what seamen term lee-way; it is the drifting of the vessel lee-ward by the under-current of the sea. It is by the daily observation of the sun, whose altitude is designated by the reflecting glass of the sextant (with an imaginary line drawn from the center of the earth, to the center of the sun, which forms the basis of the intricate problem), that the variation of the ship from her direct course can be corrected, and her exact whereabouts in the deep be plainly pointed out. So I remark that the daily observations of the child of God should be taken on the ocean of time, where sin is rife and its pressure is brought to bear against him, often causing him to drift from his direct course heavenward. We must take the Bible, which is our sextant, and peer into the pure and shining disk of the Sun of Righteousness, view his lineaments, and reflect his image upon us, so that we may discover our drifting, and regain our position on the way to the desired haven of sweet and unending rest.

Thus we describe life's wonderful voyage to be difficult and often dangerous, and it requires nice government and engineering to urge our way through all obstructions. But if we are as vigilant and sagacious as officers and seamen are in the natural enterprise of navigation, I have no doubt but we shall ultimately reach the harbor. Every department of business in this life requires close attention, persevering energy, and often, fatiguing toil. If natural enterprises require constant exertion and an exercise of these respective traits, do we not justly conclude that the spiritual enterprise will require the same? The more interest we manifest in our sacred cause, the more success will we meet with; and the more God's servant hath, the more he will receive. God loves to help those that help themselves, and he giveth more grace to those who utilize what they have.

Well, my time is being so absorbed in the religious work that I almost forget to inform my readers of the fact that we are rapidly nearing the Sandwich Islands, where the monotonous spell of the seafaring life will be broken and new courage imparted, particularly in the divine life. I am longing for intelligence from home, and expect a reply to my letter, written to mother from the Islands on our way from the Arctic region, *en route* for Lower California. All these expectations, if realized, will afford a new incentive to my wandering life, I trust, especially if the letter indicates that my cherished friends are still alive. We have had, since we left the Marquesas Islands, the usual ups and downs that characterize nautical life, of which, by this time, my readers have a pretty fair insight.

We have been keeping up our meetings as regularly as practicable on shipboard. Some of my adherents are still sanguine in the work, but some are exhibiting a feeling of lassitude and I have unpleasant apprehensions of their falling into sin again. But I cannot do any more to prevent it, that I can discover at present. I expostulate with them, both privately, and when our little number is assembled, and we pay our tribute to the Lord. I feel just as deep an interest now in keeping our little band of seamen together in the Christian work, as I used to feel in keeping my comrades together when engaged in the sportive element of sin; but I had much more success then than now. That was more easy, natural and congenial to our carnal propensities. But the divine life requires a constant repelling of the carnal tide, and that, as already explained in this work, is difficult to do, especially on board of a ship where our range of territory is so small, and we are obliged to meet our opposers all the time.

I am obtaining some experience in religious government, and finding out practically what it is to keep myself balanced and help balance others. When I was young and irrepressible I used to harness myself, and do as I pleased, apparently; but now another has harnessed me and leads me whither my carnal inclinations would not go. I find it much easier to go with the current of nature than to restrain our passions by grace, and counteract that course which was indulged in so long and became so natural. When I was arrayed in my regalia, and was marching to the timely beating of a drum, with my associates of the band to which I pertained, and we were discoursing the harmonious strains of music, until the welkin was made to resound with the melody — well, that was friendship, and sociability, and enjoyment in the carnal element, but I cannot be liberal enough to call it religion. I love my old comrades in a higher and purer sense now than I did then; but my love now comprehends their eternal good. When operating simply in the social ties of friendship, my love for their welfare was only confined to this mortal and mundane sphere.

When I see them again, if God permits me to live and enjoy this privilege, I want my life to evidence my carnal separation from our former sportive element, in which I performed my part vigorously, and evince my initiation into the new, divine element, which, if persevered in, can bring no regrets, and will ultimately merge me into a sphere of immortal blessedness. I would much rather employ my time and talent in a work whose character is of endless duration, than to be gratifying my animal emotions in an enterprise, the results of which are only mortal. I conclude that in so many instances the old Adamic nature is just covered over with a little religion, and it is not long till old Adam tears the cover and gets to the top. The only way to keep him down is to strike the death-blow in the start, and never allow him to be resurrected again. If we begin to pander to the old, carnal passions that he controlled, and humored us with so long, you may come to the conclusion that our religion will become a mixed affair. That is the trouble to-day,—things are too much mixed. Old Adam has become a brother right among us, and he is a very sensitive old man, too, and is soon offended if you do not humor him on the religious plane. You might just as well humor the devil, too, as to humor him; and the only way to get rid of him and the devil is to place yourself on the true, Christian basis, clothe yourself with the armor of God, drill until you become dextrous in the art, and wield the Sword of the Spirit effectively, and then cut to kill. Don't merely go through with the manipulations, and after all do no executing.

This is a wonderful warfare, the most stupendous that I ever engaged in, and we must fight to kill, or there is no use in fighting at all. We want to be sure that we have the Adamic element well subdued in ourselves first before we attack others, or our religion will suffer severely from the darts of the repelling force.

On the night of March 27, 1865, we departed from our direct course by the compass and hauled our flying bark close on the wind. We were in close proximity with the Hawaii Island, an island pertaining to the Sandwich group. We stood off till morning, when the captain was escorted by a boat's crew to the shore, and in the evening they returned with the pilot. We were conducted within the bay, and there cast anchor. A number of ships were anchored in the bay, among them the Canton Packet, Bartholomew Goslin, and John Honlin.

We held our little meeting on the evening of March 28, in the quiet bay; while resting at anchor. This is significant in a figurative sense. I wish that all our anchors were properly inserted within the veil, " whither Jesus, the forerunner, is gone." The ship's anchor is a potent instrument and the sole dependence of the mariner in a wasting storm. So I remark that the Christian's anchor is an unquestionably sure support in the time of storm, and contains even a much firmer hold within the veil, than the mariner's anchor in terra firma. The one holds fast in heaven, but the other merely on the earth. If we could only by faith discover the superior strength and grandeur of the spiritual means and measures of the Gospel of Christ! But, while the mariner's anchor is a strong and powerful instrument, he does not, at all times, have safe anchorage. This is the case along some portions of the Sandwich Islands. On March 29 we were struck by a severe gale while anchored in the bay, and the pressure of the storm caused the ships to drag their anchors, and we were in danger of colliding. So we were necessitated to heave our anchors and put to the open sea where the vessels had plenty of sea room to be tossed and driven by the furious elements.

I wish those of my readers who have never seen a ship laboring in a storm could have the privilege of seeing it, and I would guarantee them a deeper impression on their minds than the description given even by an experienced seaman. The Psalmist David says the ship mounts up to the heavens, and then descends again in the cavity of the sea. This is a fair description. It is wonderful to see the ship rear up, like a frightened horse, over the top of a towering, foam-crested billow; her bow is directed toward the heavens, while she is hurled abruptly upon her beam ends. The previous billow makes its escape, and down she is precipitated, and her bow, or fore part, is buried in the cavity of the sea. Our fore-top-sail was rent in twain by the storm, and as soon as the wind abated sufficiently we bent on a new one. We kept tacking ship occasionally, so as not to be driven too far out to sea, as we intended to enter the bay again as soon as the warring elements were pacified.

But lest my readers should conclude that anchoring is an unsafe process at any time, let me here counterbalance our experience in anchoring at the Hawaiian Island, where the anchoring ground was unsafe, by that of a ship anchored in a terrific storm in the Irish Channel. Bro. Robert Jones, of Whiteside County, Illinois, a native of Ireland, and now a Christian mariner, relates the following thrilling incident: "Our ship was drawn out from Liverpool by a steam-tug. When we reached Ramsey's Bay, in the Irish Channel, the furious billows overtook us from the broad Atlantic, driven by a terrible storm that came suddenly upon us. The steam-tug, in order to make her escape, cut the large hawser to free herself from our ship, and hurriedly receded to Liverpool, borne by the powerful waves. We were left to the mercy of the storm, and the captain was driven to his wits' end. He crowded on all her canvas to keep her from being dashed to pieces upon the rocks; but, unable to accomplish his purpose, his last resort was to the anchor. At first she dragged her anchor, and kept nearing the craggy rocks till the strong fluke of the anchor was sunk into the earth beneath and held her secure. The ledges of rocks projected over the foaming sea, and rose to the height of 300 feet. In the rear was Holyhead Light-house, which could not be seen by the ill-fated mariners for the towering rocks. In this woeful plight we remained amid the terrific roaring of the tempest, and the furious dashing of the waves. At times the ship was entirely inundated by the pressure of the storm and sea; but still the faithful anchor held fast. The storm raged in all its fury for forty-eight hours and held the sailors and passengers in dread suspense. The third morning the sun arose fair and beautiful; but though the storm had abated, the sea still raged in all its fury."

The readers may see the propriety, then, of the Apostle's illustration of the Christian's hope, deduced from this powerful instrument, the mariner's anchor.

We saw the great volcano, and the melted lava in the form of cinders, which had been hurled down her steep slopes, and were heaped up to a considerable height at the base, showing that during its active operations it had ejected the fiery material through its crater. How wonderful indeed are these volcanoes! They are supposed by scientists to be the safety-valves of the earth; and did not the interior of the earth have relief from the accumulations of gas, and intensity of heat, it would necessitate terrific explosions. Here, again, we notice the great wisdom of our Creator, in making these necessary provisions to remove the surplus matter, even in the heart of the earth. Nature performs her functions admirably in all the departments of her complicated system, because actuated and controlled by the God of nature. In like manner the renovating process is kept up in the consummation of our spiritual character. The Word of God is compared to a fire, which purifies our being; and in the smelting process, or renovating ordeal, the alloy is cast off.

We remained outside of the bay until the morning of March 30. We kept adjusting our ship as the gale increased or decreased, now extending more sail, and then shortening again. But on the morning of the thirtieth the wind abated and we returned within the bay and dropped anchor again. Six vessels are swinging at anchor in the bay this morning. The captain and a boat's crew are ashore all day. The mate, with a boat's crew, intended to board the ship Florida, but was insulted by the mate of said vessel, and hence he refused to board her; so we pulled him back to our own ship again.

The Christian says:

> "When for some little insult given,
> My angry passions rise,
> I'll think how Jesus came from heaven
> And bore his injuries.
>
> "He was insulted every day
> Although his words were kind,
> But nothing men could do or say
> Disturbed his heavenly mind."

April 2,—Sunday,—finds us still anchored in the bay, and the boats going from the several ships loaded with their respective officers and crews, to visit each other. Several strange seamen are aboard of our craft. Among them is a native of the City of Philadelphia. It is a pleasure to meet one from so near our own native place.

We held a meeting on board our ship this evening and were favored with the presence of several of our visitors. We had good order and attention, which is a source of great satisfaction and comfort to us. It was consoling to have spent the day thus in trying to save ourselves and those who heard us. But the great misfortune is that some who started with us in this noble work are beginning to lag. This leaves a bad impression upon others and renders the way more difficult for us who are endeavoring to act our respective parts. If we could only keep all, who name the name of Christ, aloof from iniquity, infidelity would soon be obliged to stop her mouth; but the nominal professor disgraces the church more than the wicked who perpetrate their unlawful deeds outside of her limits.

I have paid my vows to God in the anguish of my soul, and though deserted by friends in whom I have confided, and though I be scandalized by them in common with those who have never known the way, yet will I endeavor to hold fast to the covenant I have made with him who will never leave nor forsake me. I have been severely tried in this floating prison on the deep, but my choice, made after counting the cost, has as yet brought no regrets, and I hope that my confidence may be steadfast unto the end.

At 2 A. M., April 5, all hands were aroused to heave anchor and set sail, to leave the bay. We designed making our exit the day previous, but the wind was not favorable. As soon as the wind blew fair in the night we took advantage of the earliest opportunity to leave. The captain purchased fifty barrels of potatoes for our subsistence, and we loaded them before leaving the bay. We are bound for the island of Oahu, on which the capital, Honolulu, is built.

CHAPTER XX.

At Honolulu once more.—Letters from Home.—A Letter to my Mother.—Departure for the Polar Sea.—Experiences while Traveling Northward.

DURING the night of April 5 we lay off from the harbor of Honolulu, and on the morning of the 6th we anchored outside the Reefs. We immediately went to discharging the cargo of oil and depositing it upon the wharf. It will be loaded on a merchant vessel and conveyed to Bedford, Massachusetts. I received two letters from my native country: one from my brother, John D. Zollers, and one from Isaac Kulp, a member of the German Baptist or Brethren church. I was quite overjoyed to receive the intelligence from the cherished land of my nativity, that mother and brothers and sisters were still alive, save one brother whose whereabouts was not known since the year 1860, when he was in Charleston, South Carolina. The rebellion cut off communication, and he has not been heard from since then. They received my letter, written from this place last Autumn, and the tone of the letters received indicate great thankfulness for my preservation, and particularly for the consecration of my life to the Lord. Though we are almost seventeen thousand miles apart, *via* Cape Horn, yet our spirits can blend in sweetest union, and our prayers ascend to our Creator and Preserver for his further care and protection, till we, by his kind pleasure, may, we sincerely hope, meet again. My sister has consecrated her life to the Lord; so writes my brother John, and the precious tidings bring the sweetest consolation across the waters. I trust that the good work will progress until our entire family is devoted to the service of God.

Bro. Isaac Kulp's letter I read with rapture, as he manifested such an interest in my welfare spiritually and temporally when I was, as yet, roaming in the wilds of sin. I thank God and him for his Christian kindness, and sincerely pray that he may be wielded as a chosen instrument in the hands of the Lord, to arrest many more wanderers upon sin's destructive course. Bro. Isaac was a successful merchant, but his heart was not absorbed in his merchandise, for it was athwart the counter that we held our Christian interview before my departure, which impressed me deeply and yielded a forcible incentive to my blessed change from darkness to light.

To-day I induced one of the boat's crew to pull ashore and assist the cooper in hooping the oil casks. I took with me some handsome seashells, which I had gathered on old California's coast for Mr. Weight, the English gentleman, who so kindly and courteously received me into his home circle, and permitted me to share his hospitality, and that of his family, when I was at Honolulu before. But I learned that he had removed from Oahu Island, and I gave my pearly memento into the care of a friend of his, who will forward them to him. Only the officers obtain liberty to go ashore to visit and explore: the crew are deprived of the longed-for privilege this time, and are kept busy a good portion of the time at some labor or other aboard. We are anchored at some distance from the wharf, and our cargo of oil is taken ashore on flat-boats and placed aboard of the ship Asia, to be conveyed to the United States of America.

We have a strong desire to meet with God-fearing people in the city of Honolulu, but we must be content to forego the privilege this time. Our letters received from home, however, give us untold consolation and we look forward wistfully to the time when we shall meet our friends in our native land, where our associations will not be prevented by maritime restrictions. I am responding, during my leisure hours, to the dear ones who have written to me. Although verbal intercourse has been long cut off by force of circumstances, yet pen and ink is the blessed medium of communication. I forward two letters from this place—one to my brother in the flesh, the other to my brother in the spirit—giving them instructions to address me at San Francisco, Cal., next autumn, on our return from the Arctic Sea. These are the orders received from the captain, whose purpose is so to do.

It was my good fortune to be one of the crew at different times when the whale-boat was employed to convey one officer or another ashore, and by that means I was favored with short interviews with my island friends. I met Mr. Boner, a warm Christian professor, who earnestly admonished me to continue in the noble cause which I had begun, signifying that they had heard on the islands of the progress we were making in the divine work. I was informed that the captain himself even gave it his endorsement; and they together seemed to credit the idea that God was blessing our religious work on the sea.

On April 10 the captain purchased two mattresses, one for myself, and another for my shipmate. This will add to the comfort of our sleeping berths. One of my religious adherents became very angry to-day, but bitterly repented after the paroxysm of wrath had subsided. The poor boys are at times severely tried. We hove anchor, and got the ship under way this evening, and I stood watch all night. The wind blew hard, and the sea was very rough.

In the afternoon of April 12, we arrived at Atawai, and the captain went ashore and purchased some potatoes and wood. While others were thus employed, I took advantage of the opportunity afforded by some leisure time, and wrote a letter to my mother. The captain has recalled his intention to sail to San Francisco from the Arctic next fall, and says now that he will return to the Sandwich Islands. Hence my letters from America will be misdirected, unless I can inform them, through mother's letters, of the change. We are still laying in a store of provisions and water for our subsistence in the frigid North. I will here insert my letter to mother from the Island of Atawai.

SANDWICH ISLANDS, April 12, 1865.
Dear, Affectionate Mother:
Ere we sail to the frozen region of the North, I will seize my leisure moments, amid the week of preparation, to pen you a brief letter. The best tidings that I can communicate to you are that I am still trying to serve my Creator, God, and others of my shipmates, to my great satisfaction, have become my assistants in the noble work. I thought that we would remain at Honolulu only two or three days, but as it happened, we remained nearly one week, which affords me more time to write and mail letters. I was quite overjoyed to receive those letters from my brother John, and Bro. Isaac Kulp. I was glad beyond measure, too, to learn of my sister Kate's union with the church and with

the Lord. Oh, that I might be with her just one golden hour, and converse about the Savior's dying love. But I must forego this blessed privilege until the Lord's appointed time.

Mother, I am earnestly praying for you. Tell sister Mary that I often think of her, and much desire her admission into the peaceful fold of Christ. How precious will it be for her to find this refuge in the golden period of her youth! The pleasures of earth soon fade away, and in maturer life we are left forlorn and dreary.

I replied to the letters which I received at Honolulu, and directed the receivers to address me at San Francisco, California, as the captain had given such directions; but he has since changed his purpose, and now says that we will return to the Sandwich Islands from the Arctic Ocean. Please inform them of the change, and tell them to address me at Honolulu, Sandwich Islands.

We anchored quite a distance from the wharf at Honolulu, and in consequence I had but little time to see my friends in that city; but having been employed as one of the boat's crew, to escort the captain and the mates to the wharf, I had a brief opportunity to chat a little with one or two of my friends. I have some warm friends in Honolulu, and I longed much to visit them, but sailors are deprived of many an enjoyable time.

I received a letter from Samuel C. Damon, the principal missionary of Oahu Island, giving me words of encouragement in my religious life. He also sent me books and tracts by the captain, to be distributed among the crew.

I am in good health. Please forgive errors of the past.

From your roving son,

GEORGE D. ZOLLERS.

After our provisions were gotten aboard, we extended our canvas to the wind, and set out for our long, and, in some respects, dreary voyage to the Polar Sea. Our only real enjoyment was found in the perusal of the Bible, and our devotional exercises aboard. My main stand-by now was my friend, George Wallace, of New Hampshire. John Nolan, who was quite earnest in the start, had fallen to the rear, and with all our persuasions, he would no more take an active part with us, his excuse being that it was too difficult to live the life of a Christian on ship-board; the oppositions to a character of humility and gentleness were too difficult to be overcome.

We had succeeded in making our cherished cause attractive to several of the Portuguese, one of whom became penitent and prayerful. The greatest work that we have to achieve in this world is to keep alive spiritually. I have read the account of exploring parties who wintered in the Arctic; and who were obliged to have recourse to methods to awaken the senses of those who became stupefied on account of the cold. The severest of any of these methods was to reprimand and even buffet the stupid and lagging to keep them from being frozen to death. If it required such rigorous measures to preserve the natural life, we must certainly be equally persistent, if not more so, in endeavoring to save the spiritual life. The spiritual existence is the finest part of our being, and its beauty and vital importance are too frequently obscured by that which is natural and tangible.

It seems to me that if I am able, by the grace of God, to hold my integrity to God and his cause here, I ought to be able to retain it when dismissed from this floating craft. Our thinking powers are all brought into requisition when some vital principle which we hold most dear is at stake. Paul stood undaunted before the tyrannical Nero, when all men forsook him; but in that hour of human desertion the Lord stood by him, and delivered him out of the mouth of the lion. We cannot expect to have a great train of attendants and defendants in redemption's cause, from the fact that, in its pure and genuine character, it never became a popular subject. Christ himself did not long command the voice of the populace. While in a spell of impulsive approbation they would take " him by force and make him a king," they soon cried out again with pitiless clamor, "Crucify him, crucify him." But it should be sufficient for the votaries of truth to know that their cause is just and heaven-approved; and though we are discountenanced and forsaken by friends in this world, we shall still have some friends on earth, and not an enemy among the shining throng in heaven.

> "Jesus, I my cross have taken,
> All to leave and follow thee;
> Naked, poor, despised, forsaken,
> Thou, from hence, my all shalt be.
> Perish every fond ambition,
> All I've sought, or hoped, or known,
> Yet how rich is my condition,
> God and heaven are still my own."

Every day we are penetrating the higher latitudes, and experiencing a cooler atmosphere than we have been wont to feel; by degrees we must become acclimated. We have been furnished with warmer clothing, to meet the requirements of the change. Our principal employment on our voyage North is mending sails and repairing the rigging of the ship throughout, so as to have the unstable house, in which we live, in proper condition when we reach the whaling grounds. We shall then have to give entire attention to that business. We constructed our canvas enclosure on the Royal cross-trees, the Royal being the highest sail on the main-mast or fore-mast. This renders the man on the lookout quite conspicuous, and affords him a commanding view over the sea, which is absolutely necessary. This canvas enclosure reaches about to the shoulders of the man on the watch, and protects his body from the piercing winds. The position of the watchman is not very enviable, especially when the cold and raw winds are blowing. He is not obliged to remain there when the winds and sea are too boisterous, as on such occasions they could not capture whales at any rate. We experience various conditions of the weather—sometimes rainy, then foggy, then a gale of wind, etc.

CHAPTER XXI.

Doleful Tidings. — Our Flight to Escape from the Privateer "Shenandoah." — The Advantage of our Retreating Movement. — Capture of a Large Whale, and some Particulars Regarding these Monsters of the Deep.

A STRONG gale arose on the night of May 3, and blew hard all the next day. A heavy sea struck our ship on the evening of May 4, injuring the waist-boat, when swung on the davits. We did some cruising, and captured several whales before reaching Behring Strait. When near the mouth of the Strait we were busily engaged on Sunday morning, with a blazing furnace and seething pots, rendering out the oil. We had our sails furled, save a sufficient amount of canvas to steady the ship while we were operating with the blubber and oil. A ship on the windward side of us bore down upon us, being propelled by a good, stiff breeze. Her approach seemed to create some uneasiness and anxiety on board our craft. The captain appeared anxious to receive any tidings she had to communicate. She proved to be a German vessel, and her commander had gloomy and unwelcome tidings to transmit to our captain. She had come in contact with a large gun-boat, which was favored with a double propelling power, — steam and sail. Her mission was to burn and destroy. She was a Confederate gunboat, fitted up while hostilities were still raging in our native country, and we were pained at the thought, that even in the distant North we must be exposed to the cruel ravages of war. She held the vantage ground in every respect. In the first place, being propelled by steam; and, secondly, she had invaded an unarmed and defenseless fleet. With her large guns pointing from her port-holes she was able to bid defiance to the harmless fleet of whalers, and in a short time she could have pierced their hulls with her destructive missiles, and sunk them beneath the sea. If she came in sight of them, they were obliged to surrender and give their cruel marauders full control.

It was evidently a severe trial for those competent commanders of whale ships who had conducted with their skill and seamanship through many a threatening gale, and who felt such a deep interest in their floating property. Oh, how they longed for a conquering Monitor in this woful crisis, as she appeared in the hour of emergency at Fortress Monroe. But no Monitor came; they could not repel their formidable antagonist, and hence had to surrender. Sometimes she would pounce, as it were, upon four or five vessels, floating near each other, and thus capture them all together. She would reserve one or two, perhaps, out of the entire number destroyed, place the officers and crews aboard these reserved ships, and permit them to navigate themselves into whatever port they desired, while the vacated vessels were burned to the water's edge. If my information is correct, some twenty or more vessels were destroyed by this invading foe. It was, however, still well that the lives of her captives were preserved. Had they been attacked by cruel pirates, their lives would have been ruthlessly taken. But it was a hard scene to witness, and the approach of the disaster was very sudden and unexpected.

But let us return to the account of our own craft. After the intelligence was given by the humane German captain, our commander ordered the try-works to be cooled down, the rendering process to be discontinued, and every sail to be unfurled and extended to the breeze, so that we might make our escape before the piercing eyes of the invaders would chance to fall upon us. At the same time we saw two vessels to the windward of us, making their escape. May I hope that providence favored us with a strong breeze, accommodated to our needs in this great emergency, and our Clipper Oriole, with her white wings spread, was soon swiftly flying before the wind in the direction of Fox Islands.

Our flight reminds me of God's non-resistant people who are commanded by Christ that when they are "persecuted in one city to flee to the next." They have a legal license to save their property and their lives, if it is possible for them to do so, and make their escape. But in the instance of the destruction of Jerusalem they had to let their property go, and flee to the mountains to save their lives. Our property is inferior to our natural life, and our natural life is inferior to our spiritual life. Hence Christians had better sacrifice their property rather than their natural life, and their natural life rather than their spiritual life.

These defenseless whaling vessels made their escape, first, because they were not equipped to effect a defense; it was not the kind of warfare in which they were engaged; and, secondly, it would have been rash and unwise for them to expose themselves to the destructive power of this armed invader, whose mission it was to destroy property without retrieve. Hence their commanders acted judiciously in making their escape, where this was practicable; and those who were captured did wisely in surrendering to their tyrannical sway, rather than trying to resist, when they would have lost their lives.

By parity of reasoning, I contend that God's people are engaged in a spiritual warfare and are not equipped and trained for the natural warfare; hence are divinely authorized to make their escape from their pursuers, if possible. Should escape be impossible, they should retain their integrity and make their spiritual life the first and highest consideration, in the event of their apprehension, and sacrifice property and life rather than sacrifice their spiritual and eternal interests. Does this not comport with the teachings and example of Christ? If not, how are we to understand his instructions, and how can we reconcile our lives with his own? Says Christ: "Fear not them that kill the body, and after that have no more that they can do." That exquisite part of our being termed the soul, the enemies of Christianity cannot reach: it is beyond the reach of men and devils. The Christian's God has the control of both body and soul; and, although God may allow the killing of the body, by sword, or flame, or piercing bullet, for the advancement of his cause and the glory of his name; yet he is able to resurrect the body and place it in unison with the soul again, in the most perfect attitude in celestial glory, or, if we despise his Word, he is able to cast both body and soul into hell.

Our last thought deduced from this marine disaster is, that we must all, without discrimination, at last succumb to the tyrant, death. This fatal enemy may pounce upon us just as surprisingly as the "Shenandoah" came upon the whaling fleet; and we will have to surrender both our property and our life. There will be no possibility of fleeing from his cold and ruthless grasp; and all our fame and wealth will have an end, so far as our interest in them is concerned. This cruel monster is effecting his ravages on land and sea. Let us be wise, and prepare for the land of bliss and immortality.

I will now refer to our retreating Oriole again, and disclose to my readers the fact that our apparent misfortune was no misfortune after all, I mean so far as being compensated with oil was concerned; for the formidable enemy, whose approach we so much dreaded, ran us right into a streak of good luck.

When near the Aleutian Islands, we lingered and cruised, until we supposed the danger was over and our dreaded foe had left the North. We spent about two weeks as fugitives, and while in this line of operation we captured the largest whale of the entire voyage. It was a large right whale, and produced one hundred and seventy-three barrels of oil.

The northern whale is about sixty-five feet in length, and forty feet in circumference. From the head to the tail it is round in formation. The jaw-bones are from twenty to twenty-five feet in length, and are curved. The upper jaw contains the whale-bone. The plates vary in length, the longest being between the center of the series and the throat; thence they taper toward each end of the mouth. Each side of the mouth contains about 200 blades. The largest laminæ are from ten to fourteen feet long, and about one foot in width, where they enter the jaw. On the upper portion of the head are two spout-holes. Their external openings form an acute angle. Through these openings the animal breathes. The eyes are not larger than the eyes of an ox; but they are quick-sighted. The hearing seems to be dull. The throat is small. The fins are from four to five feet broad and from eight to ten feet long; they

MODE OF BUILDING HOUSES AMONG THE INHABITANTS OF NORTHERN CLIMES.

serve to direct the course of the whale when locomotion is produced by the tail. The tail is horizontal, and from twenty to thirty feet in length. In it is located the strength of the monster. The color is black, interspersed with gray and white. The skin is about an inch in thickness. Below the skin is the blubber, varying from ten to fifteen inches in thickness. Some whales, like some hogs, are fatter than others. The whale, as a general thing, remains under water from twenty to thirty minutes. The maternal affection of the whale is remarkable. The young one is often struck first for the sake of procuring the mother, which will come close to it and encourage it to make its escape, by taking it under its fins. However intense her sufferings, she will not forsake it, even amid the throes of death.

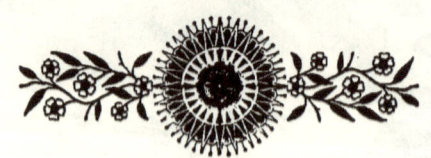

CHAPTER XXII.

A Disastrous Attack. — In the Arctic once more. — Jonah's Experience with a Whale. — How the "Would-be" Scientist is Puzzled about the Lord's Doings. — A Reasonable Conclusion. — The Lord's School of Discipline. — The Power of the Almighty, as Shown in His Wonderful Works.

IN the act of capturing this huge monster, referred to in our last chapter, one of our boats was stove by him and so badly demolished that it was lost. The great whale thrust his huge fin through the thin cedar boards (of which material whale-boats are constructed) and the boat, in an instant, was rendered useless. You should have seen the crew scramble to the rear of the boat, and overboard, for the security of their lives. They were soon rescued by the other boats, and there was no let up to our fatal darts and incisions to secure our victim, that could be valued, at the least calculation, I think, at three thousand dollars.

Our captain felt quite mortified when the privateer prevented him from entering the Arctic at the time he desired, but now he feels as though he had not suffered any loss in our retreating movement. Our clipper Oriole is good on a retreat at any rate, if she cannot do much execution in battle. We have nothing in the form of war implements aboard, save a signal-gun, to be used in times of distress; and we used it also at the Marquesas Islands, to surprise the natives, I presume, more than anything else. We did not undertake to surprise the Shenandoah.

At the expiration of about two weeks we returned to the mouth of the Strait, feeling our way cautiously, like some timid animal returning to its prey after having been severely chased. We met a few vessels that had been scattered during the consternation. The general impression of seamen seemed to be that the disturber of their peace was gone.

On our voyage out from America we were suspicious of meeting the Alabama, but she having been destroyed, another succeeded her in the molestation and plunder of ships on the great waters. So the schemes of sin and the devil are carried on throughout the successive generations; one famous marauder disappears from his active pursuits in sin's destructive way and another is ready to take his place. The rumor was here that one of the officers of the Alabama was commanding the Shenandoah.

Well, we passed through the Strait safely and floated in the Arctic once more. It seemed natural to be among the floating ice again, cautiously steering our ship to avoid these barriers as we proceeded. We had quite an experience in another Arctic term. I sincerely hoped that this term would complete the course of discipline in this portion of the world. I should have been extremely glad to reach the terminus of my nautical life, for I was tired of being driven and tossed on the sea. I knew one thing, and that was that I was not sufficiently interested in the whaling prospect to make it the pursuit of my life; it stuck to me much closer than I was inclined to stick to it. As soon as my contract for this voyage was filled, it was doubtful whether I should be found chasing these big sea-monsters any more. If I helped to catch anything I hoped it would be men. That is a prospect of higher moment, but there are also dangers and hardships connected with that.

The Savior told his disciples that he would send them forth as sheep in the midst of wolves, and charged them to be as wise as serpents and as harmless as doves. Peter was an old expert fisherman, and he had splendid tact for catching men. He made an excellent haul on the day of Pentecost.

The prophet Jonah had more experience, I presume,—not in the matter of catching whales, but being caught by a whale—than any other herald of the Lord, and it made him quite successful in catching men. But he did not seem to approve heartily of the Lord's method of securing the Ninevites; he seemed to be a sensitive creature; like some more of us, he had much to learn. I scarcely ever helped to dissect a whale without thinking of the fugitive prophet and wondering as to the whereabouts of his miserable location. The New Testament says in the "whale's belly," and Jonah himself, in his bitter prayer, terms it "the belly of hell." I have never been in the interior of a whale's abdomen, as we seldom open it for the oil upon the entrails, but I have more than once traversed and dodged around in the interior of its huge mouth, and I have concluded that there would be sufficient room in there for quite a number of Jonahs.

The throat of the right whale is small, and that is one of the exceptions the skeptic makes to the veracity of the narrative. But God has performed things, alluded to in the Bible, just as wonderful as the preservation of his sensitive and dissatisfied Jonah. The congealing of the waters of the Red Sea, and the march of his people through the dry passage is just as wonderful, and related with as much simplicity of style as the miraculous preservation of the fugitive prophet. The opening of the earth's mouth and swallowing only those famous revolters in Israel and all their adherents, and preserving the remainder, who refused to sympathize with them, is another marvelous tragedy. And so we might go on and multiply incidents.

But to return to the skeptic's weak argument. If he wants to make the smallness of the throat his leading objectionable feature, it is evident that he failed to post himself in the history of the formation of whales before he began his argument, for there are different species of whales, and they are differently formed and constituted. The sperm whale has a gullet sufficiently large to swallow a man, but the right whale, we admit, according to nature, has not. The sperm whales are supplied with teeth to serve them in the process of mastication, but the right whales are not supplied with teeth. The right whales, instead of being furnished with teeth, have the baleen, or whale-bone, orderly arranged in plates in the upper jaw, which are clothed on the inner edge with a long fringe, suspended in their huge mouth. This fringe aids in the retention of their food, which consists of small nutritious substances that may be admitted through their small throats.

If the Greek word for abdomen, or the belly of the whale, will admit of the definition cavity, as I was told by one person, who seemed to be assured that it would admit of that rendering, then I would be about ready to conclude that Jonah was entrapped by the right whale and found his temporary lodging-place in the first cavity,—the mouth. The long fringe hanging in the interior of the whale's mouth would seem to harmonize with Jonah's prayer, "I cried by reason of mine affliction unto the Lord, and he heard me; out of the belly of hell cried I, and thou heardest my voice. For thou hadst cast me into the deep, in the midst of the seas; and thy floods compassed me about, all thy billows and thy waves passed over me. Then I said, I am cast out of thy sight; yet I will look again toward thy holy temple. The waters compassed me about, even to the soul; the depths closed me round about, the weeds were wrapped about my head."

Notice the last expression in his prayer, I mean the last which I have quoted, "the weeds were wrapped about my head." That would be precisely the sensation produced upon a man's head in the mouth of a right whale. The fringe, already alluded to, suspended from the whalebone, would naturally encircle itself about the head. Jonah would also receive the benefit of the air which the whale inhaled. After descending, it arises as soon as respiration is required to take in a fresh supply of air. The contracted condition of the throat, and the inability to swallow such a large and unnatural object, would very likely provoke the huge monster to vomit him out; for he was continually coming in contact with that little throat, and the whale was not able to get rid of him, and he was even in the way of his taking in his natural food, adapted to the passage of his small gullet; and so I conclude that they were both eager to separate. The whale was about as tired of Jonah's presence as Jonah was of his situation in the whale's mouth, or cavity. The process of vomiting must have taken place in close proximity to the land, in order for the fugitive to travel on his way to Nineveh, Whales have been known to be left by the ebbing tide without a sufficient depth of water to return to the sea.

Now we have opposed the skeptic's argument almost from a basis of nature, but would say in conclusion that we are fixed upon a surer and firmer basis, which is faith in God's Word. Occupying that safe position it matters not to us, who believe in the power of God, whether his servant Jonah was in the cavity of a right whale or the belly of a sperm whale. That God, in whom we believe, was able to preserve him, and have his own created monster to discharge his captive whenever he saw that his heart was moulded to obedience.

It is a grand thing that a deserter from duty could have this temporary refuge afforded him. Although he was disobedient to God, God was merciful to him, and it was far better for the prophet to be thus arrested, and severely disciplined and humbled, than to perish in the deep, without retrieve, and to be hurled into the deeps of eternity to wail in misery for his disobedience. And not only he himself was in danger of being lost, but the thousands at Nineveh whom God chose to save by his preaching.

Here we may discover the mercy of God in correcting his children, that they may be saved and become instruments in the salvation of others. I am ready to believe that my severe schooling among whales is good for me. Though I have never been as unfortunate as Jonah, never been incarcerated in the interior of a living whale, yet I have been all around them, and even on the back of a live whale, when in the terrible contest to dispatch them. Some may think that this is only a big fish story, but it occurred while attacking them, while the sea was quite rough, and we were rendered helpless, in a measure, by the powerful waves that beat against us, and carried our boat on the monster's back; but his ponderous weight lowered in the yielding element, and relieved us from our dangerous position. I feel assured that the Lord has corrected, and is still correcting my life, and though the discipline of his mercy be severe,

> "Yet I yield, I bow, I kiss the rod,
> That saves thy servant, O, my God."

God would have, no doubt, taught me his discipline in a milder form, had I improved my knowledge of him on the land, but having been insubordinate to his will, he has allowed me at least to repair, like the fugitive of old, to the sea in a ship, the only difference being that Jonah paid his fare, and I must work my way. Guilt would more than once have driven me to the hold of the ship, to sleep in the darkness when the storm was raging, but I had to scale the masts with the seamen, and with them share the exposure to the fury of the blast. I trust that my practical schooling will serve as an incentive through life, to aid in regulating my character, and that I may be faithful to herald the displeasure of God against sin, whether found in high places or low, whether great or mean men confront me, for it is only the faithful disclosure of his Word.

In the gloom of dark desertion, when sorrow and woe dissolve the heart in penitence, then we turn wistfully toward the divinely-sacred place, and wish ourselves in the sacred enclosures once more. God will not always, even by affliction, humble the human heart, as many, in the deepest throes of anguish, pass beyond this mortal sphere with a deep and thrilling sense of neglected duty, who are not permitted, under the strokes of the correcting rod, to return and redeem the time which their prayers implore him to grant.

As Jonah found mercy of the Lord in turning the vision of his soul toward the beautiful temple of the Lord and was liberated from his gloomy prison, so let me turn my whole soul towards God's temple,—the church,—and worship as best I can in my floating prison, which is sometimes buried in the floods, until the same God who guided the monster that bore his contrite and fugitive prophet of old, shall direct our floating bark to the land of my nativity, when my heart, I trust, shall be fully moulded to do his righteous will and pleasure in the temple.

A SCENE IN THE POLAR SEA.

Thus I am rejoiced to recognize that the Bible contains a cure for every disease, while mercy predominates, and in whatever direction our afflictions may tend, we may find a corresponding incident to counterpoise our hearts in the trying ordeal.

The golden sun again shows itself in his oblique rays, in this frigid clime where the empire of night, but a short time ago, held the entire sway, but it evidently must be a source of great consolation to the inhabitants of this northern region, to see his bright visage appear again above the horizon, after his long absence, during which time they were merged in the gloom of night.

The weather during the short summer is sometimes quite agreeable; though the sun's rays fall obliquely, yet their constant descent without any intervention of night, for a time evinces some force of heat in the melting of ice, etc. The atmosphere being pure and bracing, it is conducive of health and activity; our emotional tide sometimes runs high, but the physical taxation is greater than the mental, and when the physical strain subsides, we require all our leisure hours for rest to recruit the exhausted state of the system. In a peculiar world like this, where the day is constant, we are always in danger of having our hours of repose intruded upon, as a large, spouting monster may occasion our disturbance at any time. If it were my lot to spend much of my time in this world of almost constant day, I would be pleased to have our labor more systematized, so as to afford us more regular repose and recuperation of physical and mental force.

Perhaps I may unconsciously repeat some things which I have already said, but my visit being repeated to the same place, may naturally bring about such an occurrence.

The Arctic region, for many years in the past, has been the occasion of much adventure and research. Eminent navigators have taxed their skill and hazarded their lives in trying to gain a knowledge of the condition of the sea in closer proximity to the North Pole. The wonderful circulations, occasioned by ocean currents, have been a matter of profound investigation by men of scientific attainments.

The Gulf Stream, which flows north, with its deep blue current, distinguishable from the great body of water through which it passes, both by its deeper tinge and tepid condition, modifies the air on sea and land as it traverses the mighty deep, and by some it is conjectured, to wield a modifying influence even in the supposed open sea near the extremity of the North Pole. The influx of the great rivers into the Arctic Sea, and the tendency northward of the numerous birds in the higher latitudes of the north, all contribute to strengthen the view of a more modified climate, and a polynial sea, or sea free of ice. But many of God's mystical works in nature are past finding out, yet so symmetrical and precise are the operations of nature's laws, that, when the leading principles are comprehended, we may proceed in our reasonings from cause to effect, and from effect to cause. No telling, indeed, as to what future years of Arctic explorations will disclose. Repeated experiments and scientific development may yet bring about new discoveries in the Arctic world, for I verily believe that the age of wonderful disclosures is here, and God gives the wisdom to men that his prophets have spoken of remotely in the past. The wise Daniel's prophecy purports that "in the latter days knowledge shall increase, and they shall run to and fro over the earth." I presume this language will also admit of voyages on the sea, and the wisdom or knowledge, utilized in the scientific disclosures of ocean currents, atmospheric circulations, their striking phenomena and wonderful results. It is wonderful to think of mighty currents of surprising width, maintaining a regular flow at considerable velocity, and pouring their vast volumes of water onward through the expansive deep.

Then let us turn our eyes upward and survey the atmospheric region, and contemplate the regular and irregular currents of air. What a mighty engine, of immense motive power, is the atmosphere above us!

But while these disclosures of the scientists are stupendous and grand, they remind the child of faith that the knowledge transmitted to man by the Great Creator is suggestive of the latter days, and I would infer that, according to prophecy, we are very near the millennial age; when a domain of royal grandeur shall open up, that will be far more attractive, and interesting, than this frozen Arctic Sea. We can resort to no quarter of the earth or sea, as indicated and pointed out by that wonderful instrument,—the mariner's compass,—that is not polluted by sin, the bane of the world; but when the triumphant age of the millennium shall appear, that baneful power, that mars the beauty of all earthly things, shall be subdued, and we will enjoy a climate that will not vary from intense heat, to extreme cold. We listen, with interest and admiration, to the explanations of scientists, philosophers and astronomers, as to the sublime and wonderful movements, results, and influences, in their various fields of explorations and research, and appropriate all that will aid us in our researches spiritually, and that may aid in the enlargement of our vision of faith, relative to the manifestation of celestial splendor and glory at the personal appearance of Christ.

My special work, wherever I go, seems to be to exert a religious influence over my fellow-men; and I must needs post myself, as much as possible, in the blessed Bible, for my own comfort and edification, as well as to instruct the tractable and piously inclined, and withstand the spurious arguments of the gainsayer.

CHAPTER XXIII.

The Colored Boy and the Great Change in his Character. — My Part in that Work amid the Displeasure of the Crew. — Our last Look at the Arctic. — "Just a Little More," the Desire of the Worldling. — On the Way South again. — Hardships of the Mariner.

IN the rolling deep I met with all kinds of dispositions. I presume my readers recollect the colored boy to whom I have already referred in my work. He had a special talent to divert, and interest the sailors by his comic antics. I also mentioned of having introduced to him the religion of Christ, and the deep impression it seemed to produce upon his mind. In this Arctic region I learned that the seed sown in his heart has not been lost, but that he is deeply interested in the religious work, and is trying to execute his part of the work aboard the ship, where he lives and operates as a sailor. His life is producing quite a sensation among his officers and crew, and some of them are censuring me for having inoculated the leading factor in the line of carnal amusement with so grave and solemn a spirit as that of the Christian religion. The humorous and sportive spirit having been cast out by the divine power, the hope of their gains is gone, and now they are ready to wreak out their vengeance upon me, as having been the cause.

So Paul and Silas were maltreated of yore, when the spirit of divination was driven out of that noted damsel.

I have not as yet resisted unto the blood, striving against sin, but I have resisted against frowns and sneers, and bitter retorts, and scandals. But it is evident, that wherever Christ's power is revealed in casting out devils, and saving souls, there the devil begins to wield his infernal power, to counteract the good work of the Lord, which is disclosed by the strife of tongues, and the slanderous efforts of his agents. Even our own cook, of African descent, with skin as black as jet, and hair suspended in graceful curls, could roll up the white of his large eyes, and utter his ludicrous phrases, accompanied with his naturally quaint antics, to vie with the best trained clown of the circus. He, too, felt chagrined that his colleague in humoristic efforts, had ceased his efforts in that line. His eyes glared with anger, and the tone of his voice denoted vengeance, while his words, like poisoned arrows, were hurled. But

"A poisoned arrow cannot wound
A conscience pure and clear."

God gave me the ability to vindicate his cause and repel the darts of the adversary with the unconquerable arguments of his Truth, but the poor colored boy's mind was not strong enough, seemingly, to endure the opposition, and the reflection was cast into my teeth by some that I was the main cause of his insanity. There was, however, nothing dangerous about him so as to necessitate binding or confinement. He was all the while permitted to run at large on the ship and still performed his part as a seaman, as he was wont to do, before his mental aberration. I heard at one time that, under the cover of night he descended into the cabin and preached to the officers, and warned them all to desist from their evil ways or they would be turned into hell with the nations that forget God.

It was told me by our cook that it would not go well with me if the crew could apprehend me, but I felt no alarm about that, as I knew that my work was divinely ratified, and "if God be for us who can be against us?" God is able to take care of his own work, and those, too, who are his agents in carrying on that work, and if they receive personal injuries by the enemies of truth, or even death itself be their fate, all will be well. Christ says, "Fear not them which kill the body, but are not able to kill the soul: but rather fear him which is able to destroy both soul and body in hell." If we could always measure the magnitude and importance of our spiritual interests, we would press onward in our vindications in the cause of truth and salvation, through slander, reproach, peril and blood.

I will tell the reader still more about my colored convert when we get to the Sandwich Islands for the last time on our homeward voyage. Meanwhile let us take our last look at the Arctic, for we never expect to return to give a description of its scenery, hardships, and adventures. The ships that escaped the destructive clutches of the "Shenandoah" are making good use of their short season in the Polar Sea, and most of them are having good success in securing whale oil and bone. At the expiration of the season, the ship "Onward," we are told, had secured 6,000 barrels for the voyage from June 1863 to September, 1865; that is doing extraordinarily well. The Oriole, during that time, has taken in just the half of that amount, or 3,000 barrels; other vessels, during the same length of time, have been less fortunate. The decision of the captain is, that our ship will be directed toward our native land after leaving the Arctic Region. We all hope that he will not change his mind, for "home, sweet home," in these high latitudes has a very musical sound. But some captains expressed their intention to remain and engage in the dangerous pursuit of catching whales. Even the captain of the "Onward," successful as he has been, says he must have more oil before he can consent to return. It is hard, indeed, for a rich man to get enough of the riches of this world; the more he gets, the more he wants. The rich man, who was asked as to what amount of wealth would satiate the mind in pursuit of it, said, "Just a little more." Just a little more opulence at the sacrifice of home comforts and endearments; just a little more at the sacrifice of health, and the endurance of hardships in this world; just a little more, until friends, health, life, and the interests of the soul are all gone.

Gain is a great god in our affections; "some people suppose that gain is godliness." That is a misconception; but godliness with contentment is great gain whether we are poor or rich, and as we can neither bring anything into the world or carry anything out, we ought to be wise and sensible enough to labor for the spirit of contentment with more godliness than we do for gain pecuniarily. I hope I will be as ready to leave this cold world of sorrow when the time of my departure comes, as I am to leave this frozen world of the north, and though the passage lies through a domain that appears dark and dismal to us, yet the way has been paved and graced by the presence of the Redeemer himself. Christ himself will accompany us through the dark valley, and conduct us safely to the realm of joy and blessedness forever.

But think of a twenty thousand miles' voyage, in which every zone that encircles the earth must be crossed, save the Frigid Zone within the Antarctic circle. Though difficulties might attend our way, I thanked the Lord that I was enabled to begin this long voyage with a brighter vision before me, and with sensations more buoyant than I experienced on my dismal passage from my country toward this dreary region in the Polar Sea. I have now become inured to the life of a sailor and have outweathered many a threatening gale; I have toiled beneath a burning sun in the torrid belt, and I have felt the keenness of the atmosphere in the Frigid Zone. But we rejoice in anticipation of meeting the loved ones at home.

Some of our shipmates, from the Cape Verde Islands, toward the coast of Africa in the Atlantic Ocean, were sad because a famine had prevailed on their native islands during their absence on this long voyage, and many of their friends had died of hunger. The blood that circulated beneath their dark skin caused the emotional tide to rise and beat in their hearts, as well as ours, at the thought of home and its connecting charms. But the horrid thought of friends having been reduced to starvation and misery, cast a gloom over the sensations of joy. We sympathized with them, not knowing what tidings might reach us, ere we, by God's providential guidance, might be permitted to return.

Along about Sept. 20, 1865, we directed our course toward the egress from the Arctic Sea,—Behring Strait. From Sept. 15 to 20 the whaling fleet are effecting their outward passage to the warmer latitudes of the South. Our progress was not hindered by the formidable "Shenandoah," but we had to think of the unfortunate vessels that had fallen victims to her cruelty, and could not now return with us. So, in hazardous enterprises, long voyages, and military campaigns, many sad vacancies are felt. Disappointments fill our career of mortality. The boys were full of good cheer, believing that the greatest burdens of the voyage were over, and were happy in the prospect of soon reaching home again.

We have not had the benefit of artificial heat since we left our native land,—I mean we sailors before the mast.

MODE OF TRAVELLING IN NORTHERN CLIMES.

Many a dismal night, when the piercing cold benumbed our systems, did we hurriedly pace the deck, striking our hands around our shoulders to keep our blood in rapid circulation, and I have never lived so nearly upon a level with the brute creation, so far as deprivation of the comforts of life is concerned, and coping with the rigidness of the weather. Yet withal my health has been preserved, and I am very certain that the severities of life have a tendency to keep us more humble than to be faring sumptuously every day. However, I am anxious for a change, not to fare sumptuously, but a condition of comfort, both bodily and spiritually, in our own beloved America. We could not help but anticipate the tidings of the death of many whom we knew, so there is no country on this rolling sphere of ours, where grim death is not, in some shape or form, hurling his victims into his mouldering receptacle, the grave. But "time and tide wait for no man,"—so says the old adage. Our time on earth is short, and all the comforts and conveniences that may spring from affluence, conjugal relationship, filial and parental ties, as well as the tears that may be shed at the loss and forfeiture of all these joys and sorrows, pleasures and woes, will soon be borne down the rapid stream of life, and God's children will bask in the joys of celestial bliss while the endless ages roll.

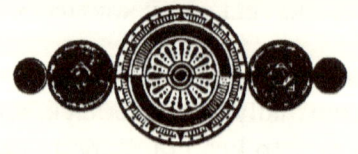

CHAPTER XXIV.

Once More at the Sandwich Islands. — Kind Reception by our Friends — Some Thoughts about Noah and his Mission. — Hospitality a Blessing to both Giver and Receiver.

WE arrived at the Sandwich Islands soon after the middle of October, 1865, and this time we entered the harbor to enjoy quite a lengthy meeting with our friends. Many vessels were lying at anchor in this peaceful haven, and the scene of their tranquility after tossings and agitation on the deep is quite agreeable. Ships from various portions of the world are seen in this harbor, and thrilling adventures are related by sailors who have long hazarded their precious lives on the troubled deep. Some of them, in shocking tempests, became humbled, and prayed God for his mercy in their deliverance; and when he guided them to the desired haven, they forsook the God who had protected and taken care of them. The Psalmist David speaks of this class of sailors, when enlarging upon the mercy and goodness of God. But now and then one retains his integrity to God when the storm is over, and forgets not the vows which his soul in anguish made.

How beautiful it is to have the mountains and fertile landscape greet our vision once more! What a striking contrast between these scenes within the tropics, and the weird and frozen scenes in the frigid belt! Our ship reminds one of the birds on the wing, soaring from a colder to a warmer climate.

Our Christian friends, on the Island of Oahu, who soon learned of the arrival of the "Oriole," made inquiry as to the welfare of the crew, knowing that religious efforts were being made on board of her. We are indeed mortified that we cannot announce every proselyte in good standing, but at the same time we do not feel any sense of condemnation in reference to delinquency upon our part. We tried to urge and admonish them to the best of our ability, but they who will not help themselves cannot be helped. Though I did not see the progress I so much desired to see, yet I feel that I was greatly strengthened and encouraged during the reviving season. But how much of the good seed only falls upon stony places, or where the thorns will spoil, is known only to him whose eye scrutinizes the secrets of every human heart. Noah had very poor success in proselyting the antediluvians, and when the deluge inundated the earth, he only had seven to accompany him into the ark. I presume some of his cotemporaries thought that it was a difficult matter to live as strict and peculiar as that aged devoted man and his household did, and concluded, perhaps, that his alarming apprehensions about the flood were only a myth, and hence they might safely forego the restrictions and responsibilities of such a godly life. But God's people are living for a grander purpose than the populace give them credit for. If they strictly adhere to the requisitions of heaven, they understand their business well, and when the confidence of the world is put to shame, their cause and profession shall be magnified.

Noah's construction of the ark was divinely authorized, and it was God's appointed means of salvation, It had to be built just as firm and strong and roomy for eight persons, as if eight thousand had been going to occupy it. Its proportions were designated, and its dimensions given. Noah was instructed as to the specifications, and commanded to build accordingly, without any license to yield to the suggestions of the people, or to be moved from God's purpose by threatenings or reward. The wise and competent master-builders, appointed of the Lord, were always charged to build precisely according to God's directions. The building of the ark, no doubt, became a very common affair, but its beauty and adaptability and saving power only became overt in the great emergency, when the roaring floods were breaking in upon the inhabitants of the antediluvian world.

The vessels, moored in the Harbor at Honolulu, and anchored within the secure enclosures of the reefs, have become an every-day occurrence to the citizens of these islands, but if, by some terrific convulsion of nature, these islands were to be gradually sunk into the great ocean that surrounds them, these vessels, adapted to their native element, would become the most precious structures to draw the attention of the perishing inhabitants, because they would be the only buildings that would present any show of salvation. Think, then, of the perishing multitudes in sight of the ark, and the hearts with anguish riven, longing for admission when their entreaties could not be granted. So it will be precisely with the ark of salvation, whose beauty and power is lost to the vision and conception of those who are hardened in sin, and those who were once moved with godly fear, but again apostatized into their carnal element. As long as they can retain any foothold at all in this world, they will feel secure and firm, and even become the scoffers, alluded to in the Scriptures, thus filling up the catalogue of prophecy, and becoming ripe for destruction on the avenging day. Noah had no commission to preach to those antediluvians, excepting at the proper time, appointed by God. Had the preaching continued, and the opportunity been granted to rescue, the ark would have been filled to its utmost capacity, but God does not propose to save people at the time his judgments are being fulfilled.

Noah had no hand in closing the door; God did that; and when once Mercy, the darling attribute of God, falls to the rear, and Justice leads the van, God will be inexorable, though the pitiful cries for relief and safety rend the air.

So, when the Master of the house has arisen and shut the door, the unfaithful shall stand outside and knock, saying, " Lord, Lord, open unto us, but he shall say, Verily, verily, I say unto you, I know you not." That interdict of Christ will debar all entrance, and every sneer of the scoffer, and every reproachful sentence of the vile and sinful will return to burden and fill with remorse and anguish its own perpetrator.

That is the way, my readers, in which I measure this short, frail, transient life, upon which salvation or destruction are consequent. I am elected to stand with the few in number if I maintain my position on the Lord's side, but that is the only safe side, and my eyes have been open to see it. If I fail to live separate from the world, I dissolve my union with Christ. I cannot live in the two elements, Christianity and the world. I must either choose one or the other.

I believe that many are trying to live in the two elements, but I certainly believe that they are trying but to fail. Some lived to try the experiment before our intelligent age, and the trial was a failure, and history only repeats itself. If I have not resolution and stamina sufficient to accept and put on a whole Christ, I do not know that it will better my condition to accept him in part. I do not want to be an agent for the devil one day, and wear the livery of a Christian the next. If I want to do that way, I might just as well do as some of my shipmates have done, — turn back and serve the Lord no more, and say with them that the life is too difficult to live on board of a ship. Christ tells us the way is difficult,—" straight is the gate, and narrow is the way,"—but that is no reason why we should not pursue it. It is the divine way; it is heaven-approved and ratified, and because the world and a nominal religion oppose it, does not invalidate it in any particular.

This world is a busy arena, where many are playing their respective parts. I am only a little atom in this vast sphere, but I can only be something as I am associated with him whom the whole world will acknowledge afterwhile. Therefore, let all mock on if they choose, let them frown or smile just as they like; I am not, as yet, deterred in the least, and though I cannot, as heroic Paul of yore, show you the scars on my physical body, to demonstrate my faithfulness to the Truth, I can produce the testimonials of a severe trial of my faith and attachment to Christ, and I feel that, by a voluntary consent of my mind, I am fully rooted and grounded in the purpose of my heart to do his will. I am glad that the Lord has disciplined and tested me, and brought me thus far upon my way, and I think I can raise at the Sandwich Islands my Ebenezer and say, like good old Samuel of old, "Thus far the Lord hath helped me, and having begun the work, he is able to complete it till the day of Christ."

It is, indeed, pleasant to have leisure time enough at this landing to visit friends and share their hospitality. Our tables aboard of our ship are very primitive affairs; they are composed of our chests, which are thus made to answer a double purpose. In the interior are placed our wearable goods and the top is used to place our edibles upon, when we dine. We have no china ware or silver knives and forks, nor have we polished utensils for style or show, but we have plain cups and plates, all manufactured of tin. This kind of furniture is best adapted to our unstable home, for it is very uncertain sometimes as to whether they will long remain where we place them, when we prepare the table. We have little strips of boards nailed around the edges, so as to assist us in keeping our furniture and victuals on the table at all during rough weather, but sometimes, with all this precaution,—re-inforced by our dextrous movements to save our edibles while we are in the act of eating, —the careening of the ship causes the whole outfit to be precipitated on the deck. When the sailors are thus baffled, a wild scene of confusion follows. But to dine with friends on a solid foundation again, where courtesy and affability have a controlling influence, is certainly enjoyable. When we have, for a long time, been surrounded by that which is degrading and distasteful, we know how to appreciate taste, system, and decorum. The contrast is so great that we are all the while impressed with a feeling of our unworthiness.

The people of Honolulu seem to take in our situation fully, and take special pains to make us welcome. I am sure that they will never lose their reward. Hospitality is a noble trait. It is beautifully incorporated in the Christian system and it should ever shine prominently in the Christian life. What a cheering light does it reflect along the pathway of life, and many a drooping and disconsolate wanderer is revived by its sacred influence. The Bible says that we shall "use hospitality without grudging." Grudging mars its influence and destroys its beauty, and will have a tendency to cripple our Christian profession woefully.

Hospitality is, by no means, all that comprises the Christian religion, but it is, indeed, a very essential part of it. Glowing oratory, melodious singing, and beautiful prayers are all empty and lifeless without the exercise of this divine trait,—hospitality. The Bible again says, "Be not forgetful to entertain strangers, for some have entertained angels thereby unawares." There is many a true and honest heart that beats beneath a faded garment, and there is many a dishonest heart beneath an elegant exterior. We should not, therefore, allow our judgment to be biased by the appearance of things.

Sometimes, when we use hospitality without grudging to some person of unassuming mien, who has been unfortunate and is leading the life of a lonely wanderer, the sequel may prove that our act of benevolence was richly compensated by the presence of the Lord in the presence of our guest, and by his instrumentality divine instruction may be imparted to the host, to stay the heart in trouble and ease the burdens of life.

We cannot measure the responsibilities of our lives, neither can we discern how far one simple act of hospitality may reach. We may entertain a mother's wandering son, for whom that mother has cared, and wept, and prayed; whose heart was broken in the hour of separation, and for whom she is burdened with grief and spends many lone and sleepless nights. During the roving years of his absence, that mother has wrestled at a throne of mercy and bears the son of her love and sympathy to the Savior who suffered and died to save the wandering and the lost. When, in some remote, foreign home, he is entertained by another whose heart is swayed by maternal influence and who is concerned for the roving sons of mothers in general, a chord of sympathy is awakened that reaches beyond the briny waters, to the old fireside at home.

Some of the mothers in Honolulu are fully awake to their duty in this respect. They have entertained so many sailors who have wandered far from home, and listened to their tales of sorrow and of woe, that they have been induced to make it a specialty, to make everything as pleasant as possible for them during their stay on the islands, so as to modify their woes and burdens, and impart consolation to the sorrow-riven hearts of their absent parents, brothers and sisters.

I shall always remember these people for their friendship and hospitality, and I pray God that we may all be entirely consecrated to his divine service. I was much impressed by Mr. Ingram's amiable qualities as well as his hospitality. He was the President of the College in Honolulu, but he now lies in the moldering tomb on these remote islands of the sea, where he was once so active and earnest in the intellectual culture of both the white and native students. May God remember him in his coming and kingdom!

CHAPTER XXV.

The Peaceful Home of Mrs. Crabbe, and her Work among the Sailors. — Extemporaneous Speaking and Its Advantages. — A Visit to the Colored Youth at the Insane Asylum. — His Melodious and Impressive Singing. — Visit to Eld. Damon. — How we may Reach the Masses and Give them a True Standard of Moral Conduct. — Keep Your Reckonings Right.

THE quiet and peaceful home of that aged lady, Mother Crabbe, of Maryland, afforded me much comfort. The fact that we once lived comparatively near each other in the United States, has in it an element of familiarity, and occasions a home-like sensation. She truly exercised a maternal care over me. How gladly would I reciprocate the hospitality if we would ever be privileged to meet in the United States! Her home was, at our last visit, still open for devotional exercises, and my New Hampshire convert, and I, as well as other religious sailors, still met there for worship. Hers was the home of the wanderer, where the tempted and tried might find a refuge from the storms of life, and the temptations of wicked men. We were consoled by her admonitions of peace, her warm congratulations in our Christian warfare, and comforted and blessed in this land of sunshine, fruits and flowers.

Mrs. Crabbe was sometimes overjoyed at hearing some of the sailors speak in the meetings. Some of them are fluent talkers. The ocean, in its changing aspects, indelibly fixed on the tablets of their memory, affords quite an incentive to those who are naturally gifted in oratory. The ocean is a practical school, whose lessons are not nearly so polished and systematic, as those taught in elocution in the refined and graded schools, but sailors are sanguine and active, and when they merge into the spirit of oratory, their native ability enables them to keep pace fairly well with the classical student. If people are not *too* highly cultured and abnormally refined in their tastes, they can, perhaps, be just as much edified by the sailor from the stormy sea, as by the cultured orator who has completed his collegiate course.

I have always been somewhat partial to extemporaneous discourses. I fear that too much exactness in the arrangement of a discourse tends to make the human part too prominent. If the discourse is animated and rendered attractive by the spirit of grace, the off-hand speech of the Bible student and Gospel minister will be fully adapted to the time and place, and the various dispositions of those who compose the audience. Peter's extemporaneous discourse on the Day of Pentecost cannot be excelled by any revivalist. Its simplicity, logic, oratory, convicting force, and his aptness and readiness to answer his convicted auditors, are admirable.

Peter's prayer, uttered at the impulse of the moment, when sinking in the deep, should permeate all our prayers in time, and it will be an excellent model to pass into eternity with. Its sincerity and freedom from alloy is self-evident, and it is the kind of prayer that all God's people will want to utter when they are about to sink into the dark shades of death.

If I were so unfortunate as to suffer shipwreck, with the ship's entire crew aboard, and I were influenced by the Divine Spirit to address them, and pray with them, before we would all sink into the deep together, I believe my impromptu speech would be precisely adapted to the occasion; if ever I would lose sight of self entirely, it would be then. The more we study, seriously and prayerfully, the Scriptures, and imbibe the spirit of inspiration in them, the better agents we will be, in the hands of the Lord, to recite the messages of the Bible. And whether learned or unlearned, if our hearts are pure and humble, God can use us to profit.

Let not ministers try to enlarge self in the pulpit, or out of it. The ministerial calling is one of grave solemnity, and it requires gravity of character and deportment to fill this responsible calling. Let humility and love be the favorite mottoes of Gospel ministers through life, and their watchwords at the gate of death; for our preaching in tone and character will be reflected in the other world. We should talk for God, and not for men, and not be moved by human applause or derision. Truth must be our theme, and God our support.

The colored young man, of whom I have been telling my readers at different times in my work, is now at the Sandwich Islands, and he has been placed in the asylum. His mind is deranged upon the question of religion. He manifests no disposition to injure any one, but is so absorbed in the theme of Christianity that he dwells upon it almost constantly. I have conversed with some of the crew of his vessel, and have seen the officers, and I find that they do not appear to hold any grudge against me now. Rumors of wars are sometimes more prevalent than wars in reality. After relating the circumstance of his remarkable change from the darkness of sin to the religious element, to Mrs. Crabbe, she expressed an intense desire to see him and proposed that I accompany her to the asylum. Accordingly we appointed a day and went to visit him. We interrogated the officer relative to his condition, and he pronounced him harmless. He spoke of him as being a very religious man and a noble singer. Often he cheered them with his sacred songs, rendered with so much freedom and gracefulness by his musical voice. He opened his cell-door and bade him come forth and enjoy our presence. His eyes immediately fell upon me, and he grasped me warmly and affectionately by the hand, and said: "George, I am glad to see you." I gave him an introduction to Mrs. Crabbe, of whom I probably had told him before. He meekly bowed and gave her a hearty hand-shaking. He told me that God had wonderfully blessed him and that he cherished and respected the advice and counsel which I had given him, and that the dark cloud that obscured his mental horizon would be graciously withdrawn by the Lord, and all would be well. He did not appear to us like an insane person, and we felt as if we were listening to good, wholesome, and well-digested religious thought. We could not help but give credence to his simple, grave and solemn message, and were impressed with the idea that his prophetic utterance was controlled and prompted by the Spirit of Truth.

God unfolds many of his wonders through very humble and unassuming agencies. Mrs. Crabbe had a strong desire to hear him sing one of Zion's beautiful songs, and urged me to make the request. I did so and he assented with pleasure, and his musical voice soon threw its soft and melodious accents into the balmy air, and his hearers were charmed with the humble attitude of the singer, and the beauty and sacredness of his song. His harmonious sounds were not indicative of a captive singing one of the songs of Zion in a strange land, for the sweet singer seemed to be at home in the native element of his song. He gave us, by the divine medium of praise, the very purest emotions of his soul. There appeared to be no disposition upon his part to hang his harp upon the willow, as expressed by the captives of yore, for his musical abilities were in the full blaze of passionate joy, solemnity and composure. He repined not at his situation, and his humble mien seemed to bespeak no regrets. The joyful sensations of our souls were stirred and all eyes were fixed on God's humble, sweet singer. The hymn was this:

> "Jesus, my all, to heaven is gone,
> He whom I fix my hopes upon,
> His track I see and I'll pursue
> The narrow way till him I view.
>
> CHORUS.
>
> "Happy day, happy day,
> When Jesus washed my sins away!
> He taught me how to watch and pray,
> And live rejoicing every day,
> Happy day, happy day,
> When Jesus washed my sins away!"

In the days of my life in the carnal element, I listened to the trained voices of theatrical singers, which elevated the emotional tide of carnality, but I do not know that I ever listened to sacred song that had a more charming influence on my heart and feelings than the sacred song by the colored sailor boy in Honolulu. The circumstances, connected with the event, had much to do with the sweetness of the song and the charm it wielded, especially upon my own heart.

When the last sweet accents of his song had died away, he arose from his humble posture on the green-carpeted earth and receded to his cell, and half closing the door he beckoned me to follow him. I responded to his signal, and found that he desired to take his affectionate leave of me, as he felt assured that we should never meet again on earth. I really felt that the divine blessing rested upon us, as he invoked the benediction of the Lord upon me, and interceded for my future prosperity. In conclusion of his humble and affectionate ceremony of parting, he asked me as to whether I was willing to kiss a colored man. In accordance with that desire, we gave each other the salutation of love, and he remained in his cell, while I rejoined Mrs. Crabbe, to return to our abode.

But how strange was the occurrence throughout! He was brought under Christian influence by my weak instrumentality and the divine blessing, and by his agency I was brought to recognize the outward token of charity, five times recorded in the New Testament and thus enjoined by Christ upon his followers. The first time I ever complied with this Divine injunction, in a religious capacity, was as above related. God shows himself in the humble walks of life, and he reveals himself in the most condescending and unassuming manner.

I shall never forget this peculiar event, and sincerely hope that I may meet my colored friend in the better land. God knows where the good seed of his Word has been sown in our wanderings on land and sea, amid heart-aches and sorrows and cares, and he can keep it flourishing until it produces the ripened fruit and the sheaves will be gathered from many lands and climes and withal from the caverns of the sea, in the great rewarding day.

Mrs. Crabbe was much moved by this visit to the asylum, and she greatly sympathized with the unfortunate colored boy and regarded him as an object of God's favor and mercy.

We also visited Eld. Samuel Damon and heard him preach again. He always manifested an interest in the welfare of seamen and we all appreciated his kindness and sociability. It requires a person who is amiable and condescending to wield an influence over common people.

The difficulty of to-day is, that there is too great a gulf between popular Christianity and the common people. Christ's meek and lowly life made him welcome among publicans and sinners. He ate and drank in their houses, and never was the life and salvation taught plainer than by the personal ministry of Christ, and his followers cannot expect to be successful unless they imitate his humble life, and present to the people the system of faith which he has given.

When the Savior condescended to seek and save the lost, the Jewish nation, with their God-given code of laws, were like the ship at sea with her chart and compass, but without that proper adjustment, brought about by daily observations, to designate her whereabouts by the natural sun in the heavens. They were furnished with an inspired record of Christ's life of humiliation. Their chart pointed that fact, as well as his exaltation, but their human creeds and commandments of men had caused them to drift from the authorized standard of God, and with their own standard of righteousness established, they were left at sea, in blissful ignorance of God's amazing love, disclosed in humble attitude to a lost and helpless world. The common people could get but little sympathy from these sanctimonious circles, and when the humble Jesus accommodated his life to their necessities, they felt at home in his presence, and heard " him gladly."

The Jewish rulers, and the nation as well, could not grasp the reason for Christ's humble attitude and common life, and they do not fully understand it to this day; but through their fall the Gentile world has been admitted.

Let the eminent professors of Christianity beware, lest the same thing befall them. We may have the Chart and Compass of the Gospel, but if our daily reckonings are not made by Christ, our spiritual Sun, we, too, will lose our bearings, and be as self-confident in our digression and blindness as were they.

It is a very important thing for a navigator to keep his reckonings right, and learn the driftings of his vessel at every available period, when a correct observation may be taken from the heavenly bodies. The navigator being baffled at times by fogs and storms, he finds himself drifted where he would rather not be from choice, but when an observation is afforded from the sun, he regains what has been lost in drifting, and then pursues his proper course. Christian professors are just as liable to lose their way spiritually, and they do often drift and need re-adjustment, as well as the mariner at sea.

We are especially in danger of drifting from the self-denying, cross-bearing way through which the humble Savior passed. And as it is much easier for the navigator to muse over the beauties and comforts of the haven to which he is tending than to encounter the warring elements to reach his destination, so it is easier for Christians to converse, and preach, and sing of the Land of Beulah than to stem the storms and floods, and keep their heaven-directed course in reaching the desired haven of rest. The Jew could see the Glorified Christ, but not the Crucified Christ, and we, as Christians may make the same mistake.

Let us, then, be conversant and familiar with every humble characteristic of Christ's life. Every humble act which he performed has its bearing upon our lives, and must be exemplified in us. He has given us "a form of doctrine" which we must obey from the heart." And we cannot afford to lose sight of the form nor the spirit that animates the form. If we do, we will be left at sea without a knowledge of our bearings.

CHAPTER XXVI.

Confusion in the Religious World.—Our Last Farewell to the Friends on the Sandwich Islands.—Thoughts of Home, as we Start on our Long Voyage.—Our Eternal Home and Its Joys.—Polynesia.—The Native from the Society Islands.—Our Short Stop at the Friendly Islands.—Kindness of the Natives.

NO one doubts that in the close of the Gospel age the economy of grace will compare in the diminution of power with the Mosaic economy. The Jews, in a national capacity, had forfeited the essence and vitality of the Mosaic code and were confused as to the import of the prophecies, while comparatively few conceived the vital current and were prepared to recognize and receive the unspeakable gift of God. So the condition of Christendom indicates confusion now. They say, "Lo here and lo there is Christ." Their religious tenets vary; their ideas are incorrect; their conceptions of Christ's vital words are no clearer than the Jews' comprehension of the prophecies. They use his name and preach its divine merits with as much zeal and enthusiasm as the Jew recited the declarations of Moses and the prophets, but the perfectly-enacted system is marred by the devices of man, and the beautiful image of Christ is hidden underneath. "When the Son of man cometh, shall he find faith on the earth?" The latitude of many of the churches is lost; their distinguishing features, to separate them from the body of the world, have been obliterated, and if there is no retracing action to regain the humble element, how can they escape the condemnation that is pronounced upon such work? The Jews suffered severely, and will the Gentiles fare any better? Did Christ accept their nominal profession of Moses? Did he ratify the actions of their representative men? Did he heed their polished prayers and eloquent discourses on the law? How many of those learned doctors knew him?

These are all pertinent questions and every unprejudiced and honest heart will agree with this. I make these investigations with feelings of solemnity and pity. I do it because they occur to my mind in the inditement of this work and because they are my honest conceptions of divine revelation. I must write what I believe, or I had better not write at all. I write these things plainly but kindly.

These incidents of my voyage on the sea, and visits on the islands, lead me out into the spiritual course, to impress upon the minds of the readers of this book spiritual truths relative to the interests of our spiritual journey. I never in my life had anything to impress my mind so profoundly as my long and adventurous voyage, nearly around the world. It seems to bear many resemblances to our momentous journey through life, which is a journey that we all travel but once.

Our visits on the islands, and associations with amiable friends were congenial to our social feelings, afforded us recreation and comfort, and gave relief to the constant strain of toil and monotony of ocean life. I shall retain in memory the incidents of this eventful voyage and make comparisons, and deduce illustrations to facilitate my passage through this mortal world.

The time came again to bid farewell to our sociable friends on the islands, and proceed on our long voyage of nearly seventeen thousand miles to the United States of America. We should, perhaps, never see their faces again in this world, and that thought filled us with sadness; but this is a world of changes, and while some friendly faces disappear, to be seen no more upon the fleeting shores of time, new ties of friendship are formed, and we become familiar with new visages as we journey on towards the domains of death and the spirit world. The sweet thought of maternal smiles and greetings, and dear associations with brothers and sisters in the old familiar circle of home, thrilled us with glad emotions, and modified the tedium of the voyage before us. We had the cordial wishes of our friends and their earnest prayers for a safe passage and secure arrival at our homes. The little plain home of my childhood, with all its familiar apartments and surroundings, and more especially the dear inmates, arose before my vision often and lent their enchantments, while far from me. The thoughts would oft occur to my mind, Shall I meet them all again? Shall my eyes survey all the scenes of home, and shall I again see the smiles, and hear the cheering words of those I love? But to experience these scenes and be gratified with these cherished realities, we must start. Though the voyage be long and hazardous, it must be carried into execution, to experience the joys and pleasures of its terminus. So is the journey of life. Our citizenship is in heaven if we have formed a union with the Godhead through Jesus Christ.

We have many friends in the better land, many of whom have passed through the shades of death before us, and are awaiting our arrival on the other shore. Thousands we shall meet there whose personal forms we have never seen but we shall view them there with our glorified vision, if we reach that happy place.

To enjoy those celestial greetings and those enraptured scenes, and the unending bliss of that bright home, we must push on in the spiritual journey, though many sorrows and adversities may attend. We are pilgrims and strangers, as our fathers were, and like them we must journey to the promised land. We ought to be willing to venture through a thousand storms to see the faces of the loved ones gone before, the illustrious vision of Christ, and the glory of the Father. However perilous the journey and dismal the temptations by the way, let us brave the gloomy trials for the felicity and glad fruition that shall crown our hope at the end.

All necessary preparations having been made for our homeward bound voyage, we took our final leave of our friends in Honolulu, and tendered our heartfelt thanks for all their kindness and sympathy. Although we prayed in their homes, yet they did not follow us to the ship, as they did Paul of old, with wives and children, and, like them, kneel upon the shore at the water's edge, and invoke the divine blessing. This would have been very nice and impressive, but it was our part to ply the windlass and heave the anchor, with our emotional feelings animated with thoughts of home, and as we were towed out of the harbor by the steam tug, and cast our lingering look upon the City of Honolulu, built on the fertile landscape by the sea, and the mountains that towered in the rear, we felt that it would most likely be our last glimpse of the attractive scenery. We felt that we would no more eat the delicious fruits upon the green and fertile shores, and that we would no more roam through the mountains nor through the streets of the city. No more would we enter the dwelling-places of those whom we cherished.

Sail after sail was unfurled as we emerged from the harbor, and were traversing the expansive ocean again. Soon our canvas extended to the wind, and under its forcible pressure we were urged along over the bosom of the deep.

We left the Sandwich Islands about the close of November 1865. Our long voyage began in the evening and after the ship was brought under good headway, and the course on the compass was assigned the helmsman, I took my seat upon the bow and was soon lost in a reverie of thought. I drew before my mental vision the wonderful voyage we were just beginning, and the dangers that might attend the four months' voyage. My thoughts were solemn as the shades of night deepened on the sea, and the towering mountains grew dimmer in the rear. Our faithful Oriole had outweathered many a furious gale, and we trusted that she might prove sea-worthy to the end of the voyage and that God would be our protector as he had been thus far. What will it be when the last farewells have been uttered to our friends in this world, and we are about to launch into endless deeps, where endless ages roll! Will our souls still be conscious when the ordeal of dissolution is past, and will we be wafted through space into the expansive and mysterious spiritual realm? Shall we rest in the fair, elysian fields, and dwell in ecstasy with departed spirits who have passed on before? If so, how wonderful will be the flight of the spirit!

The reality will only disclose the beauty and grandeur of the spirit's soaring flight, and in some respects there is a resemblance in our floating bark, bearing its living freight over the bosom of the deep. We spoke the last farewell to our friends in this world. We have lost sight of their friendly visages, so lately seen, and the distance is becoming greater between us. The great ocean is unstable and we are moving onward all the time. The towering mountains become dimmer and are receding from our vision until they will be lost in the distance, and naught but the firmament above us will be seen, and the restless, heaving ocean beneath. It occurs to my mind that there is no experience in this life that can bring our departure from this mortal sphere more clearly before our vision, and being apprised of the fact that this wonderful experience of death and dissolution must be the experience of every one, how should we strive to be ready for the solemn event! If our spirit must, then, soar to a region of darkness and gloom, when the convulsive throes of death are past and the last groan has escaped the body, and it lies still, and helpless, and pallid in the cold grasp of death, oh how dreary and lone must be the flight of that disembodied spirit! The very thought makes us shudder and long for safety in Christ.

Our future destiny for weal or woe will be the result of our thoughts and actions in this world, while the body is the home of the soul. It is well to illustrate death by impressive scenes in this mortal life, and portary the event of dissolution as graphically and vividly to the mind as we possibly can. The more we contemplate the event which must occur to all, the better our lives will be fitted and adjusted to the occasion. Life is but brief, and death is one of the inevitable things, and we cannot afford to meet that last triumphant enemy without considering his approach, the character of his gloomy mission, and the certainty of our final surrender.

Let the scenes of parting on this mortal shore, the verdure, grass and blooming flowers, all combine to teach us the short duration of life and the certainty and reality of death. Had my voyage been misspent, and my school of discipline unimproved, had divine mercy still prolonged my days in the ways of iniquity, I should now be sailing toward the land of my nativity more calloused, and deeply dyed with sin than ever, but my submission to his correcting influence has inclined my heart to measure and appreciate the sober realities of life, and to study the final destiny of the soul. Consequently, all my faculties and ransomed powers urged me to a peaceful departure, and a serene and tranquil destiny in the eternal world. Divine truth is ready to mould and purify our hearts, but if we evade the smelting furnace, and the cleansing process in this life, we shall have to meet the direful disclosures of judgment and denunciations of wrath in the other world. Hence it is our wisdom to do right and obey our Creator in this world, and fit ourselves for the next.

After the charming city, with its inhabitants, aglow with life, had all disappeared in the dim distance, the sublime and familiar aspect of the heavens above, and the swelling waters beneath were presented to our vision again. The warm breezes of the equatorial regions wafted us onward, and we were fanned and refreshed in the circulating current, but as we near the equator we merge into the intensely heated atmosphere, and suffer its oppressive heat at times.

We are now sailing through Polynesia,—the many islands in the Pacific Ocean,—and I should like to visit many of these islands if I could, while I am so near them. I used to be much interested in the study of them when I attended school, but I did not think at that time that I should be privileged to visit as many as I have already, and come in close proximity to so many more, about which I used to study in my lessons in geography.

It would not take us far out of our course to visit the Society Islands. We had a native from these islands on board of the ship at one time, and I think that I have already referred to him in my work. He had more than ordinary natural abilities, and he was an excellent seaman. He deserted our ship at Honolulu and the officers would have given quite a prize to have recovered him. I spent many a pleasant hour with him and through him I obtained considerable information in reference to the idolatrous practices of the heathen and their vile und atrocious deeds, alluded to in the first chapter of the Book of Romans. He was well posted in Scripture and had a very bright intellect. However perilous our situation, he seemed undaunted and was ready to obey any command with pleasure, though it endangered his life.

At one time I remember we were pursuing a whale, to which our boat was fastened, and the waves bore us right alongside of the huge sea monster, against our wills, of course. The captain, who did not often command a whaleboat, was controlling ours that day, and in our perilous situation, I believe that he felt more nervous than the rest of us. To show his coolness, this brave inhabitant of the Society Islands reached forth his hand and violently patted the frightened monster on his large smooth back. "You, Kanacka," said the captain, "will you stop?"

The Navigators' Islands, lying north of the Friendly Islands in south latitude 13° 30" to 40° 30"; longitude 168° to 173° west, I should like to visit, and view their lofty

A SCENE ON THE FRIENDLY ISLANDS.

mountains, fertile soil, and rich vegetation, and feast on the delicious tropical fruits, and take an observation of the well-formed, ingenious and affectionate inhabitants, and if I were controlling our craft, I presume I would gratify my desires, and visit quite a number of the South Sea Islands, for I would much rather do it, than catch whales.

We made a short stop at the Friendly Islands, within the torrid belt. They lie south-east of the Fiji Islands and are, I believe, considered a part of them. The Wesleyan Methodists became the active missionaries in 1827, and succeeded in subduing the paganism of the inhabitants. The natives are courteous, benevolent, and friendly. They have good conceptions of God, and are piously inclined. Some of them can speak English fairly well. Our coming seemed to be very opportune.

They had just been visited by a terrible hurricane, which hurled the spray from the ocean billows over the islands, and in the fearful shock of the storm the natives were greatly terrified. They welcomed our arrival and appeared to feel a sense of security in our presence. Their hearts seemed to have been greatly humbled by the dreadful visitation of the tempest. We had also felt the force of the hurricane to some extent, but did not encounter it in its wildest fury. We procured some tropical fruits,—cocoanuts, oranges and pineapples, to comfort us upon our homeward bound voyage. The natives were, indeed, very hospitable, and they seemed to experience great delight in furnishing us with the precious products of their island home. The soil appeared to be very productive.

I shall never forget the kindness of the islanders. They seemed to greatly desire that our stay among them might be prolonged, and I would gladly have spent some time with them. I presume their feelings toward us were somewhat similar to the feelings of the inhabitants of the Island of Melita were toward the apostle Paul and his associates, after they had escaped the destructive storm which resulted in the foundering of their ship. They received them kindly and kindled a fire for their comfort, because of the rain and cold. But we had not been shipwrecked, neither had we any need of artificial heat, for the vertical rays of the tropical sun produced all the heat that was necessary. We really felt that it was good to be there, and I much desired to have spent some time with these well-disposed people in religious conversation, Bible reading and prayer. The fury of the hurricane had rendered them particularly humble and they could not desist, seemingly, from alluding to its destructive power. They seemed to reverence the great and universal God, whose power can restrain the winds and the waves. I felt that it might have been in season to have labored among them spiritually.

It is our misfortune to attempt this great work so often out of season, that it affords our aching hearts great relief and pleasure to engage in the work when all things are made ready to our hand. The soil of the human heart must first be broken up, and that may be accomplished in various ways, by the roaring elements, the thunder's peal and the lightning's glare, or the sad reverses of human life that occur in the form of loss, pain, sickness, bereavement, etc. Israel of old was humbled by the sable cloud, and dreadful thunder and lightning,—the burning mountain and the quaking earth. Martin Luther was humbled and thrown into a condition of penitence by a terrific thunder storm, during which the lightning struck and killed his friend. This thrilling incident became the incentive to self-sacrifice, and a profound investigation of the Bible, by which effort he was convinced of his erroneous ideas, and induced to renounce Catholicism. We require first a shaking up to render the heart susceptible of the seeds of life, and then, if the true seed is sown at the seasonable time, we may anticipate a vigorous, spiritual growth and a fruitful harvest. Not only is earnest work required in the commencement of the spiritual life, but it is needed all along, to complete the growth.

A Christian yearns for seasonable opportunities and feels mortified when he is hindered in their improvement. No matter as to what our vocations may be, or in what department of life we may be exercising our mental and physical strength, even for financial gain, we admire seasons that are opportune, when large incomes may be realized, but much more is this the case when the pious heart is on the alert and absorbed in the spiritual interests of the soul. We greatly delight in being ushered into the presence of people who are humble, and in season for the reception of the pure words of life.

CHAPTER XXVII.

Ploughing the Ocean Once More. — At Cape Horn. — Thoughts of My Former Experience at this Point. — Pernambuco. — A Severe Storm at the West India Islands. — Approaching the United States. — At Anchor in Buzzard's Bay. — "Land-Sharks." — A Consoling Thought Regarding Our Landing on the "Other Shore."

HOW much benefit those people may have received from the few Christian remarks that I made in the spirit of meekness and love, I am not able to say, but I have not suffered any compunctions of conscience for not having endeavored to use to advantage the brief period of time allotted to me during our short stay at these pleasant islands. I did what I could, and Christ ratified the act of the woman who broke the alabaster box and anointed him unto his burial by saying, "She hath done what she could." Christ is deeply concerned for his created beings everywhere, and he wants his people to do what they can to bring them to his "grace, which hath appeared unto all men." His people are fearfully responsible to exert this religious influence wherever they go in this world. If in civilized or heathen lands we roam, let us save the exile and guide the wanderer home. Our stay at the islands, with our heathen friends, was short. Soon we prepared to adjust our faithful Oriole to the pressure of the wind again, The natives surveyed our movements, and our departure seemed to fill them with sadness. Soon we were under way again, leaving the amiable inhabitants, with all their delicious fruits, in the rear, and our thoughts would again soar on mental wings to our native home, with all its charms and attractions. Those only, who have experienced the long separation, with all the sorrows and adversities that have intervened, can know the thrills of joy in the soul, as we are daily drawing nearer to our home. There will be very few stops made on our long voyage over the seas, and if the breezes are favorable we will be daily and hourly shortening the distance, for a ship that flies before a strong wind, and is incessantly moving, day and night, is cutting down the miles of a long voyage quite rapidly.

I would often be lost in a solemn current of thought as we flew before the wind. It seemed wonderful to be retracing our course around the great continent of South America again, and I would draw the contrast between our thoughts on the outward passage and on our homeward bound voyage. When we were crossing the great waters, on our voyage from home, we were filled with grief and sorrow, but being homeward bound, our hearts were filled with joyful emotions, and the hope, ere long to be liberated from our thralldom, made us feel happy indeed.

In the month of January, 1866, we reached Cape Horn again, and were solemnly and impressively reminded of our gloomy continuance there, for almost thirty-six days on our voyage out from home. I reviewed our terrible schooling, and could thank my God with renewed fervor for his kind preservation and care over us, and that he brought us out of that dreary and dangerous region. Withal I felt glad for the rigid experience and its salutary effect. It humbled my heart greatly to ponder over all this again, and thus receive a second benefit.

I shall never forget dreary Cape Horn, the struggle of my soul, my vows to my Creator, and the yielding of my troubled heart to his sovereign will. It was a great source of pleasure and comfort to me to remember that I had endeavored to keep my vows, and that I had tried, in great weakness, to serve the Lord during my long and tedious voyage. Before I had made vows in the hour of peril, but had broken them again, but this time I executed them, which has greatly eased my conscience and given my soul sweet relief.

The distance was now about half made,—or nearly so,—from the Sandwich Islands, and our detention at the dangerous Cape was not long this time, as the wind was in our favor, and we soon doubled the Horn and entered into the waters of the great Atlantic again. It is tedious to be necessitated to sail nearly around the globe to reach home, but this is the only recourse of a ship. Our course is now directed toward the equator again. I have already crossed it once in the Atlantic, and four times in the Pacific, and crossing it once more on my home-bound trip, will make the sixth time. I call to remembrance our voyage south through this great ocean and our experiments in whale catching, when as yet we had no experience, but repeated struggles and contests with the monsters of the deep has rendered us more proficient, and we are not so apt to be thrown into confusion as then.

One of the most pleasant things in the decline of life will be that we have kept God's Word, and thus filled our obligations to him and performed our duties to our fellow-men. We will, no doubt, discover then that many of our labors will have been achieved in great weakness and imperfectness, but if only the motive, that prompted the action, was pure, and our sincere aim and effort was to please the Lord, many of our imperfections will, through the intercession of Christ and the mercy of God, be forgiven.

Our proximity to death will cast a powerful reflection upon our past life and bring it almost in panoramic form before us. To launch into the great abyss of eternity with guilty fears, will be terrible beyond description. It pays well to live right in this world, so as to entertain a hope of our acceptance with God in the end of our life.

God has given me ample time to think and to amend my ways on this long and eventful voyage on the troubled deep. Eternity, with all its amazing consequences, has been vividly portrayed to my vision by my maritime life and its awful surroundings, and I trust that the impressions may be deep and lasting and that my service to the Lord may bring no regrets in the parting hour. I have learned to love him, and all the varied conditions of ocean life have had a tendency to draw me nearer to the cross of Christ. I think I can often refer to the school of my discipline amid the roaring elements and the perils of the sea, and employ it as an incentive to urge me onward in the race of life to the celestial home of joy and blessedness forever. I hope that my training among the disturbed elements will gender a persistence and constancy in the life of Christianity, whatever opposition may yet be brought forth: and I hope that I may be a servant indeed, adapted for the most humble avocations in the Master's employ, and serve him with true fidelity.

Noah had much time to think while the floods prevailed of yore, and he was riding over the dominant element that covered the mountains and the trees, and inundated the entire earth. He had been much annoyed, no doubt, by the insults and impositions of the wicked, but they had all been swept away by the deluge. He, being a righteous man, had, no doubt, exercised a patient spirit while many of them had hurled their imprecations at him and ridiculed his foolishness in building such a peculiar craft, adapted to float on the undulating element. But the faith which God has capacitated man to exercise in his sovereign power, and the reverential fear which is coupled with it, stayed this man of God amid all the oppositions of the antediluvians until the great ark was reared before their eyes, and he and his house were saved and the selected animal creation.

All these wonderful events in which water is the leading characteristic, revolve in the mind in our meditative moments on the deep. Water is a powerful element for destruction or preservation, and Noah's separation from the wicked, and preservation by the same element that destroyed his cotemporaries, affords a figure of the Christian's separation from sin, and salvation by the divinely-authorized baptism, instituted and enforced by the example of its Author,—Christ.

Let the people of the Gospel age beware lest this valid and heaven-ratified rite be misconstrued and ignored as was the saving power and separation by the ark, and they be left to perish in their own gainsaying when the saving rites, incorporated in the economy of grace are withdrawn by the same power that arranged and placed them, with all their cleansing efficacy, in the redemptive plan. God only proposes to save by his own means and the populace, as a rule, have ever disputed the propriety and authenticity of the divine arrangement in any and every age. Let the world and professed Christendom consider solemnly the end and awful issue, which will, undoubtedly, as in every closing dispensation, only be clearly comprehended by the minority. After righteous Noah had been severely tested in the building of the ark and the oppositions which it encountered, and the breath of all animated creation was quelled and silenced by the conquering flood, and he, with his family, were floating securely over the bosom of the deep, there was a seasonable opportunity to meditate upon the power and wisdom of that God in whom they believed. Then they could form their resolutions that when the earth should be populated again, they would exert their influence for its sanctity and purity before God, by strictly fearing and revering the name of the Lord. Notwithstanding all these supposed solemn deliberations when the deluge disappeared and they proceeded in the cultivation of the earth, its increase made them prosperous and wealthy. Noah sinned by drinking to excess the intoxicating cup, and his digression from rectitude gave an occasion for a stigma to fall upon his posterity.

So with all God's discipline, to correct our lives. While sin and temptation are prevalent in the world, it is difficult for the righteous at all times to retain their equilibrium, but when they are called according to the purpose of God, even though they lose their balance at times, they may be rectified by his discipline again, though injury may result to posterity, by the offense committed.

A man of influence in the service of God evidently occupies a responsible position, and God generally tests such severely before raising them to responsible positions in his divine service. But age brings on its infirmities in the most eminent men and that should lend its influence in our decisions, lest they be rash and unwise. The customs, influences, and surroundings of the respective ages and dispensations in which good men have lived, have differed materially.

We pause in our homeward course at Pernambuco on the coast of Brazil, South America, but our ship was not conducted into the port. Only the captain with a boat and crew entered. A whale ship has not the opportunity to enter as many ports, and visit as many cities, as a merchant vessel has. However, we have seen enough of the world for once, and are ready and willing to speed our way onward as rapidly as the winds and currents of the ocean will bear us toward our cherished land. We soon had our ship Oriole under way again and were on our flight toward the more familiar coast of North America.

While sailing abreast of the West India Islands, though far out at sea, we encountered a severe gale about the midnight hour. This occasioned a reversion of feeling and drew out our nerves again to their utmost tension. A sailor's nervous system is often shocked and that is the reason, no doubt, that the average duration of the lives of seamen is so short. It is a life of excitement, of agitation and commotion, and strains the constitution. The contending elements undoubtedly diminish the strength and firmness of the vessel.

The chief-mate is seldom on deck at night, unless in a time of emergency, and this being such an occasion, he sprang from his berth and assumed the responsibility of controlling the ship amid the fury of the storm. The storm struck us suddenly, which rendered the furling of the sails a difficult task. A scene of wild confusion ensued. The mate's imperative tone in command was raised to the highest key.

Some of the men were stirred with wrath, the tempest roared wildly, and swept with fearful velocity through the rigging, while the ship was careening from one side to the other, as the foaming billows were hurled, by the force of the tempest, against her side. All the unpleasant features of maritime life confronted us again, and lowered the emotional feelings which the prospect of our nearing home had elevated nearly to the climax of joy. We were destined to experience at least one more backset on our voyage,—one more furious contest and shock of the turbulent elements. Once more we had to face the frowns of human ire and hear the hard speeches, hurled from polluted human lips. We hoped it might be the closing tragedy. It served as a recapitulation of our storm-tested voyage, of our school of severity and rigorous nautical discipline, and, perchance, stamped upon the minds of the candid and considerate, the tenor and character of the three years' tuition and practical training on the sea. "All things shall work together for good to them that love the Lord; to them that are called according to his purpose."

I accept it in this light and fondly hope that is the graduating period. One of the able and expert seamen gave the mate an insolent reply in the frenzy of the moment, which, I feared, would end in a bloody contest, but the high temperature of wrath had somewhat subsided, till the sturdy and resolute sailor descended from the yard-arm.

When the shock of the storm was over and our nerves were settled again, we increased our spread of canvas, adjusted our faithful Oriole to her course, and were wafted by the winds of heaven toward our home. The soldier shudders at the thought of a bloody battle on his journey home, and the storm-tried mariner dreads more than ever the rag-

CHRIST STILLING THE TEMPEST.

ing tempest, when nearing his native land, but when the disturbance is over and the unwelcome trial has been endured, our longings for the tranquil home of peace are increased.

In a few days subsequent to the ferocious storm we came in sight of the United States' coast, and were slowly and surely sailing on the wings of the wind toward our destined harbor at New Bedford, Mass. O reader, how charming was the vision! Our longing hearts were solaced. The long voyage, with all its checkered experiences of sunshine and shadows, sorrows, turmoils, weal and woe, was past, and soon, by God's kind permission, we could again tread the peaceful shores of the United States of America,—our own dear native country, over which the gloomy cloud of civil war was hanging when we left its borders, three years before. Now hostilities had subsided, and we could survey her rocks, hills and dales, and traverse her cherished landscape, without the dread of destructive, hostile raids. If the landing of the mariner abounds with thrills of joy in this world, what will the landing be in the celestial country? It will evidently be an experience which our finite minds are unable to measure.

We dropped our anchor in Buzzard's Bay, from which memorable place we hove it nearly three years before, when some of us were yet entirely inexperienced in the work. Now we had returned with all the advantages of practical discipline and training on the tempestuous ocean. We did not return with all our original crew. Some had deserted us on the islands of the sea and we heard of them no more. Some of them had deserted, but were arrested and brought aboard, and are now safely landed in Bedford

City. They are glad that they were rescued and have now safely arrived at their longed-for destination.

This suggests to the candid mind an important thought. How many will be missing when the Gospel ship lands at the eternal shores! How many will have deserted and will have lost their way in the meshes of sin and the labyrinths of this world!

Some will have made the attempt to desert but, through the superior prudence of the officers, will have been rescued and saved. How their hearts will swell with gratitude, as they call to remembrance the fact that, though their feet were almost gone, still they were rescued and guided by "God's counsels, and afterwards received into glory."

The ship Zion will not land with all her original crew. Some will faint at the burdens and trials of the voyage, and will experience the feelings of anguish and remorse which sad desertion brings. What a pity it is that some become weary in well doing and repine at the hardships that must necessarily attend a voyage over life's boisterous sea, and finally become hardened and rebel against the government of God, and forfeit their interest in the eternal inheritance! When all the tempest-driven, well-disciplined and loyal mariners of the old Gospel ship arrive at the celestial landing, they will be liberated forever of the burdens, fatigues, aches and pains of the soul, which they experience amid the roaring storms and the opposing elements of strife. These faltering ones must be excluded from the grand escort, by angel bands, through the gates of the magnificent city, where their eyes shall behold the King in his beauty, and their rest shall be long and sweet in the land that is far off. That time will come, just as the end of our long, adventuresome and toilsome voyage has come. In the midst of our perils and painful anxieties, the hours, and days, and weeks, and months, and years rolled slowly by, but since the desired end is reached, we can hardly conceive the reality of our arrival. So the pleasurable and victorious end of God's toiling people will come, and the woes and calamities and disappointments of the dim and gloomy past will be lost in the thrills of ecstatic joy, occasioned by the home reception in the land of rest.

Having anchored the Oriole, we cast our last, lingering look at our floating home. She had outweathered many a furious gale, and withstood the pressure of ice in the Polar Sea. She had carried us safely through nearly every zone of the world, and finally landed us safely in Columbia's land. We could see her careening movement in the storm, and her hurried flight on the wings of the wind; we admired her attractive mien under free-bent sail, and, in short, every attitude of the faithful Oriole was familiar to us, and it would be stamped upon our memories in the future, no doubt to the end of life. But we now disembarked, to see her with our natural eyes no more.

When ready to depart we were met by a large band of very cheerful, amiable and smiling merchants, who met us and took us all aboard of their schooner and we were conveyed ashore. They seemed to be greatly concerned about us, and acted as if they were especially looking after our welfare. They proposed to procure us choice boarding places, and sell us a complete outfit of wearing apparel at very reduced figures. The sailors call them "sharks." They were in the habit of stealing the march upon the sailor-boys, and we were cautioned by some genuine friends to keep our eyes open, and guard against their wily tricks.

This requires a change of tactics, as our vigilance had been drawn out in a different channel altogether, and we had almost forgotten how to watch and counteract polished, genteel-looking fellows, with glib tongues, fair speeches, and apparently benevolent designs. Mariners are tempting objects to these land sharks, who, in their appearance, exhibit a striking contrast to the sailor, in his suit of patched clothing.

It is the pecuniary gain that the affections of these polished gentlemen rest on, and not the welfare of the poor, storm-tested seamen, in their patched garments. They would cheat them out of every hard-earned dollar, before their departure for home and friends, if they could bring their treacherous schemes to bear upon them. They meet the care-worn and patched seaman just about like the devil met the Savior in the wilderness of Judea, but the only thing *they* aim to cheat him out of is his money, while there are thousands now-a-days who have stolen the livery of heaven to serve the devil in, who are ready to cheat you out of your religion and your money too. They talk like angels, but they deceive like devils. They live in the city of Babylon where all kinds of traffic is carried on in costly goods and commodities, up to making merchandise of the souls of men.

I am fully convinced that this world is a wonderful arena for playing tricks and shams, and if a man sees the appearance of an angel, let him probe and scrutinize by the Criterion of Truth and see if he does not turn up to be a devil.

The thought is grand and consoling that, if we are so fortunate and happy as to effect a landing on the eternal shores, we need not fear deception; we shall there see the angels in their native purity, and their true celestial mien, and there will be no sham movements to impose upon our credence. No devil will ever traverse that pure and unsullied landscape, neither will any of his ministers be there. It is the land of the pure and holy, and naught that defileth can enter therein. I would not desire to exchange worlds for an abode so much purer and better than this.

CHAPTER XXVIII.

Our Stay at New Bedford City. — Why We were Known as Sailors. — Attending a Religious Gathering. — Slow Growth Essential to Permanency. — Obtaining Our Pay for the Wearisome Voyage. — Departure for New York. — Approaching the Old Homestead. — A Look Through the Windows. — My Welcome by the Dear Ones at Home.

IN my mortal career there is no event that makes me think more forcibly of my arrival in the celestial world beyond, than our landing on Columbia's land after our turmoils on the sea. We met with some very warm and true friends in New Bedford City, and we spent nearly two weeks among them, as it required about that time until our ship discharged her cargo, and a proper distribution made of the respective interests of the officers and crew. During the time of settlement we had our several boarding places, and visited among religious friends, who received us very courteously and kindly into their houses. We also attended their places of public worship, and listened to several good discourses upon religious topics. We worshipped with sailors and many other fellow-mortals, who had come there from different parts of the world.

The sailors made a respectable appearance, after having divested themselves of their old, patched garments, and being arrayed once more in citizen's apparel, but we could easily be detected as sailors, by our tawny complexion and unsteady locomotion,—a result of the careening of the ship and our unstable home on the deep. It required quite a length of time to once more adapt ourselves to *terra firma*.

It needed considerable practice to adapt ourselves to the unstableness of the sea, when first introduced to maritime life, but now it required practice again to walk easily and gracefully on land. To be expert and proficient in any thing in this life, we need *practice;* even to walk, or talk, or in the achievement of mental or physical labor. All these, in their respective turns, need the practice and use of muscle and brain.

Gracefulness and adaptability in any useful undertaking is commendable. When I was practiced in military drills and marches, my step was elastic and precise, and my body was in a graceful and erect posture, but the rolling deep has thrown me out of that systematic way, and my friends on land will have to make the best of my unsteady gait, until, by practice, I become again habituated to life on the shore.

We attended a meeting in New Bedford City, where a large concourse of professors of religion had met, and we listened to the testimony of many different persons. There were some interesting messages delivered, by apparently modest, unassuming and God-fearing persons. One young man claimed the blessing of sanctification as an instantaneous work. His testimony I could not endorse. I have always regarded Christianity as affording a gradual development of character, and not disclosing its spiritual growth in sudden, abrupt transitions from one degree, or stage of character, to another.

It is possible to work up to a high pitch of feeling, but I fear it is too frequently more sensational and imaginary, than a genuine leap from one stage of Christian character to another. I am inclined to give credence to an orderly gradation of the Christian life to full stature of manhood in Christ. This view comports with God's arrangement in nature also, and there are many illustrations deduced from nature, to describe the spiritual growth. Christ's own life is an example of gradual development, and he had an experience of about thirty years, ere he reached the climax of his power.

The Scriptures teach us that Christ went to Nazareth and was subject to his parents, and that " he increased in wisdom and power, and was in favor with God and men." Christ's illustrations of the natural seed, deposited in the earth, is demonstrative of this systematic and orderly growth. It " springs up and brings forth first the blade, then the ear, then the full corn in the ear." The parable is employed to delineate the Christian character, and the incessant growth and gradual development, until it arrives at its consummate stage. Of course there are periods when the growth of nature is more rapid. Gentle showers and genial sunshine will greatly facilitate advancement to maturity, while cold and storm may retard the progress, but the principle is indicative of gradual increase toward completion.

In nature, a comparatively slow but sure growth is usually more sturdy and solid. Look at the oak in the forest, the cedars upon the mountain slopes! They are indicative of strength, firmness, and durability. Their roots penetrate deep into the earth, and their solid growth and formation capacitate them to withstand the pressure of the howling blasts. The mushroom is of a sudden growth, but the strength is meager, the formation flimsy, and the duration short. Jonah's gourd was rapid in its formation, but it withered and died when the prophet needed it most. Thus I favor constancy and regularity in Christian progress, to bring about maturity of character.

Some Christian professors, in sudden outbursts of joy, testify to strong things, and make large promises, but it bears a resemblance to the imprudent mariner, boasting of his ability when the elements are undisturbed, and the soft and gentle breezes blow. "Tribulation," says the very competent and experienced apostle Paul, "worketh patience; and patience, experience; and experience, hope: and hope maketh not ashamed; because the love of God is shed abroad in our hearts."

Storms and reverses, in the sea-faring life, habituate the sailor's mind to a life of endurance. So, by comparison, I reason that the Christian's mind and heart should become molded to the divine pattern by adversities, distresses and afflictions. The mariner's trials give experience in nautical life, and develop his character. The same, comparatively speaking, prevails in the spiritual element. The anchor is the sure stay of the mariner in the furious storm, and its firm grasp in the earth does not disappoint him. Thus, *hope* is the Christian's anchor to the soul, and entereth within the veil (in heaven). If all the essential elements are utilized in the make-up of his character, and the love of God is in his heart and controlling his actions, he need not be ashamed when relying on hope, his sure anchor.

Whenever our mind reverts to New Bedford, in future years, we shall think of the kindness and hospitable character of our friends of this city. Many of them heartily congratulated us upon our safe return thus far, after the long endurance of trials and hardships, and wished us a secure and happy arrival at our homes.

We were at length summoned to appear before the Whaling Company,—known by the name of Jones and Company,—to draw our shares of the cargo,—whale-oil and whalebone,—which we had all labored hard to procure during the long and checkered voyage. My amount was easily counted. Until all the expenditures, which had occured during the voyage, were deducted, there was. but a meager compensation left. We had to pay dearly for our clothing, and all that we purchased, on board the ship, and of course all the tobacco that I purchased for a year or more, including the last, memorable plug which I flung into the Pacific Ocean, was charged to my account. I do not know as to what the sum of it was, but I hope that there will no bills be charged to my account hereafter, for that noxious weed.

I received an order on the bank, in payment of the amount due me, and one of the polished gentlemen, who assisted in escorting us into the city from the ship, after our arrival, proposed to count the money for me, but I refused his proffered service, as I did not think it was an amount of sufficient magnitude, to justify me in employing his aid. I had $315, after my expenses were deducted, including my board bill in New Bedford City. I took the first available train, after I received my pay, and in company with John Nolan, my shipmate, started for New York City. The mournful sound of the steamer's whistle disturbed my sleep several times during the night, as we were ploughing the waters of Long Island Sound, and thrills of joy pervaded my heart at the thought of the home reception.

Next morning we were landed in the City of New York, and, after spending the day with my friend Nolan, in promenading the streets and viewing some of the grand sights of the city, I took the train in the evening for the City of Philadelphia. My heart was buoyant, when the swiftly-revolving wheels of the train were stopped within the limits of the old, familiar City of Brotherly Love. I spent the remainder of the night and the next day in the City, and purposely detained myself, so as to reach home in the evening, when the shades of night would have fallen.

I had written home from the Sandwich Islands before leaving there, that I would probably be home in the month of June, Providence permitting. I located the time for my arrival far enough in advance so as to occasion no disappointment, hence they were not expecting me for at least six weeks later, for I arrived April 13, 1866, but I meant to surprise them and I accomplished my design.

I aimed to reach home without any one knowing it in my neighborhood, but *this* scheme was defeated. The shades of night were not deep enough when I first landed in its familiar precinct, and, despite of my rolling motion on foot, I was detected by the scrutinizing eyes of Mrs. Garret Hunsicker, who just then was passing from her garden across the road to the house. Perhaps she would not have recognized me had I not passed the usual greeting, but the human voice is remembered even after many years, and when once familiarly known to a retentive mind, is scarcely ever forgotten. Mrs. Hunsicker recognized my voice, and then the greeting was ratified in good earnest, by a hearty hand-shake.

The event of my return reminds me of the charge, given by Christ to his disciples, on a certain occasion, to "salute no man by the way." They were to press their way onward, without delay, to their destination, their duties being very urgent and important. The methods of salutation then being very ceremonious and protracted, it would consume too much of their precious time. But this single instance was the only salutation performed that evening, until the affectionate greetings in the home circle.

Many solemn thoughts revolved in my mind as I trudged along on the old, familiar road. I thought of my tramps, to and fro, during almost every nocturnal hour in the years that were past, when, in the golden period of youth, my feet ran into the ways of sin. Still the prodigal was rescued, and the return was made after many clouded skies, and storms, and beating rains. I was drawing nearer home, and the quickly-beating pulses and fervent emotions of the heart are only known and appreciated fully by prodigals returning home.

Soon the familiar buildings were dimly seen. If the light of day would have rendered me visible, to the loving inmates of home, I presume I would have been met on the way, for I would have been, no doubt, identified like the returning wanderer of old.

A few more steps will cover the remote distance of twenty thousand miles from the Arctic Ocean! Is it a reality? It is, perhaps, no miracle like Peter's liberation from prison, but it is a marvelous thing. Once more I can survey the canopy of heaven above, studded with the beautiful stars, that I used to gaze at in my innocent childhood, when home, with all its attractions, was sweet beyond all else, and mother's care and presence was such a dear delight. Then my feet were not inclined to roam, and I knew not the woes of separation, and the sorrows of a roving prodigal's heart. Jesus says we must be converted and become as little children, ere we can enter the kingdom of heaven. That mild and innocent demeanor must return, and the self-important air, which is the result of sin, must be eradicated by the law of grace and the love of God. Pride, that poisonous influence that corrupts the soul, must be banished, and the heart must be purified, and reduced to simplicity and child-like trustfulness again. These scenes, alluded to, never looked more pure, beautiful and attractive to me than now, on my arrival home. They appeared just as they did in my childhood days. I was profoundly interested in every feature of my home, and I lingered, and observed, and pondered. Such an occasion gives wings to our thoughts, and the incidents and events of past years seem to be brought vividly before us.

At last I approached the window which afforded me a view of the precious inmates of the home circle. My mother and two sisters were there. A scene greeted my vision now that I had longed to behold for years. Could they have known that the roving son and brother stood without, how quickly would the door have been opened to welcome him in, but he could no longer remain outside. I must enter so that we might all rejoice together. I knocked at the door. Mother came to open, thinking that it was my youngest brother, but what a surprise! What a scene of joy and gladness ensued! The long absent one had returned! The roving son and brother was safe at home!

Our hearts were full to overflowing. Maternal love, in all its pathos and beauty, beamed in mother's countenance. My sisters' hearts were full of joy, and the meeting and greeting, on that occasion, will be remembered all along the journey of life. Our hearts were too full for utterance. My sensations were too much stirred to sit still. I traversed the familiar room of my dear home, and my mother followed me, tapping me on the shoulder and saying, "Well, George, are you at home again?"

Poor mother! How deep was the grief that had often weighed down her heart! What sad and lonely hours had she experienced during the years that rolled slowly by while her boy was absent! Often, when she retired at night, did her grief-stricken mind ask again and again: "Where is my boy to-night?" Often did the absent and roving son, who had occasioned much of her sorrow and anxiety, think of that maternal heart that was burdened with sorrow and care. But God's mercy abounded, and restored him to the home circle again, and the meeting and greeting is a sufficient compensation for the long and aching void, and the years of grief and turmoil that have intervened. Let the sorrows and burdens of the past no more disturb our hearts, for the time of gladness and rejoicing is come.

A meal was prepared for the wanderer returned, and once more, as of yore, but with more joyful emotions than ever before, could I sit and partake of the social repast, which the kind hands of mother and sisters had prepared. My sister (the eldest) was a member of the Brethren church, as my work elsewhere indicates, and had been endeavoring, in her weakness, to conduct the religious exercises at home. Now, that another member of the family had come to join in and assist her in the grand and noble work, it was a great solace to her. We could both exercise now, around the family shrine, and wield our influence for the consecration of all, to the service of the Lord. How sweet was the season of prayer that night! Ere we retired we had thanked God for the preservation of all during our long separation. Having realized his compassionate answer to our prayers, we felt his blessing upon us.

Every-where, within the enclosures of home, serious thoughts were awakened. When we retired, late at night, we still had much to think about, and hours rolled by ere we could gently sink into soft and refreshing sleep. My sleep had often been disturbed by the roar of the tempest, and the beating of the furious waves. I had slept in perilous situations, in distant heathen lands, but now the storms of my perilous voyage were all over, and all danger of intrusion upon our peace was allayed. I had been solaced with the smiles of fond greetings in the home circle, and under the auspices of a kind Providence, I had retired to my bed of repose. Free from guilty fears and the goadings of conscience, I could lie down to rest. One blessed night under such favorable circumstances is worth more than years of carnal pleasure in the wild and giddy rounds of sin.

In this very bed I had tried to sleep away my feelings of condemnation when I had returned from my midnight "revellings, and banquetings, and abominable idolatries." While I was intoxicated with those sinful and fleshly entertainments, I imagined I had pleasure, but they were fleeting as "the dream when one awaketh," and I always awoke with a guilty sensation, and when the deadly stupor, occasioned by the indulgence of the carnal propensities, had in a measure subsided, there would have to be a repetition of the same carnal enthusiasm to suppress the native longings of the soul. O what a life of thralldom! How abnormal the element! Surely the "wicked are like the troubled sea that cannot rest, whose waters cast up mire and dirt." But the long, and dark, and guilty course of sin is trodden and God has turned my feet from forbidden paths of error, and now I can rest beneath his smiles of peace to-night.

Morning dawned and I awoke from my slumbers, and saw the golden sun arise in his beauty, to perform with untiring energy, his diurnal work. The same sun I had gazed upon in childish glee, in that innocent period when my heart was free from care. Having been restored, by God's amazing grace, to that mild and pure condition again, I could view God's great luminary with the same child-like joy. All through my wanderings in the wilds of sin, that mighty orb of day had been filling the Creator's command, and had I considered his punctuality and unwearied toil, when my heart was so prone to be wayward, it might have had a salutary effect. That same sun guided us on our dangerous voyage over the troubled deep, and had there been one failure in his timely work, we should have failed in our reckoning; and have lost our way on the rolling deep. O how wonderful are the works of God! How marvelous it is to see them, too, in their true light!

How pleasant it was to arise and be with the loved ones at home, and bow around the family altar, and offer our morning oblation to God! My arrival was soon made known among my friends, and my two brothers, upon receiving the tidings, came home. My youngest brother had remained in military service till the close of the war. I had not seen him since I left him at Harrison's Landing, in Virginia, when we, as musicians, were mustered out of the Government service. I had often wondered, in my home on the sea, while hostilities still raged, as to whether we should live to meet again.

CHAPTER XXIX.

A Pressing Invitation by Bro. Isaac Kulp. — Sanctuary Privileges. — A Visit at Bro. John Detwiler's. — True Method of Bringing About Gospel Conversion. — Admitted to the Fold of Christ. — My Stay at Home During One Year. — Trip to Illinois. — Attending the Funeral of my Brother in Norristown, Pa. — Return to Illinois, Accompanied by my Youngest Brother. — Marriage to Sarah M. Rittenhouse. — Election to the Ministry in the Hickory Grove Church, and my Ideas of the Great Responsibility of the Work.

ALL of us had now met in our dear home with the exception of the second-oldest brother, whose place of abode was unknown to us all. The enjoyment of social and endearing intercourse with those who were dear to us through the ties of consanguinity, was much appreciated, but the fullness of joy and fellowship, which can only be realized through divine relationship, was not comprehended by all. I now longed for that more hallowed union with the church.

Bro. Isaac Kulp, of whom mention was made in my letter to my mother, from the Sandwich Islands, heard of my arrival, and sent me a pressing invitation to come and make him a long visit. As he was engaged in mercantile pursuits, he was kept confined to his business, and as I had more leisure time than he, I accepted the invitation, for I desired to have the benefit of his longer experience and superior intelligence in the Christian work, which I knew would prove conducive to the perfecting of my religious interest. I assisted him what little I could in his store,—in the identical store where he tendered to me his religious counsel, prior to my entrance into maritime life. My visit with him and his pleasant family is a sweet and precious memento in my Christian career. I was especially desirous to see the church assembled, and to hear the Word of God declared, for I wished to realize all the benefits of the church, by being admitted into her fraternal bonds of union and fellowship. This was the longing purpose of my heart, and had been seriously meditated upon in my penitential school on the ocean. I desired to find the church that would afford me the full privilege of obeying all the commandments of the Bible, as my desire was to put on a whole Christ.

At the first appointment in the house of worship that I had occasionally attended while in my wild career, I resorted thither, in company with my sister, whom I esteemed highly for her Christian piety. I can never forget the peculiar sensation which I experienced when I entered the door of that sacred place, and viewed the members in their meek and humble attitude. I had seen them before, but never in such sacred mien, as my eyes were never before so adapted to the vision. The very sight of the church, in her divine aspect, melts the human heart, and especially when the separation from her hallowed influence has been long and painful. My heart was deeply impressed, and my eyes were melted to tears. The Word of God was simply and earnestly declared to the comfort and edification of my soul.

After meeting I visited at old Bro. John Detwiler's residence, who was a notable pilgrim, journeying to the celestial world. He visited at our home when I was a little boy, and always showed an interest in the welfare of myself, and brothers, and sisters. He would talk to us about God and religion in such a simple manner that it attracted our attention. My father labored much for him when I was quite small, and after father's death, he showed himself a true Christian to my widowed mother and her children.

While at his pleasant home, all his kindness during the days of our childhood, and mother's bereavement was brought to mind. A number of brethren and sisters were gathered there, all of which lent its influence to make our visit especially pleasant. They all manifested a deep concern for my spiritual welfare, and we sang and prayed together, and the old and experienced brother would select portions of Scripture,—such Scriptures as were particularly adapted to my condition at that juncture,—and employed me to read them audibly for the edification of all present, but especially for my instruction, so as to be governed by the Divine Mind, by the testimony of the Bible, as to what I must do to be saved.

This was far better than to have given his experience in the matter, and simply exciting my sensations, without the solid instructions of the Bible, as to how I should proceed.

The hearts of all were moved by the simple reading of the Scriptures, and especially did Bro. Detwiler shed many tears. All the circumstances, connected with the occasion, were solemn and impressive.

I learned a permanent lesson there, of the proper way to teach those whose hearts are penitent and humble, and in a proper condition to learn the way of life,—to teach them the mind of God, instead of having recourse to our own feelings in the matter. Whatever comments we may be influenced by the Divine Spirit to make, let them harmonize with the solid Words of Life, so that all our preaching may be substantiated by the testimonies of the Bible. I believe that many inquirers are misled by not giving them the proper Scriptural instructions seasonably, as to what they must do to be saved. This Biblical testimony, produced by the instrumentality of those who feared God and kept his commandments, served to strengthen the conceptions I had already received in the school of my discipline, when my heart was penitent, and with anguish riven.

It is comforting when, after enduring divine discipline, we are found to be of one mind and one judgment, relative to the blood-purchased plan of salvation. My dear readers, truth has made me what I am, and my willingness to conform to its purging influence and not a mere external preference to the denomination with which I am identified, for other sects with which I came in contact, in my checkered life, had more opportunities to mould my sentiments and arrest the decision of my mind than the sect to which I belong. It was truth, however, that I endeavored to reach in my humble researches, rather than sectarianism, and my lonely and retired investigations of the Bible have led me into the body with which I am connected, and my choice, as yet, has known no regrets.

After meeting with the brethren, and learning more of their simplicity, meekness and humility, and their wisdom in the Scriptures, and withal, their hospitality without grudging, I plead for admission into their number. I longed to be where the altar burned with love divine, and spend with them my toiling years, and sow life's seed in joy and tears, until the harvest day would appear.

The day was at length appointed for the church to come together to receive me into full fellowship. There never was a grander scene portrayed to my faith-enlightened eyes than the church on her divine mission that day Love seemed to beam in every countenance, as in humble attitude the church proceeded in her heaven-ratified work of rescuing the prodigal. Christ came to "seek and to save that which was lost," and during his absence with the Father, he employs the church as the medium through which the perishing are rescued and brought to themselves. A church to be the church of Christ must bear the lineaments of his character and life. She must be possessed of the spiritual gifts which he imparted to her, and the divinely beautiful traits, which adorned his life during his earthly mission, must beautify the church, and thus she can be easily discriminated from the world, and her sympathy, and love, and power to rescue the lost will be greatly admired by the returning prodigals.

When her concentrated power is thus revealed to penitent and broken hearts, through the wisdom, righteousness and sanctification, transmitted by Christ, the Author and Finisher of her faith, she moves in the element of her power and the shining beauty of her love, and becomes "fair as the moon, clear as the sun, and terrible as an army with banners."

I have seen the natural army, in all the pomp and splendor of military array, moving in compact columns, with the destructive implements of war, and banners floating in the breeze, and, to a trained, military eye, it presents an imposing sight; but the church of Christ, in her celestial habiliments, presents a far more attractive view to the lost but rescued prodigals.

These were the deep impressions, dear reader, that the appearance and orderly actions of the church made upon my contrite and broken heart. Together we proceeded to the water-side, where I was "buried with Christ by baptism, and raised to walk in newness of life." I now experienced the fullness of the relationship of the Father, Son, and Holy Ghost, and the complete fellowship of the church,—the body of Christ. O that the church of Christ might ever retain her Christian identity, and continue to be assimilated to Christ! What a powerful influence she can wield over the world, and how many forlorn and grief-stricken wanderers could be rescued from the wrecks of time!

God had now answered my prayers, even beyond my anticipations, and my long and anxious wish was completely crowned. He placed me where my heart could be fortified against the raging waves of sin, and the wiles of the devil,—within the sacred walls of his church I can rest secure when the furies of hell shall rage against her battlements. May the vows that I have made, and the crowning baptismal covenant be distinctly remembered and kept, however severely I may yet be tempted and tried within the sacred borders of the church. I am now fully separated from the element of the world in which I once lived and was active, and my old, Adamic nature has been buried in the liquid grave. I trust that nature will never gain the ascendency, but that the spirit may rule and predominate through all my future life. I would labor fervently to redeem the time that may yet be assigned me to live, and I would work for Christ, for much of my precious time has been wasted in sin.

I remained at home one year, with my mother and sisters, and that precious year was diligently occupied in attending the school of Christ,—the church. I had many important spiritual lessons to learn, and my entire consecration to the Lord disclosed to my mind, how little I knew and how very much I had to learn. I saw others far in advance of myself in spiritual knowledge, and I greatly appreciated their wise instructions and pious influence. My heart was deeply absorbed in the interest of the church, and no place upon earth was so dear as her sacred inclosures. I wished that all might see her beauty and be attracted by the wisdom that adorned her from above, I sincerely desired to labor in unison with her, that our united influence, by the grace of God, might win and save many more prodigals, and, if possible, persuade the young to enter the borders of the church, ere their feet would roam so far astray over the dark mountains of sin.

In the spring of 1867 I concluded to go to Illinois, not knowing as to whether I should be permanently located there or not. I had a desire to visit a portion of the West, and ascertain what my prospects might be, by forming an acquaintance with the people in that part of the United States. My mother and sisters tried to persuade me to stay with them, as they were loath to be separated from me again, but I finally agreed that I would, by the Lord's permission, make the trip. If things appeared to open to my spiritual and temporal interest, I would remain, and if not, I would again return. This promise seemed to satisfy their minds, and they seemed to desire that the will of the Lord might be done. I accordingly came to Mt. Carroll, Carroll County, Illinois, May, 1867.

I was pleased with the aspect of the country, and with the amiable and friendly dispositions of the people, and concluded, after inspection, that I might, perhaps, pursue my occupation to a better advantage, and also labor in the spiritual field equally as well as in my native country in the East, and so I concluded to locate. I handed my certificate of membership to the little church at Hickory Grove, where I met with a warm and loving reception, and after I became acquainted with the dear members, the attachment was very strong. I soon became acquainted in the vicinity, and much admired the social tendency of the neighbors. I received an extensive patronage at my occupation (plastering), and felt quite at home, and could not see but what the Lord might have directed me to this congenial spot.

Mt. Carroll is the County-seat of Carroll County, and contains a population of nearly two thousand. I soon learned to know many of the citizens, and have ever entertained an humble and prayerful desire for their eternal welfare.

In less then ten' months after I came to Illinois, my oldest brother died of diabetes, which occasioned a dismal cloud to rest upon our hearts. His death was quite unexpected to me. I had known that he was sick, but did not think that his disease was fatal. One night, as I was about to retire, I received a telegram, bearing the sad tidings, "Your brother John is dying. Can you come home?"

I replied that I would come. This event opened up a serious train of reflections. I had talked with him on the subject of religion, and he told me of his convictions in the earlier years of his life, but, like myself, had not yielded, and now it required a strong effort upon his part to become reconciled to the Lord. This we advised him to do, as his condition, away from God, was very insecure. He congratulated me in my consecration to the Lord, but still sadly neglected his own precious soul.

How difficult it is to break off from the associations of the world, when its bands and fetters are so tightly entwined about us! How many there are like my own poor brother, who can see a beauty in others serving the Lord, but have not the stamina and fortitude to execute the work in themselves! My heart was sadly pained at the tidings, and I felt mortified that I did not urge the matter of his conversion still stronger. Perhaps, by having prayed more earnestly and having employed more persuasive means, he might, after all, have been rescued before he became the victim of death.

He was so concerned about my journey west, that he accompanied me to the City of Philadelphia, and when I boarded the train and we gave each other the parting hand, I besought him to give his heart to the Lord. "Well," he replied, "I'll see," but, alas, he delayed too long and now he is gone.

The next morning after having received the message, I boarded the train at Morrison, Whiteside Co., Ill., and when I reached Norristown, Pa., the funeral services had already commenced. I beheld with sorrow the countenance that, less than one year before, was lit up with smiles. My dear mother, sisters and brother, sat, as mourners, around the coffin, and I seated myself among them with a sad and heavy heart. He was buried in the Lutheran cemetery, in which persuasion father held his membership when he died, and where mother still held her membership. My brother's decease caused a sorrowful vacancy in the family. He being the eldest when father died, the greater responsibility fell upon him to see after the welfare of mother, and his younger brothers and sisters. This care having fallen upon him at the age of twelve years, he became experienced in that line, and was ever looked to for counsel and advice. His absence, in the cold arms of death, was greatly lamented, but in this sore dispensation of Divine Providence we had to say with aching heart, " Thy will be done." Dear reader, let this sad event impress your mind with the uncertainty of life, and urge you to make a preparation to meet the grim monster, Death, if you have not as yet made that preparation. Death sometimes delays his entrance into our dear homes for a long time. Many dangers are passed through and still we live, but he is sure to come at last and cause the sad and painful vacuum.

When I returned west from my brother's funeral, my youngest brother accompanied me, and he, too, settled in Illinois. A year after I returned to my native land. In January, 1869, I was married to Sarah M., daughter of Abraham Rittenhouse, of Montgomery County, Pa. In February we came to Illinois, and March 6, I was elected to the ministry in the Hickory Grove church, Carroll County, Ill.

This placed upon me new and greater responsibilities, and I felt myself, in a great measure, at least, inadequate to the momentous task, but tried to resign myself to the will of God as best I could. Although the way was difficult to travel, I did what little I could, under the care and tuition of my senior brother and able minister, Michael Sisler, who was the elder of our church.

I had never urged myself to the front in public speaking. Having been annoyed by a spirit of diffidence from my childhood, I would only speak when circumstances seemed to press me into it. On the sea I endeavored, in my feeble way, to comment on the Scriptures, but now the preaching of the Gospel was to be made the prominent business of my life, and it seemed to impress my mind as being a great undertaking. I felt as if it required a new consecration to the Lord, in order to be successful in such a solemn and responsible work.

A certain writer says,

> "No other post affords a place,
> For equal honor or disgrace."

I had been called by the Lord, through the medium of the church, as I had reason to believe, and I decided that I would search and obtain a knowledge of his Word, that he would give me the wisdom to apply it, and that, by a practical effort, he would enlarge my utterance, so that I might communicate his Word to the people. Thus I labored on in the ministry as the Lord would grant me ability. Paul says, "Woe is unto me if I preach not the Gospel. If I do it willingly, I have a reward, but if against my will, a dispensation of the Gospel is upon me." I felt that it was my duty to labor for the suppression of all reluctance, diffidence and embarrassment, and endeavor to be armed with fortitude and humble boldness in the execution of the ministerial work, and do it willingly under the divine sanction, and so anticipate a reward, for the work being enjoined upon me by divine authority, I would have to discharge the obligation at any rate, whether reluctant or willing.

CHAPTER XXX.

True Relationship of the Church towards her Ministers. — Marriage of my Sister, Katie, to Eld. John J. Emmert. — My Mother Identifying herself with the People of God. — Death of my Youngest, and also my Older Sister. — The Declining Days of my Mother, and her Departure for the Better Land. — My Second-oldest Brother Heard from, but his Present Whereabouts Unknown.

TEMPORALLY I had not much accumulated for our support, therefore I was necessitated to labor hard with my own hands and preach the Gospel as best I could besides. This strain on my mental and physical energies was severe at times, and has worn on my constitution.

I have ever felt as though I would like to follow the example of the apostle Paul, who labored with his hands to support himself, and some of his co-laborers, I presume, who had need of pecuniary support. At least he says that he labored for those who were with him. "These hands have ministered to my necessities, and to them that were with me." Acts 20: 34. But I do not conclude that the inspired apostle labored constantly for his temporal support. There were times, no doubt, when he was so busily engaged in the spiritual field that he could not spend any time to labor with his hauds, and we conclude, from his writings, that there were seasons when his temporal necessities were supplied by the churches. While I have always thrown my influence, by example, upon the side of self-support, yet I believe that there should be a plane of moderation recognized by the church in the ministerial work. The abuse of this principle, of the church supporting her ministers, has in some instances, made the church too reserved in looking after the temporal needs of her faithful ministers, but though a valid principle may be abused by some, the abuse of it should not prevent the *proper* use of it.

We, however, admit that great caution is requisite upon the part of the church, to supervise this part of her work, but at the same time she should not be too cautious. God has promised to give her wisdom to carry out her mission in every particular, and the ministry is an important part of it. While the church might withhold from her faithful minister that which is justly due him, she may indirectly grant license to some of her wealthy members to indulge their carnal desires in their many opportunities to accumulate wealth, and while they may be adding farm to farm, and be laying up treasures in this world, the minister, who was appointed to preach the Gospel to them, may be toiling hard to support himself and family, and forego many opportunities of doing good, because the support which the Gospel authorizes, is withheld by the rich. There are two extremes in this, as well as many other things, and the church of Christ is in danger of running to either of these extremes.

My severe training in military and nautical discipline inured me to hardships and endurance, and now being in the service of the Lord, I have felt to do all, and bear all, that may be requisite in this sacred and responsible calling. As my deliverance has been great, I feel that I owe my life and my all to God and his church, which Christ has purchased with his own precious blood.

Since my election to the ministry my labors have been, in a large measure, restricted to the little church at Hickory Grove, although I have made ministerial tours to various portions of our beloved Fraternity.

During the winter season I have devoted nearly all my time to the ministry, but during the summer, family cares, and the demands for the little church in which I have, for twenty-four years, held my membership, have demanded my labors, in unison with that of my dear co-laborers in the ministry. Upon the whole my years of ministerial work have been pleasantly spent, and I trust that I can say we worked in love and harmony together. We have not enlarged our borders as much as some of the churches in our Fraternity, but if our cords have not been lengthened, yet I hope that our stakes have been strengthened. Some of our worthy members have changed locations, and some dear and earnest workers have fallen asleep in Jesus. Bro. Christian Hope and wife, and his wife's parents and sister, were here received into church fellowship, the memory of which union is ever cherished and dear. When the great day of reunion takes place in the celestial world, and the laborers who have sown the seed in tears, will come bringing their sheaves with rejoicing, from many lands and climes, I sincerely hope that the prodigal, rescued with the few that the Lord may have given him, may be represented among the number to swell the songs of redeeming love, and share the great harvest of rejoicing.

In the beginning of the year 1870, my sister Kate was married to Eld. John J. Emmert, of Mt. Carroll, Ill., and her location in the West was the result of this union. Soon after this occurrence my youngest sister, Mary, united with the Brethren church in Pennsylvania, and we were made to rejoice greatly that she began the Christian work in the golden period of her youth. In 1873 my wife and I paid a visit to our relations, brethren and friends in the State of Pennsylvania, and when we returned to Illinois, my mother and youngest sister accompanied us.

During their visit among us, my mother united with the church of the Brethren. In the sixty-sixth year of her age she felt the necessity of this ever-blessed union and fellowship with our people, having counted the cost and weighed the responsibility of a change of church relationship. Mother was always cool and deliberate in her decisions. Amid all the reverses of life and the chastisements and corrections of a loving Providence, four of our family were now representatives of the church of our choice. This was the good effect and the fruitful result of the painful years of divine discipline, and we could say with the Psalmist David of old, that "before I was afflicted I went astray but now have I kept thy word."

My mother and sister subsequently returned to our native borough in the State of Pennsylvania, but in 1876 they returned to Illinois to spend the remainder of their days. My youngest sister was then sorely afflicted with scrofula, which occasioned her death after years of extreme suffering. The wasting malady preyed upon her vitals, and her anguish in the paroxyms of pain was heart-rending to witness, but she showed much patience, and was refined and purified through suffering, and her conceptions could grasp the deep and mournful utterances of the suffering just, in their hours of anguish and pain. She was particularly attached to the book of Job, who alludes to the bitterness of his life and the loathsomeness of his disease and who describes his emaciated condition " by his flesh cleaving to his bones, his yearning for his couch to ease his complaint, and his tossings to and fro till the breaking of the day."

All these painful features, which the devouring malady brings, she experienced, and her form was reduced to a mere skeleton, when the lamp of life flickered and went out.

Again we all merged into the shadows of death, to weep and reflect, as mourners only can, when their loved ones have gone to moulder in its dismal domains. During her long and painful illness my aged mother kept close by her darling daughter, and applied the soothing ointment to her wasting frame. Many lone nights did she linger by her couch of suffering and keep painful vigils, to comfort her suffering child in her agonizing periods.

> May her dark hours of pain,
>   So long with patience borne,
> Incite her friends the crown to gain
>   In the celestial morn.
>
> May blessings ever flow,
>   And love adorn the home,
> Whose inmates all her anguish saw
>   And heard her weep and groan.
>
> God bless my mother dear,
>   Whose life was meek and mild,
> Who toiled 'mid tears and grief and care
>   To solace her poor child.
>
> We hope to meet again,
>   In that pure, healthful clime,
> Where none shall ever groan in pain
>   Nor health nor life decline.

The next to cross the turbid waters of death was my dear sister Kate, the wife of Bro. John J. Emmert. My mother now had her home with her only surviving daughter, and when her health began to decline, her maternal care was again exerted and her helping hands administered to her necessities. My sister and her husband were workers in the church, he being the elder of the Arnold's Grove church, Carroll County, Ill. My sister Kate possessed a cheerful temperament and the bright things of life seemed to preponderate in her heart. She led the van into our beloved Fraternity, and was ever a cheerful, willing, and earnest worker in the Master's cause. Even when her faculties began to decline, under the wasting power of disease, the smile of hope and filial submission to a compassionate God, who doeth all things well, beamed in her fading countenance. Our hearts were saddened to think that another dear one had bidden farewell to loved ones. We must all become the ghastly victims, at length, to that last cruel enemy,—Death. She died of consumption March 24, 1882, aged about forty-four years. She left us in the prime of life and apparently in the height of her usefulness. But her energy in the cause of Christianity and her words of cheer, and prayers, and smiles, and tears will be retained to profit while her body moulders in the dark and silent grave. She left a Christian husband, a daughter about ten years of age, an aged mother and two surviving brothers.

Thus ended the bright and useful Christian career of one who was cherished and dear. "We all do fade as a leaf." Isa. 64: 6.

> The sun in his climax of glory we've seen,
> When nature was smiling and forests were green,
> And birds in the woodland were warbling their songs,
> All lending the charm which to summer belongs.

Those beauties of nature that come with the spring,
All fade from our vision on time's rapid wing.
The soft tints decay in the autumn's cool shade,
The beautiful leaves of the forest all fade.

How apt the resemblance of old by the seer,
Of nature's decline at the close of the year,
And man's sudden exit from life to the tomb.
Our time, oh how fleeting! How transient our home!

We follow our friends to the grave in deep grief,
To us, oh how dear, but they fade as a leaf;
They shone like the stars in the fair azure dome,
To solace our spirits and brighten our home.

The memories so solemn now soften the heart,
When friends fondly cherished in paleness depart;
Their smiles in life's sunshine, their tears in its gloom,
Recur to the mind as we march to the tomb.

The husband in sadness laments for his wife,
Who shared in the comforts and sorrows of life;
The daughter was weeping in loneliness there,
The mother's delight and her subject of prayer.

So lately her languishing sighs we still heard,
To-day her pale form in the grave was interred;
We thought 'mid our tears and our swellings of grief,
The friends in our circle "all fade as a leaf."

The herald of Truth did sweet solace afford,
'Twas "blessed are the dead which die in the Lord;"
They rest from their labors, their sorrows are o'er,
Their works follow them to that beautiful shore.

So friend after friend leaves this grief-stricken vale,
They fade as the leaf and are lifeless and pale;
They moulder to dust in death's gloomy domain,
But God shall restore them in beauty again.

Come, mourners, and rest in the promise divine,
We'll meet them again in that glorified clime;
There death's withering blight shall the bounds not invade,
No ties shall be broken, no beauty shall fade.

Some time after my sister Kate's death, my aged and care-worn mother came to take up her abode at my place of residence, and, after so many deaths in our home, and the many long and painful separations of those yet living, it was pleasant to dwell again with mother, amid the joys of family life. I felt glad that her once roving but rescued son could possess a little home for her welcome reception, when her long, weary and toilsome journey was drawing to a close. What cares, and heart-aches, and dismal vacancies in bereavement had mother known and felt! It was meet that she should experience a brief respite ere her sun would sink beneath the horizon, to rise no more in this world.

Like the prophet of yore, in his cherished home, provided for him, our mother occupied her little chamber, and we were happy in the thought that we could dwell with each other, for a few years at least. The children looked upon her as a member of the family, and spent many hours of pleasantness in their grandmother's little chamber. Especially attached to grandmother was my youngest daughter, she having been nursed and fondled by that dear one from infancy, and also a namesake of hers. The two Maria's often dined, and sweetly conversed together, and the junior seemed to greatly solace the senior in the decrepitude of old age. Her constitution was remarkably vigorous till the close of her life, and she would often lend a helping hand when my wife was pressed with cares and burdens. Mother's presence and help would cheer the hours of separation during the winter season, especially when I was absent on long, ministerial tours.

But there must be an end to all that we hold dear in this life, and our fondly-cherished friends are destined to leave us, one by one. So mother's appointed time came when the deep shades of death must conceal her from our mortal vision. She had often wished, if the Lord's will might be so, that she might quickly depart, without a lingering illness to burden her friends,—as she herself expressed it. Mother deserved the best of attention and care, for she had been so self-sacrificing and untiring in her perseverance to wait upon her children, when they were prostrated with lingering and fatal maladies. Her wish, however, was granted. Her illness was of short duration, but very severe. She died of inflammatory rheumatism, which suddenly struck a defective limb, that had occasioned considerable pain and trouble for several years. From there it penetrated to the heart, and soon set forever at rest the heart, that had continued in active operation so long, amid sunshine and shadow, smiles and tears, weal and woe. We summoned all the children to her dying bed in the early morning, and we all mourned and wept as she gently passed away. It appeared inexpressibly sad to see that familiar face so cold and pale in death,—the face that we were wont to see in the glow and activity of life and health so long. Her death occurred Nov. 1, 1890, in the eighty-third year of her age.

Thus another impressive event was recorded upon the tablets of our hearts. The end of mother's career was certainly very touching to us all. Her acts of kindness, her fortitude and courage,—all arose before our mental vision as we viewed her familiar, physical form in the cold embrace of death.

Children, remember the worth and preciousness of a mother's presence, and the care and anxiety for your welfare and prosperity! There is no love within the circle of home so pure, so deep and anxious, as maternal love. It is the first, in our infantile state, to lend its fostering care; and its vigilance, through all the meanderings of life, is untiring. When woes oppress and sorrows rend the heart, that love is nearest to console. When pain and sickness waste our mortal frame, that loving care is all aglow, by day and night. Her prayers for the wayward child are incessant, and maternal love, ignited by heaven's immortal flame, will wrestle and plead, without fainting, for the lost and wandering child.

What is home without a mother? And what a sacred and endearing place is home with the cheering presence of a fond, Christian mother! But all maternal and fraternal ties, so far as their domestic and mortal union is concerned, must pass away, and our only prospect, when we cast our last, lingering look at the grave, are the celestial greetings on the other shore, and the immortal bands that will unite us in joy and blessedness forever. Let us labor, then, while we may be aided by each other's influence and sympathies, to secure together the love and friendship that is immortal, that when all, that is visible and tangible in this mortal sphere, shall vanish from our sight, we may anticipate the grand reunion on the other shore.

My youngest brother and I are now the only two known survivors of the family, to which reference has been made so frequently in this work. I already alluded to my second-oldest brother's final departure from home in 1860, the year prior to the commencement of the Civil War. He went to Charleston, South Carolina, and when the war began, all communication having been cut off, his whereabouts was lost sight of, and his existence was involved in uncertainty till the year 1867, when I came to Illinois,

I boarded a steam-boat one day, and took passage to Burlington, Iowa, where my brother was, at one time, in business, and where he had formed many acquaintances. I there ascertained that he was still living in 1866,—that he was then in Charleston, South Carolina, and expected soon to go to Europe. That was the last intelligence we ever received concerning him.

CHAPTER XXXI.

Reflections on Temporal and Spiritual Warfare.—The Christian Mariner, and the Points he must Watch.— Fidelity to the Cross of Christ. — "New Wine should be put into New Bottles." — If God Commands, we should Go.

DEAR readers, I have carried you on my mental wings through the long and checkered journey of my mortal career. I have portrayed to you especially the most prominent incidents of my life. I have described to you my early, pious inclinations, and the longings of my heart after God in the glowing period of my youth. I have shown you how those pious emotions, in the morning of life, were subsequently suppressed by indulgence of the carnal propensities. I gave you my experience in military life, and the effect that it had to harden my sensibilities, quench the sympathies, and prevent the development of the inner man, or spiritual being. I have shown the force of military regulation and government, as being necessary to military achievements and conquests. I have deduced illustrations from military system and order, to teach and impress Christian regulation and government, demonstrating, by way of comparison, that, without orderly and methodical procedure, in the spiritual army, there can be no success.

I have taken the spirit of zeal, endurance and courage, as shown by the natural soldier in his line of military life, to urge the necessity of endurance, fortitude and zeal in the spiritual army. I have presented the natural army, with its banners waving in the air, and moving in compact columns, with glittering swords and burnished steel, and all the formidable weapons of war, as presenting an imposing scene and occasioning havoc, bloodshed and death. I have shown the spiritual army to be superior, although, to the natural eye the scene is not so imposing. The contention against spiritual wickedness in high places, requires spiritual force instead of carnal. This divine force, utilized in mighty, spiritual conquests, is only clearly understood by the regenerated heart and the trained, spiritual eye, and the spiritual conquests of the church of Christ are far superior to the conquests by military power. "He that ruleth his own spirit is greater than he that taketh a city." Christ taught and exemplified it in his condescending life of humility, self-sacrifice, love, meekness, humility, non-resistance, and patience. These are the divine characteristics for conquering opposing humanity and the powers of hell. His people are commanded to adjust variances by arbitration, and in proportion as the nations become conversant with the spiritual system, which he taught and enforced by his sacred example, they will adopt his method. In the millennial age the "swords will be beaten into ploughshares, and the spears into pruninghooks." In his spiritual kingdom they already imbibe that spirit, and exemplify the principles. "But the carnal mind is not subject to the law of God, neither indeed can be." If the princes of this world had known the wisdom of God and could have discerned the spiritual character of Christ's kingdom, they would not have crucified the Lord of glory.

"Christ was crucified in great weakness but he was raised in glory." The crucifixion of our carnal nature is indicative of great weakness, but the result is powerful, and will tend to spiritual conquest and exaltation with Christ. The spiritual army will be far more imposing than the natural, in its glorious attitude and celestial array, when Christ comes in triumph.

Reader, do you see how the indulgence of carnal pre ferment and glory impairs the vision and all the senses of our being, for the view and the conception of the spiritual grandeur and power? "Ye must be born again," and ye must be born of water and of the spirit to enter the kingdom.

My purpose in this work is to be honest and candid in reasoning, by way of comparison, and employing the hard-earned lessons of my experience in the perils and adventures of my life, to impress the superior duties of the spiritual life upon the human mind. Christ himself affords many examples of impressing spiritual instruction in this way, and if I can make the experience of my life subservient to this end, I shall be well paid for the inditement of this work. I have endeavored to draw many illustrations from maritime life, and to freight them with the burdens of my experience, while passing under the correcting rod of divine discipline; and while I was rendered contrite and humble by these sore chastisements, I aim, by the help of God to transmit their beneficial influences to others, to induce them to yield meekly to the God whom I love and adore. I have spoken plainly, and at times severely, but I trust that love for God and man has predominated in all my arguments. Military men and seamen are taught to speak in plain language, and to the purpose, for the obligations of their respective vocations are attended with serious responsibilities. And is there any calling so serious and responsible as that of the servant of God?

Life is a journey that we pursue but once, and it is a grave and momentous thing to live and pass through this sin-polluted world, and "free ourselves of the blood of all men." When the situation of the mariner is perilous, and his life is endangered, he carries the burden and anxiety of the moment in his movements, gestures, and the tone of his voice. So, I remark, that public speakers and writers,— when exploring the magnitude of sin and its deceptive influence, and the ultimate anguish and remorse which it will entail upon its vassals,—are moved to clearness and plainness in their discriminations, and show no quarters to sin, however specious and angelic its appearance, lest they should fail to exert themselves to the utmost to rescue others, and so fall under the same condemnation themselves. The Christian life requires moral courage and fortitude. It demands impartiality and strict honesty of heart. We can spare sin no more under the guise or semblance of religion, than in the overt actions of degradation and depravity.

Sin, in all its forms and phases is discountenanced by God, and it must be discarded and reproved by his servants. Christians must make themselves thoroughly acquainted with the thoughts and mind of God, and then become the sincere and honest agents in communicating his mind to the children of men. "They are bought with a price," and cannot be the servants of sin.

The Purest Being that ever graced the earth with his sacred presence offended many during his pilgrimage through it, and yet, with respect to force and pertinency, "he spake as never man spake." He uttered the truth in all its vital force and acuteness, and the sham professions of his day could not endure his piercing words. The longer he lived, the more his reputation was repudiated by the populace, till, at last, they cried out, "Crucify him, crucify him. Let his blood be upon us and upon our children." O how many luminous stars have been extinguished from this vile world, by men whose eyes, and ears, and hearts were uncircumcised and could not bear their valid and truthful messages! Sin and false religion only effect a repetition of the same dismal scenes, and repel the pure arguments of the just, until they fall upon them as a savor of "death unto death." But the beloved Christ changed not his voice, though his reputation was well nigh gone, neither can we.

The Lord tested me by many painful ordeals. He proved me in the smelting furnace, and if I smooth my tongue and soften his inspired words against "spiritual wickedness in high places," I shall incur his displeasure, and his judgments inflicted upon me, will be deep and painful. I must shine by the light of the humble Christ, who is my spiritual sun, and I must determine my spiritual reckonings by the methodical process of the Bible, and thus progress on the ocean of time. I must teach this science in its purity and genuineness to others.

Human creeds and systems will not answer to consummate the responsible voyage of life. The pleasing sensations, produced by them, and the wild raptures of the mind, are not sufficient testimony to prove the divine authenticity of the work.

The storms and reverses of the voyage will sometimes cloud the vision, and disturb the glad and joyful current of the mind, but in this hour of dark temptation, a divine hope, based upon God's Word, will be our sure support. A Christian's motto is, Christ and him crucified, in sorrow or joy, in pain or pleasure.

The strongest evidences of our veracity and fidelity to the cross of Christ will be in the time of adversity and gloom. The religion of Jesus Christ does not consist in sudden outbursts of joy amid the glow of prosperity, and a relaxation into inactivity when the emotional impulses are over, and the dense fogs and storms intervene. It indicates *progression* and *perseverance* all the time, in glad or dismal days.

> "A single, steady aim,
> Unmoved by threatening or reward."

There is too much religion in the world that is too cheap to be good. It may be compared to some of the cheap clothing that we sometimes purchase,—it won't wear. There is not a proper preparation of the heart, and the joy, connected with the first reception of the Truth, is too *superficial*. The separation from sin and the world is not effectual. Sober and candid thinkers, who are unchristianized, can discover its inefficiency. The Savior shows this by the seed that falls upon the rock, "As soon as it springs up, it withers away, because it lacks moisture." "They, on the rock are they, which, when they hear, receive the Word with joy, and these have no root, which, for awhile, believe, and, in time of temptation, fall away." It is a poor stock of religion, and yet it is quite prevalent, and generally has the preference, because of the rapidity of germination and growth. But, then, such sudden growth often comes to an end before the seed, which is deposited in well-prepared soil, obtains a good start. A heart that is not melted to penitence and contrition, partakes too much of the nature of the rock, so that the seed cannot grow and thrive.

There is nothing like preparing the soil well, before depositing the seed. Serving God too easy is like farming too easy. The result will prove a failure. Seed that springs up too quickly, amid wild acclamations, and rapturous joy, indicates danger of sudden blight and declension. It is the thinness of the soil that occasions the seed to spring up sooner. The germination below the soil, and the growth above, in fact all,—is deficient and short-lived. It is a serious and solemn thing to begin the work of grace in the heart. More sober thoughts should be given the momentous subject. Teachers should be more intent upon teaching the Word of God. By being too relax in the start, the work is rendered futile and abortive.

If the Adamic nature is not killed, the growth in grace will be a failure. Old bottles are not the place for new wine. The heart must be made new before the new wine of the Gospel can be admitted. In the Adamic hearts it will soon burst in the course of fermentation. The wine will be spilled, and the bottles rendered useless.

How many bottles are spoiled by this untimely process! This might all be obviated by a proper and judicious preparation of the heart, and the pure and genuine wine of the Gospel, inserted in due course of time, as the Word of God directs! God will not reverse his work, though men may do so. His scheme and methods of salvation were maturely deliberated upon before being presented in their pure and perfect character to the fallen race of Adam, and there will be no recantation upon the part of Divinity. His measures must be accepted, or the direful loss sustained.

Devils are sometimes driven out of the human heart, by the sincerity and contrition of the one who becomes truly penitent, but while the Satanic power is dethroned, the heart is left too naked and defenseless, and is not fortified by obedience to the Truth. When a military force defeats and conquers a garrison, owing to a superior, military force, or skill and dexterity, the army, in defense of the fortifications, is compelled to retire, but the conquerors, proficient in military attainments, will observe the necessity of strengthening and securing every part of the garrison, in order to hold their position. By comparison, I would argue, that when "the evil spirit is gone out of a man," that heart must be fortified by the divine means of grace, and receive the Holy Spirit as an occupant in the heart. He is appointed to lead us into all truth, and so we shall be thoroughly equipped to hold the infernal forces at bay, and, secured within the impregnable walls of the church, built upon the "Rock of Ages, against which the gates of hell cannot prevail."

God has given us a record of his Divine Will. In legible characters it is inscribed on the sacred pages of the Bible. The Living Word, animated by the Spirit of God, penetrates the honest heart of the candid peruser, till the vital force of all the words of life exert their saving power. This Written Word, this Transcript of the Divine Mind, is represented as the "Sword of the Spirit." It is employed as the instrument to slay and subdue with the correcting arguments the lusts of the flesh, and instruct and guide, by its counsels and commandments, the soul to life eternal. The Spirit does not operate in an abstract sense; it employs the Word to wield its sacred influence upon the human heart. The Words of Christ, and all the words of Inspiration are written for our learning, and they who are called and chosen of God are commanded to teach all "the words of this life."

John, the inspired evangelist, informs us in his Gospel, "And there are also many other things which Jesus did, the which, if they should be written every one, I suppose that even the world itself could not contain the books that should be written. Amen." There never was a life lived that was so "pure, holy, undefiled, and separate from sinners," and so perfect and full of meaning, as the life of Jesus Christ on this earth. There never was an experience, fraught with such mighty import, power and love, and yet the wisdom of God deemed it necessary to withhold the account of some of his wonderful deeds from the knowledge of his creature, man, for in his finite condition it would be more than he could contain to profit. Therefore the infinite mind of God, that could fully measure the condition and character of man, had just enough written to melt his heart to penitence, to test his integrity, and "guide him to glory."

It is pitiful to behold that there is even too much written now, for many, who profess the name of Christ, to contain. They say, "Lord, Lord," but they do not the things which he says, and even in the great day of reckoning they will recommend their own work to Christ, and say, "Have we not cast out devils in thy name, and in thy name done many wonderful works?" But Christ will reply, "Depart from me, ye workers of iniquity, I never knew you." Do you think that I am telling too much truth to be wise?

I do not want to be wise above that which is written. I have been punished severely enough by the rod of God's discipline, I trust, to make me humble enough, and faithful enough to believe and try to do, at least, all that God says. Every sentence in the military code bore its express and definite meaning, and was obligatory whether averse to our feelings or not. The imperative signification was obey, or suffer the penalty annexed to military law. Maritime law was equally binding, and our only security was to obey every command in the line and order of nautical duty. Entering the school of Christ,—to experience *his* training and discipline,—would it be reasonable to expect exemption from duty? Could I hope to be exonerated if I failed to obey his commands? You reply, "Only believe and you shall be saved." All right, but the misfortune is, we take issue upon the meaning of faith.

I adopt the language of the inspired James, to state my position, "Show me thy faith without thy works, and I will show thee my faith by my works." Faith is expressive of action, and implies obedience to God. Abraham had faith in God, and obeyed God's most trying command to offer his own son, in whom the promise was located. Enoch had faith in God, and walked with him, and it requires correct walking to walk with God. Abel had faith in God, and was not baffled or influenced by the offering of his brother Cain's sacrifice, but offered to God a more excellent one, which met the divine acceptation, and he was justified. Noah had faith in God and verified it by his loyal actions, in the building of the ark, by virtue of God's command, and thus "condemned the world, and became heir of the righteousness which is by faith." Moses had faith in God and chose the divine honor, although it inculcated humble discipline, and affliction with the people of God, rather than to be called the son of a renowned king's daughter, "esteeming the reproaches of Christ greater riches than all the treasures of Egypt."

If we are men of faith, it is not our business to question the propriety or impropriety of God's commands; we should implicitly obey them, as did the ancient worthies, and then we will have what they possessed,—faith in God.

If God commands me, I never need pause to consult consequences. When God commanded the children of Israel to cross the Red Sea, he opened the passage. When he commanded them, under the supervision of his servant, Joshua, to execute their daily marches around the walls of Jericho for seven days, and obey his directions, even to the blowing of rams' horns and shouting, his own power overthrew the walls when their obedience was fulfilled.

The colored man was right when he said that if God commanded him to jump through a stone wall, it was his place to jump, and it was God's place to make the hole. That is what I would term Biblical faith, and I do not consider that it is so plentiful in the world. Christ says, "When the Son of man cometh, shall he find faith on the earth?"

We are sometimes told that the interrogative form of expression is the strongest. I consider this a vital question, and one with profound meaning, and it should prove an incentive to every one who names his name, to depart from iniquity, and have the mind of the ancient worthies, to forego the honors and emoluments of this perishable world, and endeavor to gain and retain that wonderful, saving and heaven-approved principle of genuine faith in God.

True faith in God will be the infallible support to his humble and unassuming children amid all the oppositions that may attend their mortal life. To strengthen their trust in the divine protection, the Savior alludes to many things in nature, such as the beautiful growth of the lilies, with their natural splendor surpassing the glory of King Solomon. He speaks of the birds that have neither storehouses nor barns, and yet provisions are made for their sustenance by a kind and beneficent Father in heaven. Not one sparrow escapes his scrutinizing eye. His children are of more value than many of these.

CHAPTER XXXII.

God's Care for the Little Flock. — What our Life should be. — The Millennial Age. — An Outlook into the Prophecies of the Future. — Parting Words to the Reader. — Formation af an Elevated Christian Character, the Chief Aim of this Work.

GOD'S care for the minutest thing in his creation corroborates the unquestionable truth, that he will recognize and supply the spiritual and temporal needs of his children, who exercise a filial trust in his Word. To consummate their unspeakable joy, he will finally conduct them to his home in glory, that they may behold him in all his celestial splendor. "Fear not little flock; for it is your Father's good pleasure to give you the kingdom."

O what a promise! How that little flock must have hearkened, with breathless interest, to the gracious words that fell from the lips of the blessed Jesus, to think that they, who were selected from the common and lower ranks of society, should be joint-heirs with Christ of such a glorious inheritance! How apt and significant the figure! He does not bring down from the celestial world some profound principle; to effect a comparison, he takes something with which they were all familiar,—a flock of sheep. The attachment between the shepherd and his flock, in the oriental country, is very strong. The sheep hear the Shepherd's voice. He goes before and leads them, and they follow after. He conducts them into green pastures, on the hill slopes and valleys, and to the still waters.

The Psalmist David deduced the grand and pathetic illustrations from the natural scene of a shepherd and his

flock. The natural shepherd has a responsible charge. He has the care of the sheep, and must administer to their necessities. He must protect them from danger, while he himself is exposed to the damp and chill of night, and the heat of the sun by day. He must guard his flock from the assaults of the ferocious beasts, that prowl around at night, in quest of prey. The sheep are timid animals; they fly to the shepherd for protection.

David, the good and faithful shepherd of old, slew a lion and a bear, to save his sheep from their destructive clutches. The disciples of Christ are compared to sheep, as already indicated, and there must necessarily be points of resemblance. They are innocent and harmless like sheep. They are attentive to their shepherd's voice. They will not hear the voice of strangers. They rely upon their shepherd for support and protection from destructive foes. They fly confidentially to their shepherd, when foes are near. They will not rely upon their own strength: they are non-combative and timid concerning evil, and wholly rely upon the shepherd, to avenge them of their enemies.

But while faith is coupled with a divine and reverential fear, it is not possessed of a slavish fear. It does not fear the prowling wolves and lions. Men often partake of the nature of ferocious beasts, and are intent upon devouring Christ's little flock, but he vouches his protecting might. They cannot harm them any farther than the shepherd permits. The hairs of their heads are all numbered. He sees the injuries which they have to suffer from those who hate them, but their patience must be tried like that of the Great Shepherd and Bishop of their souls. Their life may be taken, like that of the Shepherd, but they are told not to fear them that kill the body and afterward have no more that they can do. Men can only reach the natural life, the spiritual, which is far superior, is beyond the assaults of men and devils. The Great Shepherd, who gave his natural life for the sheep, has that in his care, and the evil one cannot touch it. "Fear not, little flock, it is your Father's good pleasure to give you the kingdom." Oh, how different are the characteristics of this kingdom, compared to earthly kingdoms and secular rule!

In this work we have given the nature and character of military life and conquest, which are carried on by the use of carnal weapons amid feats of daring bravery, manifestations of human vengeance, and streams of blood; but the soldiers of Christ, who partake of the harmless nature of sheep, do not kill and destroy by sword or flame. The Christian commits the subject of vengeance solely to him who hath conquered hell and the grave. They partake of his disposition.

Christ was compared to a "lamb without blemish, and as a sheep dumb before her shearers so he opened not his mouth." He could have called for twelve legions of angels to have come to his defense, but, then, how could the Scriptures have been fulfilled? That would have been contrary to all the predictions of prophecy. God's plans were laid and his purposes fixed, and now, when the awful crisis is come, and the painful shock must be felt, and the scorn, and ignominy, and shame be realized by the Great Sacrificial Victim for sin, he would not flinch from the long-preparatory arrangement, although he must drink the bitter cup to its very dregs. In his intense mental agony he prayed that if it were possible the Father should let this cup pass from him, "but not my will, but thine be done.' In his human nature he suffered untold pain and anguish. "He was bruised and mangled for our sins, and the chastisement of our peace is upon him, and with his stripes we are healed." This is characteristic of the cross, and all his sheep partake of his self-sacrificing nature, and suffer with him in the flesh. Self-crucifixion permeates his entire life of humiliation, and is characteristic of all his words of spiritual life. Had he brought his physical power into requisition, the combined forces would have fallen before him, but the time for the disclosure of his vindictive ire had not yet come. It will be displayed in all its conquering force when he comes, without a sin-offering, unto salvation. Hence, the humble Christian's time is now here, to conquer the flesh and the devil,—not by the use of carnal weapons, but spiritual.

Like the meek and suffering Savior, the Christian must suffer the sneers, and scoffs, and scorns of men, and if the vindication of truth require it, yield up his own life also and expire, in great weakness, as did the humble Christ, but, like him, he shall be raised in glory. This is the manner in which this wonderful and glorious kingdom is to be gained, and no wonder the flock is pronounced to be small, for it is evident that few will recognize this humble and self-sacrificing method of being saved.

How many thousands of professing Christians fail to know this humiliating and condescending life by practical experience in the crucified channel! It is only daily contact with the cross that saves, and this is the practical confession that Jesus Christ is come in the flesh, when we suffer in the flesh with him. "It is only when the nations shall learn war no more," that they will fulfill that part of Christ's teachings. Only then they show the spirit which his followers imbibe, when they pass through the purifying process of the new birth, and are partakers of this element of non-resistance, as exemplified by the humble, self-denying Jesus. It was the purpose of his life of humiliation, to inure us to the same humble sphere, and assimilate us to his life. Our life must be similar to his, for "As he is, so are we in this world." Christ did not conquer with the sword, neither can his followers. I am glad that my eyes have been opened to discover this wonderful life, which is preparatory to an immortal state of felicity in our Father's kingdom. It required much training and severe discipline to induce me to an acceptation of this humble life, so diametrically opposite to the carnal element, but at last I became willing to become a soldier of the cross of Christ, and as I, after successive years of turmoil, came out of military and maritime life, so I hope, eventually, to realize a transition from this life of trials to a life of exaltation in glory with Christ, providing I am steadfast to the end of my cross-bearing life.

"It is your Father's good pleasure to give you the kingdom." This kingdom, in all its celestial grandeur and glory, will not be given reluctantly by the Father; it will not be a gift that will be grudgingly tendered to his humble and believing flock, but it will be given with pleasure. Christ has merited the kingdom and all those who have followed him in his humiliation shall share the immortal benefits of the kingdom.

This kingdom will transcend every other kingdom. "All other thrones will be cast down," as indicated in the glowing vision of the prophet Daniel, and this kingdom will have the universal sway. Nebuchadnezzar's image, representing the different successive kingdoms, was finally demolished by the stone that was cut out of the mountain without hands, and smote it upon the feet, and all the kingdoms, comprised and prefigured by this image, were superseded by this glorious kingdom, which shall be inherited through Christ, the king of glory, and enjoyed in its magnificence and beauty forever, by the little flock. The first phase of this kingdom, beyond the present economy of grace, will be the millennium or thousand years' reign. "Blessed and holy is he that hath part in the first resurrection; on such the second death hath no power, but they shall be priests of God and of Christ, and shall reign with him a thousand years." Rev. 20: 6.

At the ushering in of this wonderful dispensation, the angel will descend with a great chain in his hand, and will lay hold upon the devil and bind him, and place him in the bottomless pit, and place a seal upon him, "that he shall deceive the nations no more till the thousand years shall be fulfilled; and after that he must be loosed a little season."

What joy will thrill the hearts of the "little flock," when they unite with the vast multitude, that shall be gathered all along the line of Adam's posterity, to be concentrated in the millennial age and enjoy the felicity, attending the personal reign of Christ! Although the number of believers were few, and the flock was small throughout the successive ages and dispensations of time, yet, when all shall meet together, they will constitute a large concourse of saints, and they will reign in a superior gradation from the nations, who must experience the test at the close, or expiration, of the millennial age, when the devil shall be loosed for a little season out of his prison, "and shall go out to deceive the nations which are in the four quarters of the earth, Gog and Magog, to gather them together to battle." The number of them will be as the sand of the sea. "And they went up on the breadth of the earth, and compassed the camp of the saints about, and the beloved city, and fire came down from God out of heaven, and devoured them. And the devil that deceived them was cast into the lake of fire and brimstone, where the beast and the false prophet are, and shall be tormented day and night for ever and ever." Rev. 20. Read the entire chapter in order to obtain a clearer conception of its meaning.

This purports that an immense army will be deceived by the Satanic power, which has been so effectual in the art of deception ever since Adam and Eve were created, and occupied the Garden of Eden in their primeval condition. This will be the last effort of Satan and his innumerable army. He will then be plunged into the lake of fire, like Pharaoh and his hosts were plunged in the depth of the sea.

These hosts will encompass the camp of the saints. This discloses the beautiful and transcendent dwelling-place of Christ and his resurrected saints, during the millennial age. Satan ever wages his malicious warfare against Christ and his people, and, when extricated from a thousand years' confinement, he persists in his infernal project with consummated rage and malice. But the loving apostle John informs us, that Christ came into the world to "destroy the works of the devil," and this will be the completion of the inspired prediction. We learn in this stupendous tragedy also, that none can be admitted to dwell in eternal blessedness without purification through the testing ordeals of an overruling Providence. But the camp of the the saints cannot be invaded by this hostile army. "They had come up out of much tribulation, and made their robes white in the blood of the lamb," and they can no longer be assaulted, when clothed in their resurrected bodies, and arrayed in their celestial habiliments. They are freed from temptations and infernal raids, and this daring charge of their assailants shall end the war, and consummate all the artful and treacherous maneuvers of the great arch-enemy.

The rush and collapse of the immense volumes of water in the Red Sea settled the dispute with the Supreme Ruler of the universe and Pharaoh; and this dreadful conflagration will settle the controversy between Christ, the Redeemer of the world, and his great antagonist, who carried on his first personal dispute with the Savior in the wilderness of Judea, but it will terminate in this disclosure of his vindictive ire. " Fire came down from God out of heaven, and devoured them." This is the terrific destruction to which the inspired apostle Peter alludes, when he says, "The heavens and the earth shall pass away with a great noise, and all the elements shall melt with fervent heat. The earth and all the works that are therein shall be burned up."

The prophet Micah also refers to it, "Behold the day cometh that shall burn as an oven; and all the proud, yea, and all that do wickedly, shall be stubble: and the day that cometh shall burn them up, . . . it shall leave them neither root nor branch."

The revelator continues to record the events, after this dreadful conflagration, as follows: "And I saw a great white throne, and him that sat on it, from whose face the earth and the heaven fled away; and there was found no place for them. And I saw the dead, small and great, stand before God; and the books were opened: and another book was opened, which is *the book* of life: and the dead were judged out of those things which were written in the books, according to their works. And the sea gave up the dead which were in it; and death and hell delivered up the dead which were in them: and they were judged every man according to their works. And death and hell were cast into the lake of fire. This is the second death. And whosoever was not found written in the book of life was cast into the lake of fire."

Then follows John's sublime vision of the new heaven and the new earth, after "the first heaven and the first earth have passed away, and there will be no more sea." All things are made new and the New Jerusalem descends, arrayed in celestial splendor, with pearly gates and jasper walls, and streets of transparent gold. Too dazzling and beautiful for mortal eyes to behold, we can only be capacitated for this ultimate disclosure of beauty by the Lord's refining process. In that elysian clime the soul can exult in an untarnished atmosphere, and dwell in ecstatic *joy* forever. Its raptures will be unsullied and pure, and the vision of the immortal home will ever be imposing and brilliant. This is the awful judgment that the prophet Daniel saw in his grand and sublime vision. He says, "I beheld till the thrones were cast down, and the Ancient of days did sit, whose garment *was* white as snow, and the hair of his head like the pure wool: his throne *was like* the fiery flame, *and* his wheels *as* burning fire. A fiery stream issued and came forth from before him: thousand thousands ministered unto him, and ten thousand times ten thousand stood before him: the judgment was set, and the books were opened." Dan. 7: 9, 10.

We here have a description given that is sublime and awful, and harmonizes with John, the Revelator's delineation of this grand and notable event. Daniel presents the demolition of the thrones, the cessation of all secular rule, and the throne of God in all its celestial·grandeur appearing with the eternal, self-existing Deity in regal splendor, and celestial array. Multitudes composed the retinue of attendants, and the immense concourse which stood before him, in exact numerical reckoning, would number one hundred millions, but, no doubt, his representation of this vast throng would indicate an innumerable multitude. Daniel mentions the opening of the books, and so does the Revelator John. John portrays the dead, small and great, standing before God, who had come from the caverns of the sea, and the dark domains of death and hell. John portrays the effulgent face of the Universal King, on his magnificent throne, from whom the heavens and the earth fled away, and Daniel describes the shining and fiery display of his presence with hair and garments of pure white, representing his unsullied condition and exquisite purity. Christ appeared thus on the Mount of Transfiguration, which attitude was a figure of the immortal condition of celestial purity.

Whether the "books," in the plural, refers to the hearts and consciences of the innumerable assembly or not, is a question to be deliberated upon and decided by the studious and candid mind, but this is the best conclusion at which I can arrive at this time. Millions of human hearts, in the time of probation, are susceptible of right and just decisions, ere they are calloused by sin, or deluded by false raptures of the mind. The very turning point and digression from this normal judgment, and the lack of will-power to yield submission to the Divine Criterion of judgment, will be reproduced in all its unwelcome reality. The goadings of conscience will be renewed, and remorse and anguish will fill the soul.

Another book was opened, which is the Book of Life. That is undoubtedly the Book of the New Testament, which was sealed with the pure blood of Christ. Although Christ himself will be seated in regal splendor upon the dazzling throne, yet he will judge no man, "but the words that I have spoken, shall judge you in the last day." Oh, what intense anxiety will there be then, to know as to whether our "names will be written in the Lamb's Book of Life!"

There will be an unerring susceptibility then, of the "savor of life unto life, or the savor of death unto death." The books must harmonize, and all the vital words of Inspiration, for weal or for woe, recorded in that Book of Life, will appear in their native purity and power, and the finespun argument of the disputer will be removed. The human creeds, established and proclaimed by the eloquent tongue, under which the image of Christ, and his words of spirit and life were hidden, shall then be scattered to the winds, and Christ's pure and holy Law, retaining its untarnished identity, shall be revealed.

Oh what consolation will it afford *then*, if *our* book and the Book of Life harmonize! It may be said then, "Blessed are they that do his commandments, that they may have right to the tree of life, and may enter in through the gates into the city." Rev. 22: 14.

That will be the great day of accounts, when men shall be judged according to their works. Then the righteous shall hear the welcome applaudit of the King on his throne of glory, "Come, ye blessed of my Father, inherit the kingdom prepared for you from the foundation of the world." Matt. 25: 34. Then shall the wicked hear the awful denunciation, "Depart from me, ye cursed, into everlasting fire, prepared for the devil and his angels." Matt. 25: 41. "These shall go away into everlasting punishment, but the righteous into life eternal." Matt. 25: 46.

Now, dear readers, as we are approaching the end of this work, we hope that all the various incidents and pertinent illustrations may have their salutary bearing. Our purpose has been to make the incidents of our adventuresome life conducive to the welfare of others, in the sense of reflecting the mercy of God to the wayward and the lost. If, through the infirmities of the flesh, we might have failed, in some instances, to present our comparisons as clearly and methodically as we should have done, we hope that the leading sentiment and intent of the book may be a sufficient apology for some defects in the style and arrangement.

I have aimed to show that there is a vacancy in the roving heart of man that the world, with its charms and pleasures, can never fill; that there is no rest in the wayward course of sin, and that privation and sorrow may arouse the normal flame and restore the native force of kind words "that can never die," that lie beneath the rubbish of carnal joy and pleasure, deep down in the human heart. Oh that, by the divine blessing, it may fall into the hands of the wayward, and effect a recurrence of pious instructions in the youthful period of life, and, though remote within the barren wastes of prodigality and woe, the return may yet be effected to the Father's house.

In this wide world, where sin and sorrow reign, there is much to do for those whose spirits yearn for the gathering in of the lost. We live to execute the labors of life but once, and the serious thought, freighted with responsibility, should set our hearts aflame. First, the Truth of God must be evidenced in us, by strict tenacity to his words of life, and thus we will declare plainly our purification by its power, and that we seek a country that is heavenly and divine.

We should impress upon others, by every available means, these pure truths, whose efficacy we have applied to our own hearts. We should urge a welcome reception of the Truth upon their hearts, that they may be purified by obeying the same. He who is engaged in rescuing the perishing, is engaged in a work that meets the divine approval, and, if he braves the opposition, and continues in the self-sacrificing course to the end of life, he will evidently be richly remunerated for all the privations, temptations and toil, incidental to such a life.

When we think of the roving prodigals amid the howling wastes of sin, rescued and brought back to the Father's house, and their zealous work afterwards in the Master's employ, to save others, and then portray to the vision of faith the ultimate gathering in eternity, when they shall come with rejoicing, bringing their sheaves with them, the trials and adversities, the sorrow and tears will sink into insignificance, when compared with the "exceeding great and eternal weight of glory." We will only then discover to perfection what it is to labor for Christ, to convince men and women of sin and show them how to escape and be saved by the power of God's Word.

I have made many efforts in my public preaching to entreat the wayward to believe and obey the Gospel. I have conversed with many privately and presented to them this sublime subject of religion. For at least twenty-seven years this has been my employ, and at this advanced stage of life I can still avow that it is my favorite theme, and one which I feel safe in recommending to others. Through the agency of the pen I hope to be enabled to reach a greater number than by my verbal communication. I hope that my own prodigal life will have a tendency to convince other prodigals that the pursuits of worldly amusements and carnal gratifications can never satisfy the native longings of the soul, and that the most solid enjoyment and comfort can only be obtained when Christ is formed within us "the hope of glory."

I feel assured that the divine discipline and correction, under the supervision of a merciful Providence, have raised me out of the miry clay and the horrible pit, and placed my feet upon the rock. God has put a new song into my mouth, which is purer and sweeter than any song I had ever learned to sing before, and I hope the melody of this new song will cheer me to the end of life. I will try, in my weakness, to sing it to others.

I have given you the extent of my wanderings and my rescue from the dark and stormy way, and I have endeavored to show the mercy of God in this my great deliverance. It is my sincere desire that this work may have its salutary bearing upon those who may chance to peruse it. The growth and perfection of Christian character is a momentous work. It demands close attention and strict scrutiny. I do not claim the perfection of Christian character, but avow that I am endeavoring to progress toward the "full stature of manhood in Christ Jesus." The more the faculties of our being expand in this divine growth, the more we realize our own weakness, and it requires much discipline and training ere many of us, who have named the name of Christ, can give ourselves unreservedly into his protecting care. It requires severe discipline to urge many of us to espouse the cause of Christ. Often an application of the correcting rod is demanded to keep us balanced and advancing in the growth of Christianity, when in the church of Christ. Christian professors are ofttimes censured justly for their tardiness and indifference in the Christian work, and they are sometimes rashly and unmercifully criticised, when they are laboring hard in the divine work.

A proper balancing of Christian character is just as significant as the delicate balancing of forces in the universe, to which we have cited attention in this work. The inspired apostle says, "Add to your faith, virtue, and to virtue, knowledge, and to knowledge, temperance, and to temperance, godliness, and to godliness, brotherly kindness, and to brotherly kindness, charity." These noble and divine traits are all comprised in the Christian character and constitute its perfection. It requires a single, steady aim in the child of God to secure these attainments, and our lifetime is required for the completion of the work. Let the candid and active mind consider each of these important elements, that constitute the Christian character, and portray them in his own life. He will then come to the conclusion that it is the work of a life-time.

This formation of our Christian characters, I believe, occupies the infinite mind of God more than the balancing of forces in his natural creation, because all these forces are, or have been, put in operation by his wisdom and power, and they obey implicitly their natural laws, but the human creature is tainted and demoralized by sin, and it requires much correction and discipline to balance him by the divine means and methods of God, in his beautiful economy of grace. Love for God subdues the carnal will or mind of man, and inclines his heart to obedience to the sovereign will of God.

God has enjoined many commandments, to test our integrity and fidelity to him. Obedience to the commands of God, in faith and love, will mould the character after the divine mind and bring about the ultimate bliss and felicity in heaven, which God designs. The Prophet Isaiah exclaims: "Oh that ye had hearkened to my commandments, for now should your peace have been as a river, and your righteousness as the waves of the sea."

God required his children to be obedient under every dispensation of his Providence, and it is the only life that brings men into the divine favor. We need not pause to explain this principle any further here, as we have illustrated it fully in the various incidents in military and maritime life, but we will allude more particularly to the sequel or result of obedience. First: "Thy peace shall be as a river." The river here is employed as an emblem of peace, and it is a very apt and beautiful comparison. We might say much in reference to the beauty and utility of a river, but will try to be brief in carrying out this illustration. We have observed the tranquil flow of the beautiful river in its channel, its waters clear and transparent and scarcely a ripple on its placid bosom. In the glow of sunset, when the golden hues of the orb of day tinge the clear blue sky, and both the tranquil bosom of the river, and the glory of the heavens above, lend their united charms to beautify the scene,—can you think of a more graphic figure to impress the thought of Christian peace in the perfection of its beauty upon the mind? The full peace of God "which passeth all understanding," can only be experienced to perfection when our obedience to the commandments of God is fulfilled.

The peace, then, is deep, and constant, and permanent. It is a peace that has been tested by severe trials and is genuine. It is consummated and ready to effect the transition into a new world, where peace unsullied reigns. So our fathers and mothers in Israel passed away when their characters had been proved through obedience to God; their hearts were tranquil and composed, and they longed to be on that ocean of peace, "where the wicked cease from troubling and the weary are at rest." Christ says, "My peace I give unto you, not as the world giveth." Christ's peace is given upon his own equitable terms,—the terms of righteousness, obedience to his commandments. The world offers peace upon her own proposed plans, but that peace is not a divine peace, it originates in the world, is proffered by usurped authority and is not reliable. It is confined to this world and has no virtue or power to stay the soul in adversity, or yield serenity and composure in the trying hour of death. But the peace which Christ gives will endure the tests of persecution in the line of duty and obedience, and the more severely it is tested, the deeper will its power be felt in the soul.

"And your righteousness as the waves of the sea." This discloses the strength and firmness of character that is consummated in the course of God's righteousness. There is naught in this world that can equal the solidity of Christian character; it is far above military power and eminence, and surpasses the attainments of the learned who have passed through the refined courses of the arts and sciences, and who have built up characters that are famous and renowned in the world. The Christian character, moulded and formed in the righteousness of God, is compared to the waves of the sea.

How great and wonderful the comparison! We have frequently portrayed to our readers the irresistible and overwhelming aspect of the waves of the sea. All the combined military forces of earth could not impede their onward progress in the deep. There is no power that can control and stay them but the power of God. Christ, the Son of God, gave an evidence of his overruling power when he stilled the raging waves on Galilee. Christian character, formed in God's righteousness, overcomes the world, and this overcoming force may well be designated by the waves of the sea. The reward of fidelity to God, and adherence to his righteous requirements, will be unconquerable strength of character and peace, which cannot be intruded upon or disturbed.

THE ORIOLE (See Page 320).

Dear readers, is this not a rich compensation for our service to him who hath formed the placid rivers, and stays the proud and foaming waves of the deep? Surely, we could not wish a more glorious end than is designated in our closing text, which, it appears to me, brings to a focus all the aims and efforts of this work and depicts to our vision the closing scene in the great arena of this life. O how wonderful is the import of our apprehension by the mercy of God and how unspeakably great is the ultimate design of his love! O that his power, operating through our weak agency might have its longed-for effect! Having experienced his saving and purifying power in our own soul, we are eager and anxious to show to others his wondrous power to save.

APPENDIX.

POEMS FROM THE AUTHOR'S COLLECTION

Once More on the Rolling Deep.

AGAIN on mental wings I soar
  Where ocean billows rise and roar,
Where tempests wild in anger sweep,
And spend their fury on the deep.

Once more I merge in ocean life,
And view the elements of strife;
Once more the sailor's burdens bear,
And all his midnight perils share.

Those nights of darkness on the deep,
I ever shall in mem'ry keep,
To aid me on the sea of time,
Till moored within the port divine.

Of Zion's ship I am aboard;
Her Captain's name is Christ the Lord.
We hope to land on Canaan's shore,
Where foaming surges beat no more.

How many similar things there be,
On this and on the natural sea;
Which similar points I will unfold,
Ere yet my ocean story 's told.

We meet the weather foul and fair,
And calms and storms, as well are there;
By furious winds we, too, are driven,
While steering on our way to heaven.

Can I a solace thus afford,
To some poor drooping hearts aboard,
Till we've outlived this ocean strife
And reached the port of endless life?

Shall veteran sailors on the sea
Encounter storms with bravery?
And will the Christian mariner sleep,
Where sin's destructive billows sweep?

O Christian, wake, no rest for thee!
Dark clouds are lowering o'er the sea;
The lightnings flash, the thunders roll,
Stretch every nerve to save thy soul!

In Memory of Mother.

LIFE is sad and home is dreary,
    Since maternal love is flown,
All around seems lone and weary
    Since the cherished form is gone.

Life was sweet when in the radiance
    Of her cheering smile we lived,
But those years of rich experience
    Now are fled, and we are grieved.

Mother's life we fondly cherish,
    While she moulders in the tomb:
May her living counsels flourish,
    Till we meet in yonder home.

Mortal pleasures soon must vanish;
  Earthly comforts fade and die,
But no cloud our light shall banish
  In the cloudless home on high.

Let us hail God's sovereign power,
  Let us yield to His control,
Then, however dark the hour,
  All will tend to save the soul.

Friendship, then, by death though riven,
  Dark and lone the path we tread,
Friends shall be restored in heaven,
  God will raise them from the dead.

Jonah on the Sea.

HE slept; ah he slept in that terrible night,
  When the heavens in darkness were veiled,
And the Lord was propelling the storm by his might,
  While the seaman his anger bewailed.

The call 'mid the elements' deafening roar,
  Woke the fugitive Prophet from sleep,
But his burden of guilt was oppressing him sore,
  And he asked to be plunged in the deep.

How dismal his refuge far down in the sea,
  Where he drank of the wormwood and gall;
Till his spirit was moulded God's Word to obey,
  And prophesy Nineveh's fall.

A warning to all, who endeavor to flee
  Away from God's All-seeing eye,
We cannot escape him on land or on sea,
  And we all must surrender or die.

We are only secure when his Word we obey
    And bow to his sovereign will;
He will save from the terrors of midnight or day,
    For his power the tempest can still.

My Voyage on the Sea.

ONCE o'er the stormy sea I sailed
    'Mid nights so lone and drear,
In deep distress my spirit wailed,
    I called on God in prayer.

The winds were roaring o'er the sea,
    The waves were raging wild,
Alas! thought I, no hope for me,
    I am a ruined child.

But in an awful night of gloom
    A lucid star arose,
It shone to guide me to my home
    And mitigate my woes.

The clouds dispersed, the tempest lulled,
    The waves their fury ceased,
By that Bright Star of hope controlled
    All was reduced to peace.

'Mid gentle gales and threatening storms
    Life's sea I since have rode,
But safe in my dear Savior's arms
    I fear not storm or flood.

And when these wild commotions cease
    And all life's storms are o'er,
Oh may I gain the port of peace
    And rest on Canaan's shore.

Weighed and Found Wanting.

THE merry laughter ceased, and condemnation
 Seized on the mighty in the banquet hall,
Belshazzar quailed, and saw with consternation
The hand inscribe his doom upon the wall.

Wise men were called to interpret the forebodings
That veiled in gloom the monarch's troubled heart
But vainly do they scan the dismal tidings—
No sage in the realm their meaning can impart.

Where's Daniel now, the man of true devotion,
Who prayed to his God despite of jealous foes?
Soon comes he to the scene of their commotion
And he alone the writing can disclose.

Daniel declares it with a heart undaunting,
"It is thy doom, oh King; thy doom is sealed.
Weighed art thou in the balance and found wanting,
Who didst not heed the word that God revealed."

Truth is the balance that weighs all our actions,
And tests the thoughts of every human heart,
Just are the weights and right are the exactions
Nor can sin screen its vile, deceptive art.

Men still will violate the laws of heaven
To enforce instead their meager human creeds,
But how their souls will be with anguish riven
When in the balance weighed to test their deeds!

They now indulge in ease and sensual pleasure
Laughing and feasting in their temples gay
But, oh, their woe no human mind can measure
When weighed in the balance at the judgment day.

Now, while we live in mercy's dispensation,
Let us the Gospel Balances apply,
Or like the King, in trembling condemnation
We must sink beneath the frown of God and die.

In Memory of a Husband and Father.

LIFE still bore its even tenor
   And no omen dark was seen,
All the inmates of our circle
Wore a countenance serene.
'Mid the bleak and frigid winter
Bravely had we toiled along,
Hoping for the vernal season
With its sunshine and its song.

But how soon our prospects vanish
And dark sorrows intervene;
Ties of friendship soon are riven
Mortal life is but a dream.
Suddenly the dark-winged angel
Of grim death came swooping down,
Now our home is veiled in mourning
And our cheerfulness is gone.

Precious husband, loving father,
Vacant are our hearts and lone
Since thy cheering form is absent;
Since thy smile of love is gone.
Thou the leader of our household,
To direct, advise and plan
'Mid life's changes bright or dreary
Thou wast ever in the van.

Cherished as a friend and neighbor
In thine own dear neighborhood,
Courteous, kind, humane and loving,
Ever in a helpful mood.
But the hands that kindly aided
And the heart of sympathy,
Now in death have ceased their action,
In the dismal grave they lie.

Oh that God would be our helper
In this time of sore distress,
And control our lonely spirits
Through this gloomy wilderness;
Transient are earth's consolations,
Fading all the joys of time;
But in Christ are solid comforts
Comforts that will ne'er decline.

The Seasons.

STERN winter will soon cease to reign,
　The bleak, piercing winds will be o'er,
And spring will be welcomed again,
　　To cheer drooping nature once more.

The fields that are shrouded in gloom,
　　Surrender to winter's cold sway
In verdure and beauty shall bloom,
　　And triumph 'mid spring's genial ray.

Sweet thoughts nature's changes suggest
　　To solace the children of God,
Inciting their hope of sweet rest,
　　When life's weary journey is trod.

While meeting their sorrows in time,
    Enduring the winter's rude blast,
They yearn for the country sublime
    Where spring shall eternally last.

Oh welcome the bright, gladsome day!
    When friends long divided shall come
And meet in celestial array,
    To praise God forever at home.

Awaiting the Train.

'TIS near the midnight hour,
    The moon in beauty shines,
I think of God's great power
    While I indite these lines;
Our weary eyes from sleep refrain;
To watch the coming of the train.

As watchmen of the Lord
    The Gospel news we bear
And we in sweet accord
    These midnight vigils share,
We hope to gain a rich reward
Which God doth promise in his Word.

Oh may our tongues proclaim,
    Salvation's joyful news,
May we in Jesus' name
    The heavenly light diffuse;
Oh Lord, attend us on this tour,
And clothe us with thy Spirit's power!

INDEX.

Abusive Officers,	173
A Consoling Thought,	321
A Disastrous Attack,	262
A Dreadful Experience in an Ice-floe,	145
Advance toward Manasses,	42
A Fierce Encounter,	37
A Fluent Speaker,	23
A Last Farewell,	14
A Letter to My Mother,	158, 250
A Look through the Window,	330
A Loving Father Consigned to the Tomb,	9
A Midnight March,	26
Among Strangers,	9
A Native Dinner,	225
An Imperative Command,	206
An Interruption in our Repast,	203
A Pell-mell Retreat,	39
A Poem,	100
A Portuguese Drowned,	172
Appendix.—Poems from the Author's Collection,	388
Approaching the Old Homestead,	330
Approaching the United States,	318
A Pressing Invitation by Bro. Isaac Culp,	334
Arrival at Hagerstown,	27
Arrival at Hawaii Island,	241
Arrival at Honolulu,	125
A Serious Struggle,	12
A Severe Storm at the West Indies,	315
A Siege of Small-pox,	66
Assisted in Manual Labor by a King and Queen,	113
A Start for Old Virginia,	22
At Anchor in Buzzard's Bay,	318
At Behring Strait,	145
At Cape Horn,	310

INDEX.

A Tedious Voyage North, ... 137
A Terrible Contest, ... 13
At Honolulu Once More, ... 247
At Lower California, ... 163
Attached to a Music Corps, ... 32
Attacked by Rebels at Gaines' Mills, ... 55
Attendance at Collegeville Seminary, ... 67
At Williamsport, ... 24
A Visit at Bro. John Detwiler's, ... 335
A Visit to the Battle-field of Bull Run, ... 48
A Visit to the Colored Youth at the Asylum, ... 290
A Visit to the Island of Juan Fernandez, ... 103
A Wise Dispensation of Providence, ... 80

Becoming Acquainted with Eld. Damon, ... 129
Blockaded in the Ice, ... 145
Bravo Island, ... 85
Bro. Robert Jones' Experience in the English Channel, ... 243

Capture of Whales, and Particulars Regarding these Monsters, ... 259
Carrying away the Wounded, ... 55
Christ's Example, ... 19
Constant Vigilance Required, ... 40
Crossing the Equator, ... 199

Death of My Sisters, ... 348
Deciding to Enlist on a Whaler, ... 69
Departure for Honolulu, ... 246
Departure for New York, ... 327
Departure for Norristown, ... 13
Departure for the Polar Sea, ... 252
Departure for the Sandwich Islands, ... 122
Departure from Marquesas Islands, ... 230
Deplorable Laxity of Matrimonial Life among the Natives, ... 217
Depravity of Natives and Crew, ... 116
Description of War Scenes by Prof. Snyder, ... 48
Difficult Creek, ... 37
Disposing of the Blubber, ... 91
Doleful Tidings, ... 255
Down James River to Fortress Monroe, ... 62

Early Trials, ... 10
Effects of False Alarm, ... 39

INDEX.

Election to the Ministry, ... 344
End of Peninusalar Campaign, ... 61
Enjoyment of Home Associations after Three Months' Campaign, ... 31
Escape of Part of the Crew, ... 137
Experiences while Traveling Northward, ... 253
Exposed to the Fury of a Rain-Storm, ... 42
Extemporaneous Speaking and Its Advantages, ... 289

Fierce Assaults by Rebels, ... 61
Formation of an Elevated Christian Character, ... 368

Gen. Reynolds amidst a Shower of Bullets, ... 52
Getting Wood Aboard under Difficulties, ... 113

Habits of the Marquesas Natives, ... 220
"Halt Boys! We're Right among Them," 38
Hardships of the Mariner, ... 277
Heart-rending Scenes in the Parting Hour, ... 13
Home of Robinson Crusoe, ... 100
Hospitality a Blessing to both Giver and Receiver, ... 285
How I Got Rid of the Tobacco Habit, ... 222
How I Lost My Wearing Apparel, ... 203
How the Scientist is Puzzled about the Lord's Doings, ... 265
How to Reach the Masses, ... 294
Human Flesh Eaters, ... 114

Ineffectual Commands, ... 39
Influence of Maternal Teachings, ... 11
Initiated on Board the Oriole, ... 72
In the Arctic Once More, ... 263
In the Pacific, ... 99

Jonah's Experience with a Whale, ... 264

Kamtschatka, ... 143
Kindness of the Natives, ... 306
Kind Reception by Friends, ... 280

Land-Sharks, ... 320
Leaving Home Again, ... 32
Lessons at the Helm, ... 83
Letters from Home, ... 247
Long Marches, ... 22

Marriage of my Sister Katie to Eld. J. John Emmert, ... 347
Marriage to Sarah Rittenhouse, ... 343

Martial Music and Its Effects, ... 23
Military Training and Its Results, ... 22
Music among the Natives, ... 226
Musicians Mustered Out at Harrison's Landing, ... 62
My Confinement in the Hospital at Alexandria, ... 43
My Diary, ... 165
My Feelings, as Expressed in a Poetic Effusion, ... 75
My First Attempt at Sermonizing a Failure, ... 129
My Lonely Watch on a Stormy Night, ... 94
My Mother Identifying Herself with the People of God, ... 348
My Ride to Manasses, Unprotected from the Elements, ... 43
My Second-Oldest Brother Heard from, ... 354
My Welcome by the Dear Ones at Home, ... 330

Nature's Beverage, ... 22
New Wine in New Bottles, ... 362
New Year's Day and Its Experience, ... 165
"No Place Like Home," 10
Novel Mode of Sleeping, ... 116

Obtaining Our Pay for the Voyage, ... 327
Once More on the Sandwich Islands, ... 280
On the Way South Again, ... 277
On to Martinsburg, ... 25
On to New York, and to Bedford, Mass., ... 71
Our Arrival at the Marquesas Islands, ... 207
Our Experience in Eating Candle-Nuts, ... 114
Our First Attempt at Whale Capture, ... 87
Our Flight from the "Shenandoah," 257
Our Invitations to Officers to the Meeting, ... 194
Our Last Farewell to Friends on the Sandwich Islands, ... 299
Our Last Look at the Arctic, ... 275
Our Meetings in the Forecastle, ... 192
Our Stay at New Bedford City, ... 323
Our Stormy Passage around Cape Horn, ... 94

Pernambuco, ... 315
Plowing the Ocean Once More, ... 309
President Lincoln's Call for Volunteers, ... 13

Rebel Picket Guard, ... 25
Reception at Harrisburg, Pa., ... 15
Reclining by the Way-side, ... 23

Reconciling Myself to the Life of a Warrior, ... 19
Reflections on Temporal and Spiritual Warfare, ... 356
Reluctant Departure from Cheerful Surroundings, ... 136
Renewal of the Conflict, ... 31
Replacing Lost Goods at a Disadvantage, ... 203
Retreat from Charles City Cross Roads to Malvern Hills, ... 60
Return to Camp Pierpont, ... 42
Return to Illinois, Accompanied by My Youngest Brother, ... 243
Return to Place of Encampment, ... 38
Return to Sandwich Islands, ... 156
Rigors of Army Life in the Winter, ... 33
Routine of Camp Life, ... 36

Scenes of Death and Carnage, ... 37
Some Facts about the Whale, ... 92
Some Incidents of the Hawaii Islands, ... 245

Terrors of the Peninsular Campaign, ... 50
The Bread-Fruit Tree, ... 227
The Colored Boy, ... 273
The Declining Days and Death of My Mother, ... 352
The Disgrace of a Harpooner, ... 167
The Drudgery of a Seaman's Life, ... 169
The Guano Islands, ... 99
The Marquesas Islands, ... 109
The Portuguese and Their Music and Dancing, ... 139
Trip to Illinois, ... 343
Two Deserters Left to Their Fate, ... 104

Value of Good Anchorage, ... 241
Visit to Eld. Damon, ... 294

Why We Were Known as Sailors, ... 323
Winter Quarters at Camp Pierpont, ... 38

www.ingramcontent.com/pod-product-compliance
Lightning Source LLC
Chambersburg PA
CBHW020105020526
44112CB00033B/923